ENDORSEMENTS

Mike Brill's *An Uncertain Life: Growing Up Gay and Southern Baptist*, is a moving, authentic memoir that is so very familiar, and so uniquely told. Mike's journey growing up poor, southern, fundamentalist, and gay is at times harrowing, poignant, yet triumphant. He reveals tender family secrets, and tales of bullying and abuse that make one wonder how he survived. Mike contextualizes his story in the historical and political events that have shaped many decades. He comes out of fundamentalism and into a new intellectual and social awareness that encompasses race, gender and class. He gives credit to many influential teachers and writers, some well-meaning but flawed therapists; and finally, to "God and grace," for saving him, and preparing him for a whole life, full of love and church and friendship. His story is the story of our community, of overcoming, of becoming awake to God and grace.

Rev. Dr. Nancy Wilson, former Moderator of the Metropolitan Community Churches (MCC)

Michael Brill's story is as raw as it is redemptive. With honesty and courage, he invites us into the painful, complicated journey of growing up gay in a Southern Baptist world—and the grace-filled path of becoming whole. *An Uncertain Life* is more than one man's memoir; it is a beacon of hope for anyone who has wrestled with faith, identity, and belonging. I was moved by its candor, inspired by its resilience, and grateful for its witness.

Eric Elnes, author, *Gifts of the Dark Wood*

i

This book is as poignant as it is timely! I spent my afternoon reading *An Uncertain Life*. Some parts left me teary-eyed like "Fresh-man." It leads me to hope that this work will help others not to accept blame for actions of others. I found the book fascinating & terrifying! It's spooky that aspects of the Civil Rights Movement described, remind me of the terrible things happening now and the ideology/theology behind them.

Natalia Marquez-Sterling, OTD, OTR/L, ally of the LGBTQ+ community

Michael Brill's *An Uncertain Life* is an intimate memoir of coming out. Reading the book felt like being invited to listen to a favorite uncle tell a story that included edge of the seat, heart rending, private tales, ultimately leading to redemption. From the 'dark night' to the ecstasy of freedom in fully owning who he is, the book takes the reader on a journey of emergence, much like watching an ugly caterpillar evolving into a beautiful butterfly. Through a very personal and intimate lens, Michael Brill has documented a turning point in the life of the Southern Baptist Convention and her institutions while telling his personal struggle of coming out as gay. It is his Damascene journey toward full acceptance of himself as a beloved child of God.

Jonathan Rudy, PeaceBuilding Global Senior Consultant and author, *Sand In My Shoes*.

We've all met this guy; a happy, popular, conservative Southern Baptist, full of charm and funny stories. Mike didn't "come out of the closet," as much as he came kicking and dragging his feet, hanging desperately on to one more sweet girlfriend. But in this book, we get to hear the inside story, not just of the struggle, but of the careful step-by-step study of Scripture, seeking of counsel, and examination of his own heart. I've known Mike for years. If you like a good story, or need your own path through the wilderness, you don't want to miss Mike Brill's book.

Marsha Stevens-Pino, author, professional Christian Musician and song writer

Michael Brill's autobiographical novel, *An Uncertain Life: Growing Up Gay and Southern Baptist,* is an amazing literary work of art that weaves together the dangers of homophobia in a White Supremacist culture with the tragic, and at times humorous, journey to find meaning and joy in life. Brill's narrative beautifully illustrates life as a gay man in a post-Jim Crow South, and his struggles of seeking acceptance and love in a Southern Baptist community. Most importantly, *An Uncertain Life* provides hope for a new generation of people caught off-guard by the rise of a new oppressive MAGA culture and power structure. This is a must-read, because history, in many ways, is repeating itself.

Guillermo Márquez-Sterling, author, *Killing the Butterfly*

This book is Mike's story, but it's so many other people's stories too. It's the story of anyone who has ever been the outsider in their family, the one who swims upstream, who doesn't fit in. It's the story of anyone who has ever had trouble finding their place in this world. It's the story of anyone with a big heart that breaks open for people in need, people who are told they feel too much and too deeply for this harsh world. This is the story of anyone who has ever had to hide their true identity, anyone raised with rigid expectations, anyone who didn't feel like they could safely live an authentic life. But this is also the story of anyone with a deep and abiding faith in God, a relationship that's honest and gritty, one that sometimes feels like God's nowhere to be found, but in our core, we know we are loved so deeply beyond our wildest dreams. Mike invites the reader to pull up a chair and find our place in his story, and at the end, one can't help but be deeply inspired and encouraged about the future. Life is hard and messy and those who are supposed to love us the most often hurt us the worst. But Mike reminds us that we are a resilient people and if we can persevere, work hard, and have courage, then love, fulfillment, and belonging, can be found just a little further down the road.

Angela Wells-Bean, Senior Pastor of Pass-a-Grille Beach Community Church, UCC, with a Doctorate in Ministry focused on Open and Affirming Congregations

AN UNCERTAIN LIFE

AN UNCERTAIN LIFE

CHARLES MICHAEL BRILL

SANTOS BOOKS
EVERY STORY SACRED

CONTENTS

I dedicate this book to:

Ruby Brill, my mother, the one most responsible for me coming to know Christ.

Dr. Hazel Petersen, the one most responsible for me developing into a professional while being a committed Christian.

Grace Pritchard, the one who most encouraged me to be my authentic self, regardless of what others think.

Rev. Dr. Mel White, the one who first encouraged me to write my story for the benefit of LGBTQ+ youth and young adults from conservative denominations.

ACKNOWLEDGMENTS

I cannot begin to express my gratitude for the many people who helped me with this monumental task. The journey has been challenging, as are the times in which we are living. Twenty-three people read my early manuscripts and gave me valuable insights and suggestions for improvement. I took many of them, including a list of my family members so readers can keep them straight.

A big thank you to the first readers: Kay Marino-Munion, a retired Bank Executive, and Susie Carbray, a friend and Canadian, readers of the first rough draft who gave me the courage to continue.

Subsequent drafts were read by: Marsha Marks, retired counselor; Judy Raynor, retired school teacher; Marsha Stevens-Pino, Singer, Song Writer, and published author; Rev. Harry Knox, retired CEO of a non-profit organization and Civil Rights activist; Michael Bozeman, retired attorney; Sylvia Ball, retired Federal Reserve examiner; Dr. Vivian Fueyo, retired Dean of the School of Education, University of South Florida, St Petersburg, FL Campus; Bob Pope, attorney and Civil Rights advocate; Lawrence Konrad, activist; Dr. Sharon Groves, Faith Organizer, coach, and Social Justice facilitator; Karen Doering, retired civil rights attorney and Social Justice activist; and Rev. Dr. Helene Loper, pastor, author, and SoulForce (Participant member).

The 4th draft was read, in all or in part, by Rev. Dr. Eric Elnes, pastor and author; and Rev. Dr. Guillermo Marquez-Sterling, pastor and author; Bruce Schumann, retired nurse and wildlife conservationist and my old home church friend, Tony Jones, who sought my help in reconciling the Scriptures with being gay, which confirmed for me the need to finish this book.

Later drafts were read by Dr. Joan C. Rogers and Dr. Margo B. Holm, professors emeritus, University of Pittsburg; Natalia Marquez-Sterling, a young adult who learned of the book through her father and asked to read it; and Rev. Chitoka Webb, whom I met at Kathy Baldock's seminar held at her church, working to bridge the divide between the LGBTQIA+ community and the Christian Church.

Last but not least is Richard W. McDonald, my husband, a retired court reporter. As one would suspect, he possesses excellent language skills. He read the first and the last drafts, giving me the first and final thoughts to consider.

To all of these, whether they read the first rough draft or the last one before going to the publisher, thank you!

Two people agreed to continue with the project after their first reading of the book. I am forever grateful for their assistance and expertise. First is Karen Doering, whom I met while fighting for LGBT civil rights when my home county in Florida came under attack in 2000. After reading my manuscript, she agreed to help where she could; after the unexpected death of Bob Bare, my original editor, she agreed to take on a bigger role. Karen worked with the National Center for Lesbian Rights when I first met her 25 years ago. She is now retired, giving her the time and freedom to help with this project. I am forever grateful for her expertise and insights.

The other is Sharon Groves, whom I first met as a colleague of Rev. Harry Knox, who was working for the Human Rights Campaign's Religion and Faith Initiative. She has great insight into how to reach groups of people who often do not talk with one another. It is through her that I found Lindsay Fertig-Johnson, the talented cover illustrator who designed the clever, insightful cover.

My sincere thanks to Santos Books and to the executive editor, Dr. Conrad Kanagy, and his publishing team. He has been wonderful to work with. He likes to say that every story is sacred. He came to me by way of a referral from an author I respect, after my previous publisher unexpectedly passed away in the middle of this project. For more information about Santos Books, contact Conrad Kanagy at Santos-Books.org.

PROLOGUE

Why write my story now? That is a question I keep asking myself. Is it ego? Is it my need to be heard? Is it God's Spirit moving me? I've asked myself this question over and over again.

What I can tell you is that in late December of 2023, I started thinking about the book again after I came across the original floppy discs of my two failed earlier attempts, 22 and 24 years ago. Each night for three months, I dreamed about the book. But nothing captured the full essence of what I wanted to say and why I wanted to say it now.

Then one day in April 2024, I started writing as if I was possessed. That day and for the next 21 straight days, I wrote for 8 hours (or more). It was a drastic change from the previous two attempts when I struggled to put words to paper. This time it felt as if the book had a deeper God driven purpose and direction.

Rev. Dr. Mel White, author of *Stranger at the Gate: to be Gay and Christian in America*, first challenged me to write my story years ago because there weren't enough voices from the Southern Baptist tradition speaking up for gay, bi, and trans youth.

The title: *An Uncertain Life* is a perfect description of the many challenges I faced, but it is also a story of resilience, overcoming and accomplishing more than anyone, (including me) thought possible.

Along my journey of faith, I came to realize that KNOWING GOD LOVES ME is a power that no one can take away. With that acknowledgement, acceptance of God's love, I was empowered to become the full person I was created to be, regardless of what anybody: family, faith community or larger society, says.

This book is mostly focused on my struggle for self-acceptance. Some names have been changed as it is not my intent to embarrass anybody regarding my life and struggles coming to terms with being gay. But the struggle is not mine alone, nor the benefits. Everyone is a part of creation. After my own coming out, I could no longer ignore the plight of my brothers and sisters: black, gay, female, immigrant, First Nations, poor in rural America, transgender, homeless, etc. You get the picture: we are all in this together.

I wrote it now because we are moving backward, not forward, on this and many other critical social issues. The progress made over my lifetime is being reversed. The time to act is now. Take for example the vilification of the transgender community, who generally make up less than one percent of the global population.[i]

I must confess I initially struggled with the transgender issue more than most. I believe that all should be treated with respect and are endowed with the same rights and privileges guaranteed by the laws of our country and the U.S. Constitution. However, my own acceptance of transgender people was a challenge. I finally reached out to my friends Sandy Steward and Jake Kopmeier, both of whom have now passed. They were a lesbian couple before Jake transitioned from female to male. I told them I was struggling to accept transgender people; that I didn't understand it. They both replied that I didn't need to. They asked me to love them like I would love anyone else. Wise counsel! With that, my dilemma was solved, and I became a real friend to them and the transgender community, as I am called to do as a follower of Christ. Unfortunately, my state, Florida, is leading the way in criminalizing transgender people and those (particularly parents) who support them. It is now against the law in Florida to help your own transgender child get gender-affirming care and treatment before adulthood.

Come along with me as I tell of both the triumphs and despairs of my life journey with God guiding me through the workings of The

Spirit in my life. Learn how my faith walk changed my perspective on how God views all His children. I am writing now because we are at a unique moment in time where fear and uncertainty prevail. I want to provide HOPE and COURAGE to conservative/fundamentalist Christian LGBTQIA+ youth and young adults that you too can live your best life.

As you read these pages, you will realize that I am a fighter. I do not quit. I try and try again until I get past the roadblock. I started professional Christian counseling to overcome homosexuality while a freshman in college and continued until I finally came out of the closet at age 38; yep, I fought it for a long time! I finally realized this is one area of life where there is no OVERCOMING, just denial or acceptance. I rejected myself over and over. But nothing I did helped me escape my attraction to men. I am part of the 3.5+% (a conservative estimate) of American society with same sex attractions. I tried to overcome these unwanted attractions to the point of despair. I want my story to help others reach their own self-acceptance a lot quicker, and with less pain for themselves and others.

This book is not a fairy tale! Being honest with oneself is tough in a society bent on conformity. I lived in fear most of my young adult life. I was afraid of being a homosexual. I feared rejection by my church, my family and society if they knew I was attracted to men. I worried for my safety. Yet I will tell you now, the closet was worse than all of my fears combined!

Jesus said that he came to give life and give it abundantly (John 10:10, paraphrased). You can't live abundantly if the focus of your life is NOT being your authentic self. And because I didn't want to be gay and was trying *really hard* not to be, I missed out on many joys in life. But since coming out, though life has sometimes been difficult, it has been a life of abundant joy.

I also have another audience in mind: the people of goodwill who make up the great majority of people in this country and around the world. It is time we awaken from our slumber and realize the dangers society is facing, not just regarding the LGBTQIA+ community, but all the "politically" unpopular groups in our society being told they are and treated as "less than." My faith informs my understanding of everything, including democracy.

I had no idea that by the time I finished this, my third draft of a book that's been on my mind for decades, the very foundation of America -- who we know ourselves to be in the world -- would be shaken to its core before the book was done.

This book is my story as a beacon of hope in an otherwise dark sea of confusing voices, all saying, you are not worthy. They are wrong, you are worthy! I have it on good authority that you are a Child of the living God. Have the courage to face life. I did it with God's help and God's Grace: Unmerited Love. You can too.

Note to Readers: How Michael dealt with **The 4 Big S's** (Sex, Sin, Southern Baptist and **S**criptures) is found in the Appendix, Page 263

---

[i] Transgender – Wikipedia, [https://en.wikipedia.org;wiki/Transgender]https://en.wikipedia.org;wiki/Transgender. *See, also,* HRC | Seven Things Abou Transgender People That You Didn't Know, Seven Things About Transgender People That You Didn't Know; and "Gender identity worldwide, 2023, by country" Published by Statistica Research Department, March 3, 2025, "In a global survey conducted in 2023, three percent of respondents for 30 countries identified themselves as transgender, non-binary/non-conforming/gender-fluid, or in another way. https://www.statistica.com/statistics/1269778/gender-identity-worldwide-country/#.

CHAPTER 1

The Moment of Truth

"You will know the truth, and the truth will set you free."
(John 8:32, New International Version)

Dark Night of My Soul

I remember it well. It was ten, no, eleven days after my 40th birthday and seven days after my last girlfriend dumped me. One had been glorious, the other heart-crushing. Let me explain.

For my 40th birthday, friends came from all over the United States and from in and around Mobile, Alabama, to celebrate with me. The past two years had been excellent. After 13 years of service, I left Southern Baptist Convention (SBC) employment on the advice of friends and mentors. I was in much better shape fiscally than if I had stayed at the University of Mobile. Many in the administration, including the President, were sacked, retired or accepted positions elsewhere within a couple years of my leaving, and conservatives took over. Fortunately, I missed all that drama. Instead, I made more than $50,000 a year for the first time in my life. At New York Life (NYL), my new employer, I was among the top rookie recruits nationally with fewer than 3 years of experience. All was looking bright.

But a few days later, Sheila, a woman from the church I had been dating on and off for some time, called and said, "I'm going to tell you something and I do not want you to interrupt me or say anything."

This sounded serious. Sheila started by confessing that she loved me but said she knew I didn't love her. "I don't know what game you're playing, but it's painful! And I'm sure it's a game. You don't really want me, but you don't want me to be with anyone else," she declared. I started to defend myself, but she stopped me dead in my tracks. I could hear her fighting back tears even in the midst of her fury. She continued, "It is a game. You let me go and reel me back when you need me, then let me go again. I never want to see, talk to, or go out with you again."

I asked if I could reply. "No." She hung up. I called back. She didn't answer.

It was a stinging rebuke in my ears and tears flooded my eyes, because I knew she was right. I had strung her along and didn't want to get serious with her. But I never considered what it was doing to her.

My dishonesty with myself had caused real harm to someone I loved as a friend. While I didn't want to make love to her, it hadn't been my intention to wound her either. I was asked if I was lying to myself or the women. The answer is I lied to myself and the women I dated. That is why it hurt them so much.

That day, after 25 years of dating women, by my count nearly 300 (though some say this is an exaggeration), I decided I could not, in good conscience, date women anymore. It was not fair to *THEM*.

With my cover gone, I pondered the next steps I might take to keep doing the "right thing." But I was lonely. She had been the only phone call since the party. The partygoers had all gone back to their lives in places far and near. They had families, jobs, and other friends. I had nothing. I counted back the days since my last telephone conversation. Back then, we all had landlines at home with a red button that blinked when someone called but we didn't pick up. My phone was not blinking. Day 1: No Call. Day 2: No call. Day 3: Sheila called. Day 4: nobody called. Day 5: nobody called and so it went until day 10. On the tenth day, I finally realized nobody was going to call. The one person who might have called did and told me she wanted nothing more to do with me ever again.

To everybody else, while I was a friend, I wasn't the center of their lives. My life had only me. Nobody called because nobody really knew me. That had been my strategy for a very long time. I thought it was the right thing to do. But, as Sheila pointed out, it wasn't. In my head, I could hear a chorus of women who felt like her: Diana, Betsy, Ivy, and Vanessa, among many others. In my effort to live "Holy," I had caused real pain. This realization compounded my sense of shame and guilt.

That night, I waited by the phone, looking out the west window of my Palmetto Street turn-of-the-century-before-last home in the Garden District. At 5 pm, as the sun was just beginning to set, the colors shone through the window. At 6 pm, the sun's rays were lower and the colors bolder, but the red button was still not blinking. I thought, no big deal, somebody will call tonight...they just must, or why keep up this charade?

At 7 pm, the sky was turning dark red and purple, the sun almost set. I still thought maybe somebody would call tonight. After all, they've had time to settle down; at least they'll call and tell me what a great party it was. Nothing.

At 8 pm, the room darkened as the sun finally set, my low-grade depression began to ratchet up. My life wasn't even worth a telephone call from my friends and family, how pitiful is that!

By 9 pm, it was dark, and the last glimmer of sun was gone. I knew it was increasingly unlikely anybody would call tonight. It was getting late. Working people were putting kids to bed and getting ready for tomorrow. Now, I wasn't mildly depressed; I was very depressed. "Maybe, no, no, not maybe, I am a fraud," I said to myself. "I am an abomination unto God," I continued. "I don't deserve to live, do I?" The conversation in my head continued.

From 9 to 10 pm and 10 to 11 pm, I contemplated killing myself. My attention turned to how. Maybe a gun, no, too messy, plus I didn't have a gun. A rope? That is a good old Southern way, right? No, it takes too long to die. Maybe pills would be better, at least cleaner.

From 11 pm to 12 am, deeply blue, I was still pondering my fate. By then I knew that I was a failure, a total fraud. But how could I be honest? Then, people would know I was gay. That word, "gay," sure didn't seem to fit. I didn't feel happy at all. I felt awful acknowledging that I was that terrible thing called a "homosexual."

I had prayed and prayed and prayed for God to take away this temptation. But God had not answered my prayers. I had been faithful, not acting out with any number of guys I was attracted to. I was still a virgin at 40, unless you counted an episode when a "friend" forced himself on me. As an adult, I now know that forced sex is neither healthy nor appropriate. But at that moment in time, I was confused because, in my heart, I had wanted to participate.

Confusion and depression are a dangerous combination. I knew a great deal about suicide at this time, having graduated with a degree in Psychology and Religion from Oklahoma Baptist University (OBU) and a Master of Divinity with a concentration in Social Work (MDiv/SW) from Southern Baptist Theological Seminary (SBTS). So yes, I knew I was at the end of my rope.

From 12 a.m. to 2 a.m., I continued to contemplate how to kill myself, finally concluding that I needed to get infected with HIV because that way, I couldn't hide, and everybody would know my shame. At this dark place in the wee hours of the morning, I remembered Dr. Will Baker's words. He was the chaplain at The University of South Alabama Medical Center and pastor of a local Baptist Church. He had also been my counselor for a couple of years but stopped seeing me, in his words, "until you are ready to move forward." When he stopped seeing me, he said, "Call me anytime, day or night, when you need me. You will know when that day is." Today was that day.

So, in the early morning of September 13, 1997, I finally called Dr. Baker. He answered and made me promise not to do anything for the rest of the night/morning. I promised. He said he would see me in Fairhope, across the bay, five hours later at 7 am. Those hours were the darkest of my life: indeed, this was the Dark Night of My Soul.

The Moment of Truth

One of my favorite scripture passages is: *Ye shall know the truth, and the truth will set you free.* (John 8:32, King James Version) But the truth wasn't what I wanted. Through the years, I had been told by various people in one way or another that I was gay. Roy, my friend knew. So did the Psychiatric ward nurse at the hospital in Louisville, Kentucky. She told me that I was gay and that I should accept this as the way God created me to be. But I rejected the truth from her.

I rejected the truth from Mark who proclaimed his love for me while in Seminary, another sad story of me betraying my values by harshly rebuking him. Vanessa told me she knew I was gay because I never tried anything physical with her when we were dating. I dumped her after that comment. Even Dr. Baker's assistant, whom I saw once or twice when Dr. Baker wasn't available, told me straight out that I should admit I was gay and move on. I stopped seeing her as a counselor after that. So, it was clear I had received the message but refused to hear the truth. Now, time was up, and it was now or never.

I entered the medical center in Fairhope, where Dr. Baker had his Baldwin County office. He was there before I arrived, which was good because I was as nervous as a cat on a hot tin roof. He asked me if I had tried anything. (Meaning actually, attempting suicide). No, I said, "I promised you I wouldn't, so I didn't. But I wanted to."

He acknowledged how seriously he took my call the night before. I apologized for calling so late but said, "You said I could."

He assured me it was all right that I had. He asked me what had happened to trigger this event. I told him about the party, the girlfriend's call, and that I felt like a fraud. He stopped me at some point and said, "Let me get this straight: you are saying you are gay?"

Embarrassed, turning red, I said, "Yes."

"Can you change?" he asked.

"No," I replied, "I don't think I can. I've tried and tried, and I'm still attracted to men."

So, to recap, he said, "You are gay, and it can't be changed, is that right?"

"Yes," I replied.

Next, he asked me if I was a Christian. I was braced for this and replied, "Yes." He then said, "It seems to me if you are gay, it can't be changed, and you are a Christian, the question you ought to be asking is, how do I live this out in my life?" He further opined that if this is who God created, then it is a gift, but I must live life well.

I was relieved that I hadn't been condemned but frustrated just the same. I remember my reply like it was yesterday, "So now, after all these years, I'm supposed to be happy about this?"

He laughed and said, "Yes, you are still God's child, gay or not."

He concluded by saying that God was still walking with me and would be through this, too. It would be just another step of faith, like all the others. I had my doubts, but I trusted him.

The closet door was finally opened, never to close again. I left feeling like a burden had been lifted; the worst part was the prison of my own making - that stupid closet.

So now you know this part, it is time to learn the rest of the story and how I got here in the first place.

CHAPTER 2

Life, Death, and in Between

"Death is never wanted; even the suicide does not choose it because it is filled with happy meaning, but because it seems less violent and painful than living."
Rev. Dr. Calvin Miller

Meet the Family

In the deep South, where I was born, the most significant acknowledgment that you were welcome was when someone invited you to their home as a guest to "meet the family." Then you would know you were welcome. So now you know you are welcome, come meet my family and enter into my world.

The year I was born, 1957, is best remembered as the year Russia sent Sputnik into space and sent America into a panic that our foremost enemy was winning the Cold War. It was a time when few women worked outside of the home. It was also not unusual that women, including my mother, Anne Claire Lindsey Brill, didn't drive.

Family picture

Mother was a beautiful woman, of that there can be no doubt. However, according to my grandmother, Nanny Shaw (not her biological mother), she was trouble from an early age. Anne was born during the Great Depression. Her biological parents, the mother a teenager, and the father in his 40s, came to Mobile, Alabama by hitching a ride on a freight train from New Orleans. This, of course, was a scandal. Her biological mother died in childbirth, and her father, who didn't know what to do, gave Anne away. Little is known of him except that he was a watchmaker of German descent.

Anne was first given to Nanny Shaw's relatives. They had a big family with many children in the middle of the Great Depression, and were already struggling to keep from starving, so they gave her away to a woman I affectionately knew growing up as Nanny Shaw. Dad always called Nanny Shaw a "hardshell" Baptist because she was against anything fun. And it was pretty much true: no drinking, no dancing, no smoking, no card games, no dating (unless approved by her), and, apparently, no adoption. Every time Anne thought it was about time for her adoption to be submitted, Nanny found a reason not to go through with it. It was clear that my mother never felt loved or wanted. Nanny Shaw, on the other hand, felt that Anne was a gift from God for her lost stillborn baby, and she was determined to raise Anne "in the ways of the Lord," much to Mother's chagrin.

So, as soon as she could, Anne did everything her mother had warned against, including smoking, drinking, and dancing. She was a wild woman. Men were attracted to her from the beginning. It didn't take long before she was out of the house and married. Soon, she had her first babies: twin girls. Not long after that, she was divorced. But in an apparent twist to the usual story, Mother refused to take the twin girls, who were raised by their father instead, according to Nanny Brill, the keeper of family secrets. Incidentally, the twins blamed my father for not wanting them, while the opposite was true.

Apparently, my father, Carl William "Bill" Brill, had dated Anne before her first marriage. After her divorce, they started a romantic relationship again. Soon after, they were married and began a family of their own with the birth of Carol Lynn Brill in March 1955. Carl William

Brill, Jr. was born in October of 1956. This would be her second child with Dad and Mother's fourth child of the decade.

I did not know about Mother's first two children until I was in college and asked Dad for Mother's death certificate for a speech I was giving on Death & Dying. I had inadvertently opened Pandora's Box to a family secret. Over the course of my life, many family secrets broke out into the open, each time wreaking havoc. Nanny Brill, one of my strongest supporters in a family with few such people, told me to tread carefully. Dad had initially refused my request but eventually gave in, saying I could be as stubborn as a mule.

"He Looks Like a Rat"

Southerners are born storytellers, and every family has its own stories. Some stories are warm and wonderful. Others, not so much. This is the first story I remember about me while growing up.

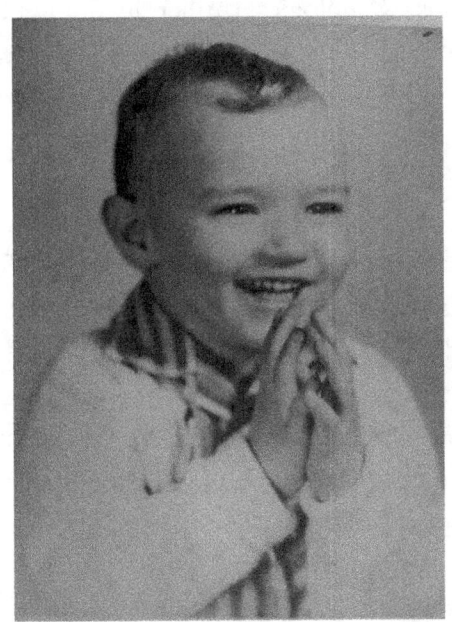

Mike as a child

Eleven months after giving birth to Little Billy, I, Charles Michael Brill, was born three months premature on September 3, 1957. I weighed just 2 lbs., 11 ounces, and soon became the bane of Mother's existence. From the beginning, I was trouble. Few babies born that prematurely in the 1950s lived—those who did often suffered numerous maladies. I was no exception. I was NOT fully developed when I was born. I stayed in the hospital incubation ward for three months, and I was ugly. You know how people always say this or that child is beautiful? Well, in most cases, they are lying. Most babies are not that cute, except to their parents. Occasionally a gorgeous baby is born, but no one said that of me. One of the earliest family stories was when Dad wheeled Mother to the viewing area to see the preemies, a woman standing nearby pointed me out and said, "I would hate for that to be my child. He looks like a rat."

Thus, I came into this world with an uncertain life ahead.

About a year and a half later, Mom and Dad's last child, David Lindsey Brill, was born in late January 1959.

Nightmares

Have you ever had a nightmare that was so scary you couldn't go to sleep? As a child I did, frequently. In fact, I was forbidden to watch *Hush, Hush Sweet Charlotte* because every time I saw the severed head come rolling down the steps in this psychological thriller, I wouldn't be able to get it off my mind or go to sleep. If I somehow managed to sleep, I'd walk and talk in it. For me, the scene lingered in my mind and caused me nightmares. Not that this movie was the only reason I had nightmares, but it surely didn't help.

The 1960s were one long nightmare for our beloved United States of America. African Americans were finally seriously standing up for their constitutional rights but with great resistance from the Jim Crow South. In that decade, we would witness the assassinations of our president, John F, Kennedy; the Attorney General, JFK's brother Robert Kennedy; and Dr. Martin Luther King, Jr., among others. We would also see college students murdered in Mississippi and Black Churches burned in Mississippi and bombed in Alabama.

It was a long, dark night for many, including my parents, who had to worry both about our country and their family. It didn't take long to learn just how difficult life would be for us.

Like his father before him, my father worked for BLP Mobile Paints. While very young, Dad was offered a promotion to manage the store in Huntsville, Alabama, best known for Redstone Arsenal where the Saturn Rockets were developed that first launched man to the Moon. The move to Huntsville in 1963 was drastic and exciting, but it was also a time of growing unrest in the nation.

The modern Civil Rights Movement kicked into high gear in Montgomery, Alabama two years before I was born when Rosa Parks refused to give up her seat on the bus to a white man in 1955, which was against the law. Few knew then what that one act of civil defiance would lead to.

In the decade that followed, Alabama experienced significant racial violence, including towards the first Freedom Riders (non-violent protesters who were black, white, young, and old). The Ku Klux Klan (KKK) bombed their Greyhound Bus just outside of Anniston, Alabama on May 14, 1961. Although another bus arrived safely a few days later in Montgomery, the Cradle of the Confederacy, those riders were beaten by a mob once they got off the bus while the police stood idly by.

The Civil Rights Movement was just starting to take off in Alabama when George Wallace was elected governor for the first time on a platform of Segregation Now and Forever in 1962. He or his wife would be my governor for the next 18 out of 20 years. Lynchings continued with two more in the state that year. According to Tuskegee University, from 1882-1968 in Alabama, 347 people were lynched; more than 86% of the victims were black. Alabama trailed only Mississippi (581), Georgia (531), Texas (493) and Louisiana (391) in lynchings.

The nation took notice of the brutality of the segregated South. The first March on Washington took place on August 28, 1963 when hundreds of thousands of African Americans and allies descended upon our nation's capital to be heard. While in D.C., Dr. Martin Luther King, Jr. gave his famous "I Have a Dream" speech to those in attendance and watching on TV, raising hope for a better tomorrow for Black Americans, all Americans. But the reality on the ground was far different from the ideals of a society where all are free to be themselves.

On September 15, 1963, not long after we moved to Huntsville, Alabama, a pivotal moment occurred when a member or members of the KKK bombed the 16th Street Baptist Church in Birmingham, killing four young girls. The distance between Huntsville and Birmingham was about 100 miles, too close for comfort! Though I was unaware of this tragedy then, I'm sure my parents knew. This was a time when both communities, black and white, were aware of the risks of "stepping out of line" in the deeply segregated South.

I write about Civil Rights because it is the backdrop for all social interactions while I was growing up. The South, never known as a flexible region, enforced social behavior harshly. Black people knew this better than any. But they are not the only ones to face the wrath of self-righteous "keepers of the status quo." I would learn this painful lesson later in life.

I'm sure it was a time of high stress for Dad and Mom, with four small children in tow, to move from the far southern end of Alabama to the state's northernmost prominent city, especially with so much trouble in between.

But it was a great time for Mom and us kids when we moved to Monte Sano Mountain, overlooking Huntsville. Mom even wrote in a letter to Nanny Brill that Huntsville integrated without violence though that didn't matter much on the mountain because "we had no negroes" up there. While Carol Lynn, Billy, and David thrived up on the mountain, I did not. Nightmares became a regular feature of my existence. They were so bad that my parents could not wake me out of them. Once, I remember hitting a big glass window that looked out towards the backyard as hard as I could while screaming in my sleepy, trance-like state. They were worried that I might sleepwalk out of the house, with good reason: it happened several times.

During the first year in Huntsville, though I was technically old enough to start first grade, my parents decided to keep me out an extra year, a wise decision by them not to have me compete with my bigger, stronger, and smarter older brother Billy who would have been in the same grade. I started the first grade the following year at age seven.

Mom and my other Grandmother, Nanny Brill, shared letters during our years in Huntsville that later gave me insight into the family from Mom's perspective. Carol Lynn and Billy thrived with them getting involved in extracurricular activities, Mother wrote to Nanny Brill in September 1964. In that same letter, she wrote that "Mike still likes school even though the teacher believes in strong discipline," adding, "he hasn't had to go to the bathroom (punishment) yet." However, it was only September 24th, less than a month into classes.

Later that year, Mother wrote again about how well Carol Lynn, Billy, and David were doing. But for me, she wrote: "I asked his teacher how he was doing, and all I can get is that he has the 'sweetest smile'."

Mother never said how I was doing, because I wasn't doing well. She sarcastically wrote, "Maybe he'll be able to smile his way through life." (Nov. 1964 letter).

In another letter, she wrote that I insisted on riding my bike to school, slid, fell, got wet, and came home. "He came walking back into the house kinda like a monkey - arms swinging wide and legs bent so they didn't touch. He looked so funny." Not once did she write any anecdote like that about David, Carol Lynn, or Billy.

It was also during this period that my parents, not knowing what to do about my lack of social development and nightmares, began to seek help. First, I went to Dr. Foley in Huntsville and then for testing at Vanderbilt University Hospital in Nashville, Tennessee. The Doctors asked my parents to continue watching me for "spells," and of course, I had three more after the testing. The doctors told my parents I was "borderline," though Mother didn't explain what that meant in her letter to Nanny Brill. Meanwhile, the rest of my siblings were doing well, except David got bronchitis. Later that spring, Mother wrote: "Carol Lynn was in 'Music from Around the World,' Billy was in the rhythm band, and David has really developed a terrific interest in the Sun and the Planets."

All she wrote about me was that her mother, Nanny Shaw, still wanted me for the summer. These childhood years are painful to remember, but they were also the best of my growing-up years.

By 1965, I began having slight seizures during the day. By summer, I was back to seeing a psychologist. In the meantime, Susan, one of four foster children raised by my dad's parents, Nanny and Pawpaw Brill, wanted to come to Huntsville and finish school with us. However, this was not possible because of me. Mom wrote: "Not that I wouldn't like for her to stay, but we've had a consultation with Mike's doctor at the mental health center here since then, and she doesn't think it would be advisable right now. It seems that Mike is more seriously disturbed than we had thought. She says that he is a 'bright but emotionally disturbed child.'"

In another letter, Mom writes: "Mike is still Mike. He has good and bad days, I guess we all do, so maybe he is just being normal, only it seems that when his days are good, they are really good, and when they're bad they're horrible."

On top of this, the doctors were increasingly leaning toward epilepsy as my diagnosis, which they considered a "very serious" condition and, with it, a diminished, uncertain life.

Butterflies & The Big Lie

Have you ever seen a butterfly? Of course you have. They are beautiful, delicate things. Have you ever had butterflies like when you were in front of a crowd to speak or were called into the principal's office for some offense? I've experienced both, so too has our nation.

On November 22, 1963, President Kennedy was assassinated. When Lyndon Johnson became president, white Southerners hoped he would be more sympathetic to segregationists since he was from Texas. To their dismay, under his leadership, Johnson got the Civil Rights Act passed on July 2, 1964, with help from Robert Kennedy, then the Attorney General of the United States.

Even more outrageous to many white Southerners was Johnson's support for the Voting Rights Act, which passed on August 6, 1965, prohibiting states from imposing qualifications or practices to deny the right to vote based on race. Although I was unaware of these developments at the time, as I was only 8 years old, these laws significantly impacted the Nation, the South, and my family.

As for my well-being, matters declined throughout our years in Huntsville. Moving there had given my parents butterflies, I am sure. Desegregation had caused both parents to be greatly concerned as Gov. George Wallace embroiled Alabama in the Southern resistance to equal treatment of black citizens.

However, another matter gave them even more butterflies: me. By 1965, my parents were at their wits' end about how to help me. I had gone for testing the previous two years, and the doctors were still trying to figure out what was wrong in my head. By 1965, I started counseling sessions with Dr. Adams to help me channel my "aggressive impulses" toward more socially acceptable practices. Mother wrote that July that Dr. Adams would continue to work with me because I had "suicidal rushes."

Dr. Adams gave me a nature and butterfly collecting set in the counseling process. This interested me, and I began making a butterfly collection almost immediately. I remember thinking they were delicate, "just like me," because you couldn't touch their wings (skin) because they would rub off, just like my skin when I was born. Soon my collection included Swallowtails, Buckeyes, Monarchs, and many other butterflies and even a few moths, especially a Lunar Moth.

One day, running after a butterfly out in the neighborhood, I encountered a stray, mean dog. The dog scared me, which made me remember him.

A few days later, I was hunting butterflies again when I came upon a beautiful Yellow Swallowtail, one of the prettiest. That's when it happened, the big lie. I hadn't meant to tell a lie. I hadn't meant to jump over the fence. I was just after a big, beautiful butterfly. While out with my net, I was in my own little world of peace and tranquility. I could be out for hours, trying to catch them, take them home, and put them in my display. They were beautiful. Indeed, to me, they are a beautiful part of creation.

Our next-door neighbor was an older woman who liked us but clearly didn't want us children in her well-manicured lawn. However, the big, beautiful butterfly had a different idea. Our yard lacked most flowering plants, as young feet regularly trampled it. The neighbor's yard, by contrast, had lots of flowering plants. Of note were the Tiger Lilies, all vibrant orange and very enticing to pollinators. I wouldn't catch him at this rate unless I tried something else. So, when he landed on that Tiger Lily, it was my last chance, if only it wasn't on the other side of the fence. Between me and him was the neighbor's chain-link fence, the kind with the two-point prongs on top. I figured that because I was a good climber, all I needed to do was quickly hop over the fence and catch him...and what a catch it would be! Surely, no one would notice these couple of minutes. Would they? However, the best-laid plans of mice and men ... it turned out much as an adult would expect, but not a eight-year-old. I got to the top of the fence ok, but I couldn't get down. Eventually, fearing I'd be caught, I yanked my leg over, but it snagged on the top prongs and ripped a gash in the back of my leg. Horrified, I ran to Mom; she would know what to do.

Lucky for me, when I came running inside (about to die, I thought), Mom asked what happened and said it looked like a dog's bite. Great answer, I thought! She put alcohol (that hurt) and then peroxide (better) on it and bandaged me up. I thought I was "home free" until she asked me how it had happened. Of course, I couldn't say I climbed over our neighbor's fence since it was expressly forbidden. And Mom had mentioned it looked like a dog bite ... and then I remembered the old mean dog that had wandered through our neighborhood. Innocent and harmless enough, I claimed the stray dog bit me. After all, I was smart. I couldn't name a neighbor's dog, so that stray I had seen while trying to catch butterflies fit perfectly in my tall tale; as Mother had said, it looked like a dog bite to her. Years later, I turned this story into a sermon: "You reap what you sow," but ironically, Dad never believed I had lied all those years ago.

I almost forgot the rest of the story. When Dad got home, "next steps" were discussed, and he went out and bought traps to catch the dog that did not bite me. With the money spent, I was really scared to tell the truth. The next step after that, on the advice of the doctor, was to start rabies shots. From July 27 till the end of the summer, I had to get 23 gauge/25 MM shots. Now, my parents were worried that I had rabies to go with whatever else was wrong with me. Topping off an already bad summer with me, a Yellow Jacket stung David while we were on a camping trip to Kentucky, and he had to be hospitalized. To my parents, their lives looked uncertain. But mine looked even more so.

Let's Play Ball

As time passed, Mom and Dad became extremely concerned about me, along with the doctors and both of my grandmothers. The theory at the time was that the mixture of oxygen given to premature babies in the 1950s was linked with psychopathic behavior in adults, according to an article Mother referenced (given to her by Nanny Shaw) in her letter to Nanny Brill. That's when the bombshell hit the family: I, Michael, was really sick, sicker than anyone had expected. I was falling out of chairs and not remembering, having nightmares, and walking in my sleep. I didn't play well with others, and most concerning of all, I didn't relate as either male or female, and, according to Dr. Adams, if this persisted I would become a "homosexual." The year was 1965, eight long years before the American Psychiatric Association (APA) voted to declassify homosexuality as a Mental Disorder (12/1973) and nine years before homosexuality was removed from the Diagnostic and Statistical Manual of Mental Disorders 3rd Edition (DSM-III), clarifying that homosexuality was not a mental illness. While not appropriate for eight-year-olds, it would have been extremely helpful to have this information in my teen years as I started struggling with my sexuality, but as usual, this became a family secret.

Dad was determined to ensure this didn't happen to his little boy. After all, Billy was doing great in Peewee Baseball and David was showing a manly interest in science. Back then, it was expected that men were scientists and women were teachers. All these messages were subtle but told me, actually all of us children, what our expected roles in society were to be.

This led Dad to take immediate action. From the age of 7 to 13, I played baseball. One year, I played football; two years, I played Basketball; and in middle school, I ran track and was quite good at it. But Dad never came to see any of my track meets or basketball games after my football disaster, as I was an embarrassment to him.

I was so bad, as the joke goes, "How bad were you?" So bad I was picked last. So bad that my team forfeited the game before I took the field. That was the case with me. In the seven years I played Little League Baseball, I never made it out of the minor leagues, even the last year when Dad was the coach of a "major" league team and picked his players. He chose my younger brother David instead. I was crushed, but in his defense, David was a much better player. In all my years in Little League I caught three balls in right field (the position with the least action) and had three hits over seven years.

As bad as baseball was for me, football was worse. I played peewee football one season and was put in for ONE play at center. I fumbled the snap, got pummeled, the other team recovered, scored a touchdown and we lost 6-0. Dad was so embarrassed he didn't talk to me the whole way home. If I could have crawled under the seat, I would have. What do you say to your dad, who is so embarrassed by your performance? The answer: nothing. I sat in the car looking out the window, hoping to get home quickly to retreat to my room away from his embarrassment. What did he do after the fiasco? He did not allow me to play football ever again.

Then there was basketball. I played in the community park league during my middle school years. I remember we played a predominantly black community center and lost 62-6. It wasn't my sport either. Dad's effort at making me into a "real man" failed miserably.

Runt of the Litter

After the long, hot, difficult summer of my rabies shots, fall returned, turning the leaves all shades of beautiful colors soon after school began again. I started my second-grade year (1965-1966 school year) on Monte Santo Mountain. It was not a happy time for us. Dad was miserable as the store manager for BLP Mobile Paints and finally decided to leave. In the middle of the school year, he accepted a job with JetCo as a sales representative, but we stayed on the mountain until school let out before moving to Conyers, Georgia.

The move to Huntsville had proved disastrous for Dad. Selling the house up there was even worse. By the time we arrived in Georgia, we were close to broke. The precious resources used in Huntsville to improve me were gone.

The mountain was wonderful for Mom and the rest of us, as everything was within walking distance. It was a close-knit, friendly community. That is not to say I didn't have all the troubles mentioned earlier. It is just that these were the best of my growing-up years, as difficult as they were for me. Matters only got worse with the move to Georgia.

Conyers, Georgia in contrast, was red-neck country, unfriendly to newcomers, and spread out in 1966. Remember, mother didn't drive. The town was 25 miles from Atlanta and too far to even walk to a grocery store. We also bought a Mobile Home. Mother hated the trailer. It sat on a sloping lot with one end on pillars about 20 feet in the air. One evening, a storm blew in from the west and rocked the trailer back and forth throughout the night. We were all terrified. Mother determined then that we had to move again.

We stayed in Conyers for just one school year (1966-1967) before moving again, this time to Decatur, Georgia. Mom and Dad found a house on Ansley Street within walking distance of the school, the bus line, and the grocery store. This helped as it gave Mom transportation options, especially with Dad now traveling more as a sales rep.

When the move to Georgia happened, the letters between Nanny Brill and Mom ceased. So too my appointments with the doctors in

Nashville, Tennessee, and Huntsville, Alabama. The family pretty much resolved itself that this is the way it is going to be with Mike. They adopted a "sometimes you must just let nature take its course" attitude.

The pressure on Dad to keep the family together was significant, as Mother was very unhappy. I was no longer the only problem; Dad, like male eagles, was expected to take care of his nest and young. If one had to be sacrificed, it would be the runt of the litter.

As an amateur wildlife photographer, I know that when baby eagles are born, the runt is often denied food, picked on by his/her siblings, and almost never makes it alive to the end of its first year. But in 1966, I didn't know any of this. I just knew I was forever going to be the runt; I was always the "sickly, nervous one," unlikely to succeed in life.

Then, the bottom fell out. Pawpaw Brill passed away in the fall of 1966. His passing rocked Mom's life and sent our family on a downward spiral.

A Terrible Time

The years 1962-1968 were a terrible time for me, my family, and the country. The Civil Rights protests, from sit-ins to Freedom Riders, climaxed in Selma, Alabama on Bloody Sunday, March 7, 1965, when hundreds of black non-violent protestors and some white allies joined together and attempted to march across the Edmund Pettus Bridge from Selma to Montgomery. On the way out of Selma, the marchers were met by state and local police who used whips, tear gas, and billy clubs to attack and severely beat the hundreds of civil rights activists as they began the march. For the first time, the nation watched the brutality of Wallace's segregationist rhetoric in action on national TV. Words have meaning, then and now, and white supremacists heard Wallace's message loud and clear ... but so did the American public who were shocked by the horrifying violence on their TV screens that they had only heard described previously. John Lewis, who later became a U.S. Representative and is an icon of the Civil Rights movement, nearly died on the bridge that day. Ironically, Wallace's strategy of brutality backfired for the first time and gave a reluctant President Johnson reason to sign the Voting Rights Act of 1965 three months later.

When Martin Luther King Jr. and the Southern Christian Leadership Conference (SCLC) began its "Birmingham Campaign" of non-violent protest against segregation and white supremacy two years earlier in 1963, Alabama fought back, literally and figuratively. Birmingham at the time was one of the most segregated cities in the U.S. The South, never a region that liked to be told what to do by the Federal Government or "outsiders," railed against King, the Freedom Riders, and the non-violent movement generally. They labeled King a "troublemaker" and "outside agitator" (King was from neighboring Georgia).

On April 12, 1963, eight prominent white clergy wrote "An Appeal for Law and Order and Common Sense," posting it in *The Birmingham News* and other media, urging blacks to stop engaging in demonstrations and protests with King and other civil rights leaders and instead leave it to the locals to work with the (all-white) local government and through the courts (with their all white judges), to resolve the issues.

In response, four days later King wrote an open letter addressed to the eight white clergy in which he eloquently and respectfully stated his case in his "Letter from Birmingham Jail." King said that while people have a moral duty to follow just laws, they have a *responsibility* to break unjust laws through direct action rather than waiting indefinitely for justice to come through the courts. He explained that he was invited to Birmingham by SCLC's local affiliate "because injustice is here," referencing its stark racial divisions, brutal police, unjust courts and many "unsolved bombings of Negro homes and churches." He also noted that those who live in the U.S. can never be considered an "outsider" anywhere within its borders.

He pointed out that "Injustice anywhere is a threat to justice everywhere" and that "Whatever affects one directly, affects all indirectly." King conceded that due to previous failed negotiations, he and demonstrators were using non-violent direct action to create a constructive tension to compel meaningful negotiation. Because, said King, "We know through painful experience that freedom is never voluntarily given by the oppressor; it must be demanded by the oppressed."

By 1966, the black-led civil rights movement based on direct, non-violent action began to fade, and other groups with different ideologies and strategies took over. Malcolm X had been assassinated the year before, and following his death, the Black Panther Party was formed in 1966 to protect African American neighborhoods from police brutality. A series of urban riots followed from Los Angeles to Detroit. The Black Panther Party was a self-proclaimed socialist organization and, like other socialist organizations before it, found itself in the crosshairs of J. Edgar Hoover's Federal Bureau of Investigation (FBI).

Meanwhile, the Brill family continued to struggle following the death of my grandfather, Oscar Brill, in 1966, followed by my mom's death in 1968.

Thank God for Aunt Julie & Nanny Brill

As one can imagine, I didn't take change very well. The move from Huntsville was difficult enough, but during the summer between moves, we also made an extended trip back to Mobile to be home with Nanny Brill during Pawpaw Brill's last days.

The summer of 1966 was a sad time for our nuclear and extended family. We stayed with Nanny Brill for three months as Oscar (Pawpaw) Brill succumbed to throat cancer. It was painful and slow. But once again, I was the problem. It was decided that Billy, Carol Lynn, and David could stay at The Big House, an antebellum home turned farmhouse, but that it "was best for all concerned" if I stayed with Nanny Shaw's sister, Aunt Julie. The adults realized that Pawpaw Brill's health was declining and that I needed to be in a "friendly environment," as I was always "emotional," and by '66, all the adults were very aware of just how serious my condition was. Hence, I was shipped off to Aunt Julie, who had been 100 years old for as long as I could remember. Secretly, I was thrilled not to be with everyone else. Besides, Aunt Julie had always taken a special liking to me. So, for the summer and into the fall I was the house guest of Aunt Julie at her small Chickasaw, Alabama home, where I was her prince charming.

At her home, I truly felt special and accepted for the first time. Aunt Julie was the opposite of her sister, Nanny Shaw, in every way. She had lived in New York City whereas Nanny had never lived anywhere but in and around Mobile, Alabama. Aunt Julie not only gave me a safe place to stay during a very difficult period but was also willing to play with me. We played "Brillville" with her old photo film cans and plastic tomato holders. She taught me all about imagination and how to entertain myself using the simplest of things. We also discussed "running away" together to New York, where we could be anybody we wanted to be. As a nine-year-old, this was a magical adventure, and it spared me the emotional trauma of Pawpaw Brill's death, something no one believed I could handle.

To help me deal with the pain during the waning days of his life, Aunt Julie gave me one of her most beloved treasures: a picture that changes color in different light. We agreed that I would not take it from her until I was old enough to take care of it and keep it safe. True to her word, she gave me the picture to take home during our regular Christmas visit in December 1976, the year I graduated from High School and began attending college.

Living with someone for three months can teach you a lot about them. I learned that Aunt Julie's family considered her a renegade, and she had been "sent to Mobile from New York for her own good" by her children, primarily Winston, her eldest son. Later, when she died at age 77, Nanny Shaw burned and destroyed all records of Aunt Julie's life. I asked Nanny why she did this. She replied, "Nobody needs to know about her life."

She was SUCH a disgrace to her sister, my grandmother, that she tried to let Aunt Julie's memory die with her. This led me to surmise that she might have been a prostitute or some other "shameful" thing, but I never verified it. I didn't care. She loved me! For that, I am and will always be grateful, love her, and remember her.

Nanny Brill became my other ally in the family, advocating for my benefit. That summer, she and Mom got into a serious conversation about how Mother had wanted me so badly, only to now treat me as less than her other children. Nanny was also the dispenser of critical family secrets that, later in my life, would be instrumental in me becoming the person I was created to be. Nanny Brill made Dad promise to give me the letters between Mother and her after she passed away.

At this time, though, Nanny Brill's sage advice spared me the sadness and despair of Pawpaw Brill's final days and spared the family from having to deal with an emotionally distraught child during such a difficult time.

Oscar Brill died on October 29, 1966, after a long struggle with cancer. He worked for BLP Mobile Paints for 40 years and they closed the company for half a day so all could attend his funeral, according to my grandmother. All felt the loss, but especially Mother. She had a special relationship with Pawpaw Brill, and he with her. His death was sad for all of us, but tragic for her.

Gone with the Wind

1968 started out exceptionally well for the Brill clan. We attended the showing of *Gone with the Wind* at the Fox Theater in historic Five Points of Atlanta on New Year's Eve 1967 and came out at midnight with horns blowing and people cheering in the New Year. It was my happiest memory of the year!

Soon, however, everything seemed to go wrong. First, Dr. Martin Luther King, Jr. was shot and killed in Memphis, Tennessee on April 4, 1968. Atlanta, King's hometown, was very tense after his killing. Mom and Dad thought Atlanta might burn down as it did in *Gone with the Wind*. Hundreds of African Americans passed by our home on the way to Ebenezer Baptist Church to mourn his passing. He had been the de facto leader of the Civil Rights Movement that called for equal treatment of all Americans under the Constitution.

A few months later, Robert Kennedy, the brother of slain U.S. President John F. Kennedy and the front-runner for the Democratic Nomination for President, was shot and killed on June 6, 1968. Additionally, the Vietnam War was top of mind, with lots of casualties, and was regularly discussed among my classmates. One even said we weren't going to college because we were going off to Vietnam. We were only in the 4th grade, yet we were discussing the war there. It should have been the farthest thing from our minds, but it was not.

My siblings and I had other pressing matters. Mother kept slipping off, going out of town, and leaving a maid to watch us kids while Dad was working away from home as a sales representative. Carol Lynn even called us kids together and asked us all to pledge to be good so Mom and Dad would stay together.

Mother had become a big fan of Dave Garrett, whom she met at an Atlanta Nightclub, and her interest in him apparently grew. He was a comedian and singer with a growing reputation. Mother's out of town trips continued unabated during the spring. Tensions between Mom and Dad were very high.

Mother

While Mother and Dad had always been concerned about my mental state, it was Mother who was now on the verge of a breakdown. On three occasions, she terrified me: 1) She made Carol Lynn wash dishes past midnight, screaming, "They are not clean on the outside;" 2) She made me eat Chinese noodles until I finished all of them, sometime after 9 pm; and 3) After I asked her to buy catsup, she bought 32 bottles and made me stay in the closet and count them until I was sure we had enough.

Last, the neighbors on the east side, the Loves, thought they had found Mother's real father because they met a watchmaker of the right age and of German descent. Apparently, the Loves set up a meeting. Whether it took place or not, I never learned for sure. But all these things together: The move, Pawpaw's death, the comedian/singer, and possibly finding her real dad, were just too much!

In July, David and I were stopped as we walked home from Oakhurst Baptist Church's Vacation Bible School, the first Baptist VBS we ever attended, and not allowed to go home. Police cars were at our house, but we had to wait at a neighbor's home until the coast was clear; together, we waited. Only Carol Lynn was allowed in. I protested that it wasn't right that Carol Lynn got to go in just because she was the oldest. Billy told me to shut up! The neighbors tried to calm me down, but I knew something was wrong, very wrong. Finally, we were allowed to leave and raced to the house.

I remember walking in and noticing Dad sitting on the white couch. That alone said something was terribly wrong because we were only allowed on the white sofa for special events like Christmas. Dad asked us to sit down. Carol Lynn was already sitting next to Daddy and crying. Tears rolled down his cheeks as he started to explain what had happened. It was all so strange because he had never cried in my presence before.

Daddy told us that mother had passed away from a heart attack and had gone to heaven; she wanted us to know, "She loved you and would be looking down from heaven over you."

Then we all cried. In truth, I felt nothing. I was numb. I couldn't understand it. Mother was here in the morning and gone by the afternoon. It wasn't fair. She had left us. Maybe I was angry? Perhaps I was sad? Mostly, though, I was stunned. My not-so-terrific life was even worse now, that much I knew.

No other details about Mom's death were forthcoming, then or ever, from Dad. But secrets, family secrets, always find a way of getting out eventually. I believe secrets in a family are poison, by the way.

Soon, we moved back to Mobile, Alabama to live with Nanny Brill and her foster son Gary in The Big House. Aunt Beverly and her two children, Mickey and Bobby, lived in the small house "out back."

It was hard on all of us, but especially Nanny Brill, who, in essence, became the mother to 7 kids, while Aunt Beverly (recently divorced and depressed) and Dad (recently widowed and depressed) dealt with the tragedies in their own lives.

While Nanny had her hands full trying to manage all these children, and Aunt Beverly and Dad each grieving in their own way, I took the death of Anne Claire Lindsey Brill, my mother, very hard. It is hard to say whether I took it harder than my brothers or sister, but I took it hard.

CHAPTER 3

Purgatory

"...Purgatory is not everlasting."
St. John Vianney

Living in the Closet

For much of my life, I lived in a closet. From 1968 to 1970, I lived in a literal closet. Dad and Nanny Brill decided that I should have a "room of my own" for the benefit of all involved, so I was given the "small bedroom" next to Nanny Brill, which was essentially a storage closet.

Brill family history centered around 1951 Pleasant Avenue, an antebellum home turned farmhouse. It was a mystical place, replete with trap doors, secret passageways, and spooky ghost stories. It was also a place for major celebrations, including Victory Day in 1945, three years after Nanny and Pawpaw bought it. To say we loved this house is an understatement. The Big House, as we referred to Nanny Brill's home, was located on five acres from Pleasant Ave & Rondo Road to Three Mile Creek. The property's front two acres were a designed Pecan Orchard with neat rows of trees. The middle acre is where the homestead sat, with Nanny's prized Rose Garden behind the Big House. Behind the rose garden sat the Little House, where Aunt Beverly and her two kids lived. The last acre was open land from the Little House to the creek.

This big, converted farmhouse included a huge front porch with a rocking swing attached to the ceiling. On the back of the house was another porch as big as the one on the front where Gary, Nanny Brill's foster son, had his bedroom.

Inside, downstairs, there was a long center hallway. Antebellum homes always had a central hallway to allow for airflow from front to back. Nanny's house was no exception. Branching off from the grand hallway was a TV room/library on the right and a kitchen. On the left was the formal parlor, where Nanny had her nine hand-painted window shades from just after the Civil War, the prize of all her possessions. This room was mainly off-limits except for special occasions. Then, midway, some pillars narrowed the grand hallway and led to the formal dining room. This room could be closed off with pocket doors.

Upstairs were three huge bedrooms, a sitting area near the stairwell, a bathroom, and the "trunk room" (think of a sleeper cab in a semi) that had been converted to a bedroom. This was my room.

The summer of 1968 wasn't a happy time for me. I needed this sanctuary away from the ugliness in the world. In that room, I kept my prized possessions: The Butterfly Collection, my four-band channel radio that I received that Christmas (my best Christmas present ever), and my stuffed Camel named "Camelly."

When we visited The Big House, we kids used to play and sneak around in the secret passageways. But by late summer of '68, there wasn't much play left in me. Sensitive by nature, I had had enough of life. Death seemed to be the only certain thing. Death was certain for those I loved: Pawpaw Brill dead ('66) and Mom dead ('68), both before I turned 11. Death was also in the news, Robert Kennedy and Dr. Martin Luther King, Jr. were killed that year. Then there was the Vietnam War, which was not going well, with lots of casualties. No wonder death preoccupied my mind.

I took Mom's death exceptionally hard. I couldn't reconcile myself to the fact that she was gone. Clinging to her memory, I kept all the ribbons from the funeral in my little closet room. Nanny Brill was very concerned that this wasn't a normal reaction to death. Indeed, it was not. Death engulfed my mind and was ever-present. I was also walking and talking in my sleep more than ever. Nanny was worried about my safety, with good reason; I managed to walk down the stairs, outside The Big House and into the yard once that summer before waking up. I also started acting out by developing a "Pet Cemetery" in Nanny's rose garden.

It was the worst year of my life, in a life with very few good years to date! I was miserable. My life was MORE uncertain now than at any time since my birth. The same could be said for our republic as riots (Los Angeles, Detroit, Birmingham and others) and assassinations echoed throughout the land.

Rain, Rain, Come on Down

Reality set in after my mother's funeral that my life, my family's life, had changed dramatically and irreversibly forever. Mother wasn't ever coming back. My immediate family now included Gary, Bobby, Mickey, David, Billy, and Carol Lynn as siblings and Aunt Beverly, Dad, and Nanny Brill as parents. This was ok except that as it turned out, everybody matched up well with somebody except me: Billy and Gary, Carol Lynn and Mickey, David and Bobby. And then there was me.

I was lonely at Nanny's house on Pleasant Avenue in the Toulminville neighborhood of Mobile. The area was becoming increasingly African American. The year was 1968, and black and white people did not socialize together back then, lest the white "Citizen's Council" come for a visit. But none of that made sense to me. Dad had always preached to treat all people, including black people, with respect. Besides, no one at Nanny's house wanted to play with me. So, I made friends with neighbors at Bragg Hill Apartments next door. This seemed too good to be true. They were nice neighbors, but I soon ran into trouble. I asked if my friends could come over and play. Nanny wanted to know who "my friends" were. I said they were from the apartment complex. Then she asked what color they were. Never once had color mattered before, so I said they were black. The answer was NO. I couldn't understand it. Nanny, who was still working for Toulminville-Warren Street United Methodist Church where most of the church members were now black, said no. "It isn't a good idea."

"Why?" I asked.

Her Answer, "Just because, end of discussion."

On this one, I lost the battle. Nanny was unyielding. She said it was best, even if I didn't understand it. It would be years before I realized this was reinforced racism caused not by belief on my grandmother's part, but by fear of retribution.

This meant "my friends" now consisted solely of family, none of whom wanted to play with me, Gary, in particular.

Gary, the youngest of the foster kids, was also the meanest. He didn't like me. He would do things for David & Bobby, but especially Billy. But for me, he would do nothing. Well, almost nothing; he did torment me. He even made up a song and sang it. Of course, it caught on with Bobby, David, and Billy too:

Rain, Rain, Come on Down
So, little ole Mikey will drown!

More than once, Nanny got on to him for being so cruel, but the more she did, the worse he got. He played a game with Bobby and David where if the coin he tossed came up heads, David would win. If it came up tails, Bobby would win. If it landed straight up and down, Mikey would win. Of course, I never won, except that one time when the coin landed in a crack in the floorboards on the back porch, landing straight up. I was elated, but Gary said that the floor had interfered with the coin and, therefore, was null and void. I was crushed. Gary was elated. Bobby won the prize on the next flip; a model pirate ship Gary had assembled.

But it wasn't just David and Bobby not wanting to play with me, nor Gary's hatred of me, but also Billy's determination to make my life a living hell. Since moving down from Georgia, Billy had become aggressive towards me, like I suppose most big brothers are to younger ones, though I do not remember him being that way to my younger brother David.

He tormented me nearly every day with few exceptions while living at Nanny Brill's home. First, he would catch me, then decide what my torture for that day might be. One day, it was eating dirt. The next day, he hit me until my shoulder was red, or slapped my face over and over again just to make me mad, or made my hair be in knots. Later in life, I asked him why he was so mean to me. He said, "You were so funny when you were angry." In essence, he enjoyed watching the show. This happened nearly every day until I found relief through my radio.

Saved By the Braves!

Living at Nanny Brill's house did not allow me to make friends. Loss is a terrible thing. Loneliness, its companion, is also terrible. Such was my life in the fall of 1968 until we left in the fall of 1970.

But something magical happened that first Christmas after Mom died. Santa Claus (Dad, who was feeling guilty for being away with so much traveling) bought me a four-band radio that let me listen to stations far away, while sitting in my little private bedroom.

In that room, with ribbons from Mom's funeral on display, I learned that after dark when many stations signed off the air, I could pick up new signals from faraway places. I was transported far from Nanny's house to places like Havana, Cuba, which came through on the Cuban National Radio Station loud and clear. While I couldn't understand what they said, I enjoyed the up-tempo music. Sometimes, they spoke English to help Americans better understand them and explained how we were an "imperialist nation." Soon, though, I discovered English-speaking stations in exotic places like St. Louis, Cincinnati, and New York. I decided that one day I would go to all these places. Maybe Aunt Julie could join me in seeing them? I told her all about it when I saw her next shortly after Christmas. She was thrilled just to hear from me, but her face lit up when I mentioned New York, New York!

Eventually I learned how to find specific stations like KMOX in St. Louis or WWL in New Orleans. These places seemed exotic and far removed from the dull and depressing life at The Big House. Before long I located the station in Nashville that carried the Grand Ole Opry. Back then I didn't like country music, but this radio show was different because, between acts, they aired the funniest and dumbest commercials I had ever heard. During this learning process, I found stations from Des Moines, San Antonio, Pittsburgh, Chicago, and Miami.

Life got harder the longer I stayed at Nanny Brill's. Gary and Billy were unbearable, so I had to figure out how not to get picked on, at least as much. In the spring of '69, I found WUNI, a local station that carried the Braves. The year before, the station carried the St. Louis Cardinals. But when the Braves moved down from Milwaukee, they decided to air the team closest to Mobile, Alabama.

Baseball has a very long season with 162 games. I religiously followed MY team during the year on my radio. Since I had no companions my age, I adopted the Atlanta Braves as my new friends. During the summer, I was allowed to listen late at night. When the Braves went to Houston or St. Louis, the games started on our time, Central Time. When they went east, it started and ended an hour earlier. But West Coast trips began and finished 2 hours later. This was a problem, especially for Nanny, as her room abutted mine. She demanded that I turn off the radio by 11 pm at the latest. I turned it down, but she could still hear it. She made me sleep on the floor in her room without my radio several times.

In 1969, the Braves won the West Division with Phil Niekro, the knuckleballer, who won 23 games that year. He was my hero. Later in life, I saw him get career wins #298 and #299 with the Yankees. Disappointingly, he won #300 away from New York, where I was living and working at that time. He was later inducted into the Baseball Hall of Fame and is remembered as one of the greatest knuckleball pitchers ever.

When not listening to the Braves, I played Monopoly with Mickey, Carol Lynn, David, and Bobby, but it wasn't much fun as I lost most of the time. Sometimes, when invited, I rode my bike with Bobby and David to Crichton, a nearby neighborhood. But I was slower than either of them. Bobby and David liked to "jump the curb," but I usually didn't try, afraid I would fall. But one day, on the way home from Hart's Fried Chicken where we each bought 5-cent biscuits, I got up the courage, jumped the curb ... and busted my tire. Bobby and David left me and I had to walk my bike back two miles by myself. Needless to say, I wasn't invited on any more runs to Hart's Fried Chicken. Thus, most of the time, I was alone.

Remembering Aunt Julie's lessons on imagination helped me cope with loneliness.

But death was my real companion. My room was still filled with the funeral ribbons a year after Mom's death, and Nanny encouraged me to depart with them many times. Each time, I refused. One day, while traversing the five acres of Nanny's property, I came across a dead bird. I thought, "How sad," that the bird had no one to bury it. I asked Nanny for a box and buried it in her rose garden. Nanny said she thought that was sweet of me. So, a few days later, when I came across a stray cat that had been hit and killed by a car, I buried it in the garden, too. Over the summer, my pet cemetery grew. Nanny became increasingly concerned about my obsession with death and finally declared the pet cemetery full and closed to new additions.

This illustrates just how close to the edge I really was. The Braves gave me hope, but my life had fallen into a kind of macabre rhythm. By late summer/early fall, something broke the rhythm of my existence: A storm was coming, a big storm.

The Storm's a 'Comin!

Luckily, I had my four-band radio, which was not your little hand-held one either. It had an antenna that could be pulled up or put back down when not in use. It could also run on batteries or be plugged in. During the summer of Hurricane Camille, it became one of our family's most important tools during hurricane season. Mobile, Alabama had been fortunate that no hurricane had made landfall since the devastating 1926 storm.

The storm brewing off the Atlantic Ocean came just in time to re-occupy my mind, given Nanny's injunction against new graves in the pet cemetery. She declared it full in early August. A few days later, the National Weather Service out of Coral Gables, Florida began reporting that a tropical wave had formed 800 miles from the Caribbean islands, which lay due west. Most people didn't think much about the storm at the time, but Nanny Brill did. She was concerned from the first report. She said, "The Storm's a 'Comin' 'cause I can feel it in my bones."

Her proclamation interested me and made me curious: how did she know the storm was coming to Mobile?

Each day the following week, Nanny tracked the storm's movement as it approached the Caribbean Islands. The storm was named Camille and tracked just south of Haiti as a tropical storm, not yet a hurricane. Next, it hit Grand Cayman before moving north. Up to this point, people in the northern Gulf Coast were mildly concerned, but it was still hundreds of miles away. Often storms on this track hit the islands and then move westerly, hitting Mexico or southern Texas. Many assumed it would do the same this time.

Camille achieved hurricane status west of the Cayman Islands on August 14 and rapidly gained strength as it clipped the western end of Cuba. As Camille crossed over into the Gulf of Mexico from the Caribbean Sea, the family grew increasingly anxious. Weather reporters from WUNI-Mobile, where I listened to the Braves that summer, broke into games to give updates about where Camille might be heading, announcing she was a threat to become the worst hurricane ever to hit the United States.

On August 16[th,] the storm became a category 5 hurricane, the highest classification on the Saffir-Simpson hurricane scale. Panic set in all along the Gulf Coast from Pensacola, Florida to New Orleans, Louisiana, for she had already become a killer storm and was moving towards warmer, open waters where hurricanes thrive.

During the day, a reconnaissance plane flew into the eye of the storm and clocked winds at more than 200 miles an hour with a barometric pressure of 26.61 millibars and heading down. With these readings, Camille would be the strongest, potentially most dangerous storm ever to hit the United States. As Camille approached the coast, we transformed The Big House into a Central Command Center, bringing supplies for the invasion. Someone asked me if the windows were boarded up too? The answer was no because they were over 8 feet tall with 140-year-old leaded glass. Also, the windows had shutters for just this reason. They had survived before, and they would again. At least, that is what Daddy and Nanny Brill hoped. Bathtubs were filled with water, and batteries were bought for my radio, candles and matches ready for when power was lost.

Aunt Beverly, Daddy, and Nanny Brill debated whether to stay or leave. After much discussion, they decided to "ride it out" as it could come ashore anywhere along the upper Gulf Coast. They figured the Big House had lasted over 140 years as of 1969 and had endured hurricanes before. She would make it through this time as well. We children thought this was a grand plan as it had a party-like atmosphere as we waited for the storm to choose who to devour. We failed to understand the magnitude of what was about to happen. On the morning of August 17, she lay just 250 miles south of Mobile Bay. It was increasingly likely that she would choose the port city as her entry point.

Nanny and I had been following the storm every day. The storm updates were important to me before, after, and, if necessary, during the Braves games. The Braves and Philadelphia were playing when the power went off. The adults heard me listening to the game on WSB out of Atlanta after our local station went off the air. They made me forfeit my radio for the greater good. (Incidentally, the Braves lost 6-0 to the Philadelphia Phillies that day in one of the lowest-attended games, with fewer than 10,000 people in the stands.) But alas, I digress, the radio proved vital as all local stations were knocked off the air due to the storm. The adults relied on reports from WWL in New Orleans and WSB in Atlanta for updates.

By evening, Mobile and all the upper Gulf Coast felt the first of Camille's outer bands. Each hour, they increased, growing stronger and stronger.

At one point Nanny and Dad lamented their choice to stay and feared the house might implode due to the declining barometric pressure, the second lowest recorded for any hurricane to hit the United States. Only the Labor Day Storm of 1935 had a lower pressure. We kids watched out the big windows through the cracks in the shutters as Nanny's beloved two-acre Pecan Tree Orchard bent to and fro, with branches sometimes reaching all the way to the ground. Winds howled, the house shook, and the adults prayed that we might be spared.

Ultimately, Mobile was spared the worst of the hurricane, but Camille was a deadly destructive storm, taking 256 lives with over 5 billion dollars in property damage.

While we missed the brunt of the storm, we had over 6 feet of flood water from Three Mile Creek in the backyard and up into the Small House where Aunt Beverly and her kids lived. All the boys swam in the water the next morning, including me, until I climbed on a fallen tree limb, joining three snakes already perched there. I decided then and there that maybe swimming in flood water wasn't such a good idea (Billy & Gary's). Nanny was most displeased and hoped that none of us had gotten infected with hepatitis!!! Fortunately, we didn't.

Finally, Camille did one good thing. The Pet Cemetery was washed away in the storm and never returned. The storm proved a perfect metaphor for my life to that point: a path of destruction and misery wherever I went.

CHAPTER 4

New Life

"If anyone is in Christ, he/she is a new creation..."
(2 Corinthians 5:17, New King James Version)

Change is Inevitable

We learned that change is inevitable in 1969 when Dad started dating again. We were all opposed. The first woman he brought home for us to meet faced immediate resistance. But we knew it was unrealistic to believe Dad would remain single with four kids at home. Carol Lynn was rapidly becoming a woman and now wanted to be called Carol. She needed a woman to guide her through this period of her life. Billy was becoming increasingly complex for Dad to handle alone. Little Billy, as the family called him, had fallen under the influence of Gary, which was not a good thing. Dad always had a soft spot for him, so having another adult might help with discipline.

In our own grief, we never stopped to consider how lonely Dad was. We never stopped to consider how sad he must be. We never stopped to think about what life should be like for him going forward. We were kids more concerned with our needs than his.

Daddy was a young man in the prime of his life. Back then, he seemed old to us, but he wasn't really; he was only in his early 30s. He was away a great deal of the time because of his sales rep job, as it was his best shot to get ahead. It also gave him a little freedom to be a young man. He had sexual desires like everyone, and being away from us kids provided him an opportunity to "test the waters." After searching for a while, he decided it was time to start looking for a woman to spend his life with, after Mom.

Dad was the most democratic parent imaginable. He realized that if a relationship was going to succeed, he needed the buy-in of his children and the woman's children, if she had any. Dad brought anyone he was seriously considering home to meet us. He dated all lovely women. Most were very sweet and motherly, and thus, we rejected them. One was too nice; we didn't trust her. Another was too motherly, which we didn't like, so we rejected her as well. Another wasn't pretty enough, and Dad rejected her. After all, he had some say in who he would marry.

Sometime later that year, Dad introduced us to Ruby Whigham, a woman he had known at Murphy High School—the same school both my parents had attended and where Carol was now a freshman.

We were all wary of "this new woman" at first, but she was kind, had three daughters herself, and Dad seemed to like her very much. Carol and Billy expressed an early positive opinion because she was hip. Slowly, I warmed up to the idea that Carl William Brill and Ruby Dell Whigham might marry. I knew that living at Nanny's house was not pleasant for me, but I didn't have any idea what life would be like with more people in it.

Dad and Ruby were married on September 4, 1970, one day after my 13th birthday. That meant moving again.

We celebrated their wedding by decorating Dad's white car with shoe polish. We didn't realize how difficult it was going to be to get it off until AFTER the wedding and honeymoon. But we soon learned it takes a whole lot of "elbow grease."

Dad seemed happy for the first time in a long time. Carol was glad for Dad, but was not pleased about losing her beloved Murphy High for the less prestigious B.C. Rain High. Billy, likewise, had voted for Ruby but wasn't happy with her rules. David was fine. And I guess the real question was, how was I? I was pleased that Daddy was delighted. I was happy to be leaving Nanny's house, but I wasn't happy, period. I wasn't sure about Ruby. She seemed nice enough, but she wasn't Mom. I didn't want to forget my REAL Mother. Soon after the wedding, Ruby showed us she was tough, but I liked her. And I liked her girls, Renae and DiAnne. They were friendly, but I didn't know how to act around them. I remember going to a Mardi Gras parade early on with "the whole family" and holding Renae's and DiAnne's hands the whole time. They were nice about it, but I heard them later telling Ruby how annoying I was. Ruby asked them to be patient, but it was clear neither was happy about the whole ordeal. We were 1-3 years apart in age, but I was light-years behind them in social skills. If one were to rate my chance of success on that New Year's Eve in 1970, it would still have been an uncertain future for an uncertain life.

"Down The Bay"

Ruby and Bill were married right at the start of the 1970 school year. This meant moving from north Mobile's Toulminville area to "Down the Bay," off Dauphin Island Parkway, south of I-65, all the way to Hollinger's Island Bridge with Mobile Bay to the east and Dog River to the west, near Uncle Bud's Brill IGA grocery store.

Carol was very upset about changing high schools and cried a lot. And it didn't take Billy long to express his opinion that the marriage was a mistake. DiAnne and Renae weren't pleased with their new pesty little brother. Still, we all moved into a rental house in Gulfdale, a neighborhood entered by Brill Road. We thought we were somebody special because we had a road named after us. But the home was small for six kids and two adults, about 1,600 sq ft, with three small bedrooms, one bathroom, a kitchen, and a living room.

I hadn't shared a bedroom for two years. It was tough to bunk with David and Billy again, especially since Billy was meaner now. He ruled the room.

Carol found herself sharing a room with her two new sisters, something she had never done before. Maybe it was just my imagination, but it seemed like the girls needed more space to co-exist.

Renae and Carol were rivals of a sort from the beginning. Carol loved Murphy High, which had an excellent reputation, whereas B.C. Rain High, our new school, was known as an underperforming school for poor kids. Carol, an outstanding student with lots of friends, had been thriving at Murphy High. But now she was starting over at a new, less prestigious school where she didn't know anybody. Renae was her age, but the opposite in nearly every way. Oh, Renae was brilliant like Carol, but that wasn't her primary concern or interest. She was a cheerleader and very popular. Ultimately, B.C. Rain High proved to be suitable for Carol, too, maybe not as good as a more academically challenging school would have been, but she was on the Scholar's Bowl

Team her first year and made the Honor Roll ALL THE TIME. By the way, she is the only one in the family to earn a Doctorate.

Still in elementary school, David excelled in science and showed a particular interest in the planets and photography. He was and is very bright, the smartest among us. He is Mensa smart. (Mensa membership requires members to be in the 98th percentile or higher on standardized, supervised IQ or other approved intelligence tests.) He was also very quiet and never seemed to get into trouble with our parents or, more importantly, with Billy. That was a feat in and of itself.

But in DiAnne, I found an ally. She also struggled with school, was not outstanding in sports, and was not a cheerleader. What she lacked in those areas, she made up for with the most wonderful ability to provide emotional support and encouragement to people. I decided I liked her the best of all my siblings.

For me, B.C. Rain High School was a dream come true. I went to high school in the 7th grade! How cool is that? No other high school in the Mobile County Public School system had grades 7-12. But attendance hadn't been high enough to warrant a standalone middle school "down the parkway," though one was planned and in the works. So, there I was in high school. I loved it. My attendance at Rain was an embarrassment to the rest of my siblings, except David, who was still in elementary school. This showed up particularly in gym class, where I was picked last for teams and often picked on.

Renae only tolerated me at school because Ruby leaned on her to do so. She unknowingly provided me with my first sex education lesson. All my male friends thought she was "hot." They kept asking me how I could sleep at night with such a good-looking sister in the next room. I thought that was gross! I had never even thought of sex with anyone, much less my sister. "That is just sick," I tell you, "Just sick."

Several of the guys realized I didn't fully understand what they were talking about, so they showed me pornographic magazines of naked women to help me grasp the nature of their problem. They said they would always have a "hard-on" if she were their sister. These pictures seemed dirty to me. Still, I protested. Renae is my sister. Brothers don't have sex with sisters. This confounded them. They didn't understand why she didn't turn me on.

But there were several bonuses to having Renae as a sister. For one, she was tough like her mother and took no crap off anyone, including anyone picking on me. Second, she was very popular. That helped, at least a little. Third, she always had the best-looking boyfriends.

First Crushes, Who Knew?

I'm a late bloomer and have been my whole life, puberty included. Shortly after moving in with our new sisters, something extraordinary happened to me. Renae brought her boyfriend(s) home. One caught my interest: George, a junior and star of the football and basketball teams. During basketball season, Rain High School went to the regional finals to play Blount High. We lost in triple overtime, and I cried for hours at the injustice of it all. George played well! He was my hero. We should have been going to the state championships. But alas, we were not. I was inconsolable. My hero had lost.

My stepmother lost patience with all my crying and told me to get over it. Secretly, she must have wondered if I might be unable to adjust to this new living arrangement; not that they could have done anything about it, since there were no extra resources to be found. (I wouldn't learn these facts for another six years). However, I did stop crying lest Ruby "give me something to cry about."

George came over often, and I always found a way to stay around them. He was kind about it and probably taken aback by having someone so young look up to him so much. And boy, did I look up to him. At this time in my development, I had no idea what was happening inside of me whenever he came around. Renae, on the other hand, didn't care what was happening to me inside or out. I was ruining her time with HER boyfriend. She complained to Ruby, who made me "go outside and play" whenever he came around. However, I usually managed to see him before he left the house.

At or near this time, Ruby, whom I started to refer to as Mom in 1971, gave me my one and only parent sex education lesson: "Any boy can jump into any girl's pants," she told me one day when it was just us, but "you should only do it after you are in love and are married to that girl." To say I was confused is an understatement. I didn't know anything about "jumping into a girl's pants," and believe me, I didn't want to. That sounded totally disgusting to me.

Confused by Ruby/Mom's instructions, I asked my guy friends in Gulfdale to explain what she had been trying to tell me. Frank, a boy down the street who was nearly as socially awkward as I was, met me clandestinely at the park to show me graphic pictures of men having sex with women. Earlier, I thought photos of naked women were bad, but these were worse, totally disgusting, and I ran home immediately.

On the other hand, I couldn't get George off my mind. Sometime later, probably after he graduated the following year, he and Renae broke up. I was brokenhearted because he stopped coming over. Soon, though, she was dating William, another good-looking man.

William was a senior in my freshman year and was selected for the Homecoming Court, as was Renae. Like her earlier boyfriend, I found myself admiring his handsomeness. He was friendly, strong, masculine, and kind. William and I once discussed how beautiful women were (like Renae) and, in contrast, William said, men are ugly. I officially agreed, but deep down, I felt he was wrong. I held this secret for years.

It did not dawn on me until years later that I had a crush on these guys as severely as any teenage girl would have on the captain of the football team or a straight guy would have on the head cheerleader.

Rev. Mel White wrote eloquently about this in *Stranger at the Gate: To Be Gay & Christian in America*. To paraphrase, he said that we are attracted to whomever we are attracted to. That is not a choice. How we choose to respond to that attraction is a choice. There is a reason advocacy groups use the initials LGBTQIA+. Sexuality takes many forms: Straight, Lesbian, Gay, Bisexual, Transgender, Queer, Questioning, Intersexed, Asexual, etc. I believe that a person should be free to love whomever they love. If society doesn't grant that fundamental freedom, then we are not truly free!

Methodist vs. Baptist

One of the most significant changes in our lives due to Dad's remarriage was Ruby's insistence that we go to church every Sunday. Before the marriage, we went with Dad to Westside United Methodist Church, but we could often talk him out of making us go. David and I were confirmed into the Methodist Church in 1969.

Once married, Dad and Ruby had to decide which church to attend. We Brills were raised Methodist, but the Whighams were raised Baptist. As head of the family, Dad set the rules that we would live by. As a democratic sort, he called the family council together to vote on which church to attend. The Whighams favored the Baptist Church, which had the most youth. But the Brills favored the Methodist Church. We voted, and Methodist won 4-3 because Dad, the judge, recused himself.

We started attending South Brookley United Methodist Church. All was going well until I got into a fight with my Sunday School Teacher over the nature of hell. She said there was no literal hell. I told her, "There is a hell!"

I came home mad from church and asked for a revote. I flipped to the Baptist. Now, the vote was 4-3 in favor of the Baptist Church. My swing vote was another blow in my relationship with my father, a lifelong, though not active, Methodist.

Thus, with that one democratic vote, we became Southern Baptists and began attending Riverside Baptist Church. My brothers and sisters were as happy as they could be attending *any* church. Billy didn't care if it was Baptist or Methodist; it was still church. Renae, DiAnne, and Carol were smart enough to go along, but were never very involved in activities like the youth group. For me and later David, it gave us a whole new avenue in which to develop friendships.

Riverside Baptist was the strongest and most significant church on the parkway. What I didn't know was what else came with the change. Mother made us attend Sunday School and Sunday Night Worship (The Methodist Church didn't have Sunday night services). Plus, if she liked the Evangelist for Revival Meetings (Methodists didn't have those very often either, whereas Baptists usually had two a year), we also had to go to those meetings.

This particular year, January 1971, we had a visiting preacher from Arkansas, Rev. Jack Hazelwood. At Sunday dinner, Mother announced that we had to attend this year's revival meeting because "he was the one who would inspire us young people to God." With moans and groans, Carol, Billy, DiAnne, and Renae complained that this was too much to be expected. Mother was unrelenting, adding, "It will do us all good to go." She was right about the preacher. He was unlike any I had ever heard before. He was a crazy man. He was bold, young, handsome, and brash. I liked him. It wasn't just me either. Slowly, he won over the youth, and attendance climbed each night, which is unusual for a revival. By the end of the revival, the sanctuary was filled. However, my siblings weren't impressed. They were there by order of Ruby/Mother. I first heard Marsha Stevens-Pino's song "For Those Tears I Died" at this revival. It spoke to me. I wouldn't know it then, but eventually, our paths would cross, and she and I would become friends.

The revival started on a Sunday morning and lasted until the following Saturday evening. During this revival, I began to fall "under conviction" that I needed to accept Christ as my Savior. This built each night, getting stronger and stronger. During the last service, I was white-knuckled, holding on to the pew as hard as I could, waiting out all the verses of "Just as I am," and there are a lot of them, believe me. I thought about the evangelist's last sermon that night and all the following week. I contemplated Brother Jack's words of hope in Christ. I thought about my life. I thought about my need for forgiveness and Jesus' promise to be a friend in times of need or when I strayed. The following Sunday, after enduring a week of conviction, I went forward and accepted Christ as my Savior. At that moment, I became a Baptist and a Christian.

It was yet another dramatic event in my life and my family's life. Dad, not given to much religion, did not take well to my conversion. For him, it was yet another betrayal of our family's historical faith. It was also a serious point of contention between Ruby and Bill. But Dad, true to his word, allowed the family to continue attending the Baptist Church because he was the only one who wanted to go back to South Brookley UMC.

My relationship with Dad became even more strained. He had gone along with attending the Baptist Church, but wasn't pleased with my decision to join it. My dad was a lifelong Methodist, and his brother Donald was a Methodist minister. But I did join, and our relationship hit another new low. It remained so for years.

Riverside had a young, dynamic pastor in Dr. Jerry Oswalt. He was the pastor when I came forward after the revival. Most importantly to me, the church had a vibrant youth group with activities I could attend.

I remember the first time I attended the youth group. Ruby drove me in her 1965 Chevrolet Impala. We entered through a different entrance because we had just moved to our own home, a $3,000 fixer-upper. I was fine until it was time to get out of the car, then I froze. But with Ruby's persuasion, I finally got out, and she drove away. Suddenly, I heard a man I didn't know ask me if I wanted to shake the hand that shook Jesse James' hand. Timidly, I held out my hand, and he instead pulled me to him and gave me a big BEAR hug. He introduced himself as Brother E, and a lasting friendship began with that introduction. I had found a group to which I could belong. He only had a third-grade education, but a heart as big as Texas. I was hooked from that day forward on the youth group.

Soon, I became concerned that maybe I wasn't really saved. I was still the same boy before I accepted Christ. I didn't feel different. I didn't act differently. I didn't look different. After a few months, I decided, following a sermon on the Rapture, that I needed to be saved again lest I be left behind when Jesus returned. I walked the aisle again.

The following Sunday, and many Sundays after, I went forward accepting Christ over and over again. Baptist Theology doesn't hold that a person loses their salvation from week to week, as implied by Mom's mother (my third Grandmother, Church of the Nazarene). Baptists are "once saved, always saved people."

One Sunday evening service, after many weeks of accepting Christ, Dad, embarrassed by my repeated trips to the altar, begged me, "Please don't accept Christ again tonight."

I didn't, but I was worried that I might be headed for hell or left behind in The Rapture should Jesus' return happen before I died. (Evangelicals often preach about the Rapture, but not much on the first seven chapters of the book of Revelation. Those seven chapters are clear in their message: Be faithful until the end. It just doesn't have the same punch as cars crashing into one another as God's faithful go to heaven, leaving the sinners behind.) As a youth, these sermons scared the hell out of me. Ruby/Mother decided it was time for a "Come to Jesus Meeting" after the service.

She was kind but forceful in asking me questions that made me think about my faith. She asked me if I believed that Jesus was God's son.

"Yes!"

She asked if I had asked God to come into my life.

I said, "Yes" again.

She asked me, "Is God trustworthy to do what he says he will?"

"Yes."

Then she paused before asking me her last question, "Have you done what God asked you to do?"

"Yes."

Then she knocked it out of the park: "Either you trust God, or you don't."

With that, bawling my eyes out, I finally came to accept that God LOVED ME! Sure, I had done bad things, but the Bible said that if we ask God to forgive us, he would. I had asked for forgiveness for my evil ways: lying, getting into fights with my brothers, particularly Billy, and being angry. And for not trusting God to forgive me. That is what grace is - God's unmerited favor! I realized that God had forgiven me the first time I asked. And God did that because GOD loved me and would always love me no matter what I did (as Brother Jack had preached, God would love me even when I strayed); that is the promise of salvation made possible by Jesus' resurrection. That night, I changed. And that night, I was changed, changed for good. In the Tony Award-winning Broadway Show *Wicked,* there is a song that ends with these words:

Who can say if I've been changed for the better?
I do believe I have changed for the better,
and because I knew you, I have been changed for good!

"For Good," by Stephen Schwartz.

That night, I knew without a doubt that I was loved by God, regardless of my past, my backwardness, my failures, or what anybody else thought of me. Because I knew Christ, I realized the God of All Creation loved me. With that knowledge, I was changed for good.

Integration to Graduation

The Federal Government finally enforced desegregation in Mobile, Alabama public schools for the first time in the 1971-1972 school year. We were the last major city in the southern United States to adopt this measure. All around us, families were pulling their children out of the public school system and enrolling them in new Christian Schools, including a new school at the second-largest Baptist Church on Dauphin Island Parkway. My parents would have nothing to do with a segregationist Christian School. But the tradeoff was that David and I would be bused to a black part of town near Williamson High School, not far from Nanny Shaw's home. (With students now being bused to Rain High, 7th and 8th graders no longer attended Rain, so we went to Middle School.)

My parents were comfortable with David and me being bused because Bill Gunter, the former assistant principal at Rain High School, had been promoted to principal at George Hall Middle School, where we would now attend. Hall was built as an elementary school, so it wasn't appropriate for middle schoolers. For instance, it had bathrooms at the back of each class. It was different but proved doable.

What I learned about integration was that economic class played a significant role in determining who got bused and who didn't. Wealthier white schools had black students bused to them, while poorer white kids were bused to black ones. Therefore, David and I were bused to Hall Middle School. However, it was only a slight change. In my 7th-grade year, the school (Rain) was 70% white and 30% black. It was the only significantly integrated school in the Mobile Public School System back then, before mandatory integration. After busing began, Rain High became 60% white and 40% black, which is not much of a difference. Why was that? It had to do with economics. If you were poor enough, you already lived in an interracial community. The population "down the bay" had been racially integrated for years because it was a poorer part of town where housing was more affordable.

Integration was happening throughout the country at this time. In many areas, as black families moved into better white neighborhoods, many middle- and upper-class white families moved into more predominantly white areas. This was known as "white flight." But down the bay, we didn't have much of that happening.

Neither David nor I had ever attended a school where white kids were the minority until we went to George Hall Middle School, where we were now being bussed. The school was about 55% black and 45% white. It was a rough neighborhood, and the worst fights I ever saw happened at this school. I remember two girls going at it harder than any fight Billy ever got into, which were sometimes brutal. Mr. Gunter waded in to break up the fight, and one of the girls slugged the hell out of him. But he was not one to back down, and with help, he subdued the girls who were later expelled from George Hall.

But some good things happened to me at Hall Middle School. For one, I was now a Christian, and both black and white kids respected my strong faith. And at Hall, I won my first race for student government. I think it was the first time I had ever won anything.

With Nanny Shaw

I still missed Rain High but tried hard to make the best of it. I even tried one last sport to make Dad proud of me, track. Surprisingly, I was good at it. The coach said I had the body of a long-distance runner. At that point, I probably weighed 100 pounds soaking wet and was not much over 5'4". But I had strong legs, so I was assigned to run the mile. It was the first sport where I actually had some talent, and it didn't require coordination.

Since birth, the left side of my body has always been more coordinated than my right. But with running, you just run. In fact, racing in the Southeastern Relays that year, the largest and most prestigious meet in the county, I came in 3rd place for the mile in my age group! But Dad never came to see a track meet, including that one. After the season was over, I quit. I was hurt that nothing I did ever impressed him. Angry, I decided then that I was done with sports.

The following year, I returned to Rain High School. Mr. Gunter had been promoted again, this time to Principal at Rain High. As a result, he was my assistant principal or principal from grades 7 through 12.

Now a true freshman, my teachers wanted to know if I was like my sisters or like my brother. Billy was blazing a trail of destruction in his wake as I returned to B.C. Rain High. Carol and Renae, on the other hand, were now juniors. Carol was an honor student with her sights on college. Renae was the head cheerleader, homecoming queen, and the most popular girl in school. Their rivalry continued, but never really got ugly. They were just on different paths. So, who was I the most like?

The truth is, I wasn't like any of them. I never got in trouble as the good Christian I was trying hard to be, nor was I nearly as popular or brilliant as Renae or Carol. I was closer to DiAnne than the others. But I was happy to be myself and back at Rain High School. Having made it this far was exciting!

As high school continued, life became better for me. I started to gain confidence, was elected to the Student Council, and led "Prayer Around the Flagpole," the first Christian Student Movement in public schools. It was then that I got into some trouble, this time with our Church Deacon Board.

The students at the Flagpole were from several different churches, including both black and white kids, which was new for most of us in the South. One day, a fellow student and youth leader at the Black Baptist Church, Ramona, approached me about our youth groups meeting up. I thought this was a terrific idea, but I told her I had to get approval from our Deacon Board. My Uncle Earl was the head of the Deacons, and I made my pitch at their next meeting. The Deacon Board resoundingly concluded it was a bad idea. I couldn't understand it. "God loves all people, right?"

"Yes," they responded.

"Then why is it not a good idea to meet our fellow Baptist Christians from down the street?" I wanted to know.

"It just isn't."

I protested but lost. That day, I learned that just because people or organizations say, "I love you," "you are welcome here," or "all people are to be treated equally," it doesn't always mean that's what they truly feel.

I reported back to Ramona that my request had been denied. She replied, "Bless your heart, Mike. You are trying, but you just don't get it, do you?"

This frustrated me because I was trying. But she was right. I didn't understand how deep-seated systemic racism and discrimination really were.

The day I finally came out, her words echoed in my head as another "ah ha" moment. Some 21 years later, in September 1997, I realized the truth of what she had been saying. I, now a member of a discriminated minority group, with nothing I could do to change it, was hated and/or feared simply for being who I am.

While in High School, I wanted to share God's love with the world. I didn't want to "just talk a good game" but actually to show love to others. I found a way to do that by joining a club called "Friends of Exceptional Children," a group dedicated to helping special needs children with activities designed specifically for them. To help accomplish this, we held fundraisers, which I threw myself into wholeheartedly. During one fundraiser, I sold 54 dozen boxes of Krispy Kreme Doughnuts, more than the rest of the group combined. I was beginning to thrive being back at Rain.

Meanwhile, our family was still struggling. I could write so much more, but let me summarize by saying our family was almost always in chaos. Billy eventually left home in the middle of 11th grade for the Army after admitting he was drinking and taking drugs. My mom's oldest daughter, Debbie, moved back to Mobile with her husband and oldest child. She had a second child who died a few days after birth, which crushed her and rocked the family. Shortly before her marriage fell apart, she had another child, Ashley. This was also a difficult chapter in our family's life, as Debbie and Mom would fight for years over Ashley's custody.

Dad and Mom disagreed about girls going to college. Carol went anyway, but the fight between my parents was intense.

My relationship with Dad did not improve, taking another hit when I accepted a call into the ministry.

Somewhere along the way, I was told that most people only use 10% of their brains. Ironically, that gave me hope because I decided I would have to use more than 10% of mine to get through. This is now considered a myth, but it inspired me to work harder and accomplish more.

My faith in Christ became my anchor in the midst of troubled seas as the wild waves of unrest, drugs, alcohol, accusations of favoritism, anger, disappointment, and death buffeted us. My faith saved me, well, not really my faith, but God's Spirit watching over me and guiding me through these treacherous, uncertain waters.

My future at this point was still uncertain, but at least I saw the possibility of something good happening. My life had noticeably improved since my salvation.

65 on 65

I was a "keeper of the rules" kind of guy. In my first year at Mobile College (more on that later), I prided myself on obeying the rules. This had been my mode of operation since the middle of High School. So, when I was driving on I-65, and the speed limit was 65, I drove 65 mph in the fast lane. I did this because I thought I was "keeping people from sinning." I received confirmation that this was not well-received. Several drivers gave me the finger. Others yelled at me. It took a while before I realized that I was causing more sins by blocking the flow of traffic on the interstate.

This simple story illustrates my High School and early College years as the keeper of the rules. During High School, as I've indicated, I became very active in the life of the Church. Then, in the middle of those high school years, I felt God moving in my life. I was pretty freaked out about it. What would people think? Does God really talk to people? I had a lot of questions and sought help from our youth minister, Rev. Cecil Dees, and learned about "being called into ministry."

I didn't want to be a preacher. I fancied myself as an attorney. But here I was being called with what I understood at the time were three choices: Minister of Music. I couldn't be that because of my limited musical ability. Second was a missionary. I didn't think I would like or do well living in a hut in India or Africa.

The last one was "a preacher" because I could talk. Lord knows I could speak, ask my brothers and sisters. It seemed the best fit. In consultation with our youth minister and then the pastor, I learned to "wait upon the Lord in prayer." I did, asking God to direct my life and lead me where he wanted me to go. At this time, I didn't understand The Spirit's nudging or "walking by faith." After months of waiting and struggle, I told the Church I thought God was asking me to be a preacher. That public testimony was another "ah ha" moment in my life. I had no idea what this calling meant at the time, but I was willing to follow. Dad wasn't thrilled. But with that decision, my life took off like a rocket ship.

I preached my first sermon at the Mobile Rescue Mission. I think it was ten minutes or less. Still, it was the beginning of my calling.

My growing faith wrapped me in a cocoon of peace and contentment. I met Betsy at the first revival I preached at East Borrow Baptist Church near Talladega, Alabama. We started dating that summer, beginning what would become a long and painful courtship. At the time, though, I interpreted it as God's answer to my prayers.

This section started with a story of me "keeping the rules." I was a good rule keeper: Do not dance, check. Do not curse, check. Do not smoke, check. Do not drink or take drugs, check. Do not have sex until married, check. Do not gossip, well, I still had some work to do on that one, but mostly check. Do not lie, check. Obey all other rules, check.

This last one caused the most grief to others. I was trying so hard to be good that I became intolerant of others who were less so. All my siblings will attest to that.

As proof, I can tell you how many times, after my conversion, I got in trouble with Mom; exactly twice. Once, I was 15 minutes late for curfew, but I wasn't driving. Still, being late was late to my mother, and I was grounded for a week. Mother said I could have called her, and she would have picked me up from the party. I would have died if she had done that. But still, I had broken the rule, and punishment was the cost. The second time I was so angry at Dad, I cursed him. It was the only time he ever hit me, backhanding me hard across the face, leaving a red mark. My mother told me how disappointed she was in me and how I should have known by now how to respect my father. If I disagree with him, I should pray for him. But he was so darn aggravating sometimes that I just lost my temper. I told Mother I was sorry for letting her and God down in both instances.

I did everything asked of me by Mom and Dad, even when I felt it was unfair. Dad regularly assigned me chores (but not the others) nearly every week before he left town, as he was gone Monday through Friday. That seemed unfair to me. One day, I finally asked him why. He said because I didn't fight him on it and just did it. I was both mad and proud:

mad because it was unfair treatment and proud that I was such a good son, even if he didn't particularly like me. He had been disappointed in me forever, it seemed.

Looking back, I realize I inadvertently did more to dissuade my siblings and others than to encourage them in their faith. Nobody likes "a know-it-all" and a "self-righteous goody-two-shoes." That was me. I now realize I "missed the mark" and caused many bad attitudes, thus "sins," through my self-righteousness.

Mike's Got a Secret

By my sophomore year, my crushes on George and William had passed, and I started dating girls, often double-dating with Jesse, my best friend. But I was uncomfortable with Jesse's aggressiveness on dates. I suppose he acted like most other red-blooded straight American males. On dates, he kissed, pawed, and tried getting by with as much as possible without getting in trouble. I thought he was being bad and prided myself on being restrained. Jesse was concerned with my "inability to perform in the kissing department." He told me that I needed to "get with it" if I didn't want to be 30 and not know how to do it properly.

That summer, I kept dating girls, sometimes double-dating with Jesse, but mostly not. Betsy, from north Alabama, was the most promising. But I dated a lot that year: Diana, Jolene, Jeanette, Karen, Nonie (before Jesse got serious with her), Julie, and Vickie, among others (names from my prayer journals).

But during the summer between my sophomore and junior year, I made a fatal mistake with Jesse, who was two years older than me and had just graduated. We were on a mission trip to West Virginia. We were all bunking on the floor of a community center building somewhere. I went looking for him and found him sleeping. He was wearing bib overalls with nothing underneath, with the flap way down past his naval, showing just a bit of hair between his naval and private parts. I snapped a picture; he awoke very angry at me for doing that. I apologized, of course, but I knew deep down that I had done a VERY BAD thing.... maybe the worst thing. Why had I taken his picture?

As the good little preacher man (not a boy anymore), I knew I needed to seek out help again upon returning home. I went to our pastor, now Brother Bill, to tell him that I still had a problem and needed his guidance on what to do. We had already started having sessions the summer before.

When we started, he was kind and listened to my struggles about being more interested in guys than girls. He explained that with my background, absentee father (Dad, a traveling salesman, gone Monday through Friday every week), and the passing of my biological mother, I had not developed past the normal development stage that all boys go through around ages 10-13.

The best thinking among Christian psychologists at this time was that I needed a male best friend to bond with to move past my temporary interest in guys. He explained that many guys experimented sexually with other guys around the age of my first infatuations (I hadn't understood what was even happening at the time). But now at 17, I needed to move to a more mature stage of development. He gave me numerous books to read on overcoming homosexuality. They concluded that homosexuality was a developmental issue. They reiterated, as he had in our first few sessions, that it was in my best interest NOT TO TELL ANYONE about my attraction to males.

Rev. Mel White refers to this in *Stranger at the Gate* as the deadly "code of silence." In my mind, this meant it was a deep, dark secret. Brother Bill and I met for several sessions, praying together that God would take away these evil thoughts. In later sessions, he said that this was the Devil tempting me like Jesus had been tempted in the wilderness. This was my wilderness. Another time, he told me that I, like Jesus, had my own cross to bear, and this was it. He said with God's help and my faithfulness, I could overcome the sin of homosexuality.

Later, in the summer before my junior year, still struggling with homosexuality, he suggested I find a truly masculine man to be my best friend and bond with him. That would cure me. He was sure of it. Jesse had been my best friend for years, since the beginning of high school. We did most things together, including double dating. But who was I to question our pastor? Besides, Jesse had graduated and was seriously dating and working full-time. We weren't spending much time together as he spent most of his free time with Nonie. Maybe Brother Bill was correct, and I did need a new best friend. If he said I did, then I must.

It just so happened that Brother Bill had the "right" guy in mind: Roy, whose family had just moved to the area and joined the church. It was a bonus that Roy had cancer and needed a friend as well. He was 24, and I turned 18 that September. The pastor introduced us, and I found him to be everything he described: strong, masculine, handsome, and sick with cancer.

I felt like I hit the jackpot with Roy. Not only was he all those things the pastor mentioned, but he was also a former Army soldier, having been discharged due to his cancer. As we talked, I learned he had to go to Houston, Texas, for experimental cancer treatment, and he asked me to accompany him so he wouldn't be alone. My parents weren't so sure, but with the pastor's help in convincing them, I went with him to M.D. Anderson Hospital in Houston for his treatment. I felt like I was doing something significant in God's Kingdom. It was a long drive and a difficult visit. He had melanoma cancer; back then, a death sentence. It was scary to be in that hospital as everyone was VERY sick, from the old to very young children. I felt that my presence there was beneficial for Roy.

We bonded strongly on that trip, and nothing of a sexual nature happened. Upon our return, I rode my bike or drove down to his house every day after class. The more we got to know each other, the more the conversations turned to girls, dating, and sex. I surmised that was what the pastor was hoping for.

The new youth minister, a young man just out of seminary, asked and got permission to hold youth group discussions on sexuality. I thought this was a significant accomplishment for our church and sorely needed. But on every central area of controversy, he would say something like, "I'm sure none of you are struggling with that." "That" being masturbation, premarital sex, pregnancy, abortion, or homosexuality. Of course, we were all struggling with some of these. It was a missed opportunity to have a genuine, factual discussion about sex and sexuality in a safe space.

What Now?

Accepting a call into ministry the summer before made for an exciting start to my junior year. I wanted to go to a "real Christian College." Mother didn't think it necessary for me to go at all. My Sunday School Teacher and principal, Bill Gunter, and my pastor thought otherwise. Together, they begged to differ with Mother, and she reluctantly gave in.

My pastor strongly favored Moody Bible Institute (MBI) in Chicago, his alma mater. It instantly became my first choice. Mr. Gunter felt strongly that I should attend an accredited college or university, which MBI was not. His opinion carried great weight with my parents; I considered it "wise counsel."

My parents had "less grand" plans for my college choice: local or at least near, meaning either William Carey College (WCC) in Mississippi or Mobile College. Both were Baptist Higher Educational Institutions. Of those choices, William Carey was my new first choice because Dr. Jerry Oswalt, our former pastor, was the Chaplain there.

My English Teacher heard I was thinking of going to William Carey College, as my parents had envisioned: something close, less grand than Chicago. Mrs. Lambert wasn't impressed with WCC but said it would be "a good school for you as a Baptist." Of course, I couldn't let that stand and asked her what she meant. She said she hoped that "when you are an educated man, you won't be a narrow-minded Southern Baptist anymore." That made me so mad that I went on a research expedition to find the highest academically ranked Baptist Schools while also honoring Brother Bill's injunction to find a "truly Christian School." I decided to look from Alabama to California because Brother Bill thought the Baptist Colleges to the east were already too liberal.

I decided to research Baptist Colleges and Universities utilizing "The Blue Book," an authority on Colleges and Universities that included data comparisons by SAT/ACT scores, acceptance rates, and academic standing, among many other factors. With more than 24 Southern Baptist Colleges and Universities to choose from, the highest ranked were Baylor, Samford (SU), William Jewell, Ouachita Baptist, and Oklahoma Baptist (OBU). After reviewing The Blue Book, MY new top choices were Oklahoma Baptist, Ouachita, and Baylor.

That summer between my junior and senior years, I preached at a revival in Slidell, Louisiana. While there, I saw a poster of Oklahoma Baptist University. I immediately felt that was where God's Spirit was nudging me, as expressed in the language of Rev. Dr. Eric Elnes. It was another "ah ha" moment for me, but my parents begged to differ. While I disagreed, I still believed that children are to obey their parents, and they were still my parents. I would give up my dream to go to OBU on one condition: if I didn't like Mobile College, where we (Mom, Dad, and I) agreed I should go first, I could transfer after my first year. Mom and Dad, thinking there was little chance of that happening, agreed. But they also said I could go to Samford if I were dating Betsy seriously.

My parents knew very little about the process of going to college. I had to keep telling them what I needed to do and what they needed to do. For instance, I had to take the ACT Test for admission. I did it twice, scoring "average" both times. It was enough to be accepted into most colleges, but not enough for scholarships.

I wasn't dating Betsy seriously enough in my junior year for my parents' blessing to go to Samford. I applied to and was accepted by Mobile College (MC) during the fall semester of my senior year.

Yet another family secret exploded during this process. Dad and Mom had different levels of enthusiasm for my going to college. Mother supported it reluctantly. Dad was more supportive as long as I did all the work. After I was accepted into MC, Dad was required to fill out the government Financial Aid Form. He refused. The Admissions Counselor at MC told me I couldn't get financial aid without that form. Still, Dad refused.

This brought back old wounds of favoritism toward Carol, whom he supported in college. Now, he wouldn't even fill out the required paperwork for me to get help. I begged. He declined. Finally, I asked him why he was being so hard-nosed on this. He said, "Knowing what I make is not the government's business."

But my ability to go to college depended on this form being filled out BEFORE graduating from Rain. Finally, Bill Gunter convinced him to fill it out. He promised Dad that the information would only be used for financial aid purposes.

Maybe I shouldn't have looked, but I did. Dad and Mom combined earned a total income of $15,000 in 1975, with five kids still at home. It made so much more sense to me why he was reluctant to share that information. I pondered how they had managed to feed and clothe us all while working and making so little. My heart softened just a little towards Dad that day. But it was yet another poison pill, another family secret.

Big Man on Campus, Now Leave

The fall of 1975 looked like the best year of my life as I entered my senior year at B.C. Rain High School. Everything was turning out wonderfully. I had a new best friend in Roy. I was a Senior Class Sponsor. The previous summer, I had competed in the Alabama Baptist Speech Contest, tying for first at the associational level and coming in third place in the state. I ran for and won "Commissioner for a Day." As it turned out, it was Rain's time to be "water and sewer," so I became the Sewer King for a Day!!!

More importantly, I had my own contemporary Christian Music Program, inspired partly by Marsha Stevens-Pino's songs, especially "For Those Tears I Died." As I came on the air, I said:

Welcome everybody to the next half-hour of contemporary Christian Music,

This is Mike Brill, and this is the "Let's Just Praise the Lord" program On WMOO Mobile's Christian Radio Station, 1550 on your AM Dial.

I had worked at the radio station for a couple of years and finally convinced the station manager, a member of my church, to let me host a half-hour of Contemporary Christian Music. He was reluctant at first, but soon the show was getting good ratings. By the start of my senior year, I considered myself a Big Man on Campus at little B.C. Rain High School.

Radio program flyer

Much good had happened since 1970, when I first set foot on campus. Back then, I felt I was a nobody; awkward and afraid of my own shadow. Now, look at me. I was successful by the Grace of God.

Next, I decided I needed to get into the National Honor Society (NHS). In my junior year, I didn't get inducted like my elite friends, including Diana, whom I dated off and on. I learned through the grapevine from a teacher who believed in me that another teacher was blocking me. Determined to get in, I mounted a behind-the-scenes campaign. Apparently, the student president of the society knew how badly I wanted this and thought it was funny to see me squirm. Regardless, I became the last inductee admitted into the B.C. Rain Class of 1976 National Honor Society. Only then did I know my campaign had been successful. With that success came confidence to try harder to get into a better school, and I applied to Samford University, where Betsy was attending. We were dating off and on, but enough for my parents to bless us, which gave me an approved reason to apply. But I really thought being in Birmingham at Samford was better than staying in Mobile. After all, with this last feather in my cap, my chances of admission had improved. I was a Big Man on Campus; surely Samford would see that.

I was accepted, but because I was late in the application process, I was wait-listed, which meant I had to wait for a slot to open.

Ben C. Rain High School
Senior Class of 1976

After I was accepted into the National Honor Society, Carl William Brill did something I never thought he would. He said, "Son, I'm really proud of you." It would have been a remarkable step towards healing if he had stopped there, but he didn't. He added, "We have to talk about what happens after this summer." He knew I wanted to go away to college, but I didn't expect this conversation. He said that while he was proud of me, his responsibility for me was over, as I was now a man. "You must make your own way in the world," and then the clincher, "I expect you to be out of the house by fall." Shocked, stunned really, I felt defeated on my most triumphant day. It felt as if Dad had punched me in the gut again! It was a bitter moment in our relationship. I asked Dad why Renae had been allowed to stay past her graduation. And why was DiAnne still there? "Because they are girls," he said, "and girls can stay until married." That answer made me madder than a hornet. Once again, Dad and Mother favored everyone over me. It brought back old grievances like Dad co-signing for Billy's first car (which he wrecked) and refusing to do the same for me. My life was looking up, but my relationship with Dad hit rock bottom.

CHAPTER 5

Growing Up

"We delight in the beauty of the butterfly, but rarely admit the changes it has gone through to achieve that beauty."
Maya Angelo

Fresh-Man

Growing up is hard, at least it was for me. After all, Dad had declared I was a man now. After his NHS talk, I didn't have time to feel sorry for myself. I worked hard to raise money to get ready for college and move out. My new first choice was Samford University where I applied late and was waitlisted. My second choice was Mobile College, where I had already been accepted. That is where I ended up my first year.

When Nanny Brill, always an ally, heard what Dad had done she was not pleased. Determined to "make it right" she offered to rent me her very small garage apartment. The plus side was she lived much closer to the college than my parents. So off to college I went, thinking I was still the BMOC, but actually I was a greenhorn.

Freshman is a good term to describe my first year away from home. While greatly improved from my early teen years, I was nonetheless naïve in so many ways. This naïveté set me up to be "fresh" or "fresh-man," depending on the situation.

I continued to read books about dating, relationships, and, of course, overcoming homosexuality. And I continued dating Betsy long distance, and Diana too. But I also continued my friendship with Roy, even though he was a long way from Nanny's house. Overcoming homosexuality became a frequent topic between us. But nothing helped me come to terms with it: not reading, not the pastor, not Roy. I was still attracted to men. In hindsight, which is always 20-20, Roy wasn't helping at all.

While I enrolled in Mobile College, I did not want to attend this school. But sometimes, God takes us on routes we do not want to go. Such was the case here. I was a hero of sorts at college because I had my own radio program and owned my own car that I bought with my own money.

In the beginning, Mobile College proved to be very difficult for me. They expected me to think through what was being said in class and decide for myself if it was true or not. An English Teacher, Dr. Garner, was particularly hard on freshman "preacher boys" who typically could not write or speak well. When she returned my first English paper it had so many red marks it looked like it had been in a fight and lost.

Then, as usual, I got into trouble for of all things, dancing in the Canteen. Baptist Colleges were very strict on dancing, drinking, and sex among students. But here we were, the freshmen in the Canteen, dancing. In the beginning, almost all the students were dancing, but one by one they stopped until I was the last student dancing. Dr. Hazel Petersen, Dean of the Department of Education, stood behind me and waited until I turned around and saw her. Hands on hips, she asked my name: Charles Michael Brill. She said, "Mr. Brill, I think it is in your best interest to go to class now and I'd better not catch you in such activity again on this campus. Do you understand me?"

"Yes, ma'am," I replied.

I didn't know it then, but she would become one of the most influential people in my life and the sole faculty member from Mobile College to make a positive, lasting impression on me.

I was confused by the religion faculty members who regularly questioned widely held assumptions, only to affirm later they were true. In one particularly stressful lecture, a young faculty member, Dr. Avant, said that he cried as he studied the original Hebrew texts on the Virgin Birth. He was honest about his struggle with it. His honest reading of the Hebrew text was that it "only says that she was a young woman," with no mention of her virginity. This was an apostate proclamation to many of the "preacher boys." But it struck a note of truth to me. I wondered what else the Hebrew scriptures (Old Testament) really say that differed from what had been taught in Sunday School and at Church. The "preacher boys" blasted him. It was the second time I remember being disturbed by people of faith whose actions weren't Christ-like. It would not be my last.

Roy and I kept in touch, but we were soon missing each other. He was still sick but not yet showing any outward symptoms of the cancer. We discussed life, death, school, and sex. Following the pastor's advice, Roy and I had bonded but it hadn't relieved my interest in guys. Therefore, I found a Christian professional counselor, Dr. Gary Minter, to help. This began nearly a decade and a half of professional counseling. I was confident that this was the missing piece to overcoming homosexuality.

Roy grew up near the college and he and I became closer friends. He was the one I turned to when I started struggling with these academic questions. He was now 26, to my 20, certainly more worldly and the one I could ask questions others refused to talk about. We also discussed my family relationships, but he had little to offer since he had not experienced anything like it in his family.

But on sexuality, he had lots to say. First, he told me that "most guys have sex before marriage, and that is normal." He even mentioned that at some point before marriage, most guys get involved with other guys, which is "pretty much normal, too." I could hardly believe my ears. Here he was, a committed Christian, openly expressing the opinion that MOST people have sex outside of marriage, even males with males. At this point, emboldened, I finally gathered the courage to ask if he had been sexually active. He said yes without a hint of shame or embarrassment.

Sometime later that year, I met Mark, one of Roy's buddies from the Army who was on leave from silo missile duty in North Dakota. This became my first "real" sex education class. From Mark, I learned that Roy had experimented with "guy sex" but felt guilty whenever he did. Mark was brash, a badass, and downright handsome. He caused deep, disturbing feelings in me. He was more than happy to share his sexual exploits and stories, though none were of a homosexual nature. Up to this point I was still a virgin; I soaked up these stories like a sponge. The only sexual activity I had done at this point in my life was masturbate, which was frowned upon but tolerated in Christian circles.

By Christmas, Roy started mentioning that maybe we should move in together, as friends, of course. He knew of a house behind a fish market in Eight-Mile, Alabama where he grew up, that we could rent together for less than Nanny's apartment. At Christmas Break, I told Nanny I appreciated her apartment, but Roy and I were going to rent a house closer to school. She was against this idea, but since neither she nor my parents were paying for any of this, they didn't have much leverage. They did not outright forbid it but asked, "Are you sure this is a good idea?" I could see no reason why it wasn't. After all, it was the pastor's idea for us to be friends in the first place and I enjoyed his company. Of course, moving in with someone is very different from going over to visit, but I was naïve about all of this.

We rented the house which was vacant because it stunk so badly when the fish arrived. The experience started off well. I was now an adult on my own. By this time, Roy knew all about my homosexual tendencies. He had them too, his friend Mark had confided. Roy gradually became more and more explicit in our conversations, asking me what made me "get hot" when thinking of guys. I told him neither of us should think of guys that way. Still, he prodded me to tell him more.

Eventually, I gave in and told him that I think of big, strong guys taking charge. I knew I had crossed a line and broken my pact with God to be strong and NOT give in to the Devil regarding homosexuality. I was thinking evil thoughts, and the scriptures implied that evil thoughts were almost as bad as doing evil deeds. I continued my counseling with Dr. Minter, trying gallantly to overcome homosexuality yet again.

Roy, however, reacted differently. In the weeks that followed, he became more aggressive towards me. One night we went for a drive, way out in the country. He told me he had a surprise. I went along happily until we stopped on a dirt road far from town. He told me to get out of the car. I had no idea what was up. What was the surprise? I did as he asked and got out. He turned off the car but left the lights on and then told me to strip. "What? No way. Here?"

"Yes!"

I refused. He said it again, "Strip!" I refused again. He was 6'2", 210 lbs. compared to my 5'9" 128 lbs. He wrestled me to the ground, and I fought like hell. We were both covered in the red clay dirt from the road, and he stripped me naked. After it was over, he literally picked me up and put me where the headlights shone and made me stand still so he could look at me. He was happy with what he saw. He then came over and wiped the dirt off me. I was confused. I was horrified and excited all at the same time. Then he directed me to put my clothes back on and get in the car. I complied. I didn't know what else to do, so I cried. He apologized for being so aggressive but then asked me if I liked it. He didn't wait for an answer. He said he knew I did because I got hard. He was right.

Nothing happened for a while after the first event. I thought a lot about that night, wondering how he knew. I figured I had tipped him off with that comment about big, strong guys. I wondered if it would happen again. Did I want it to? I wasn't sure. I was conflicted. My counselor suggested that I take more precautions with Roy to avoid situations where this could happen again. But that was hard to do being roommates and leasing a house together.

On the one hand, my body seemed to react positively to him, to it. On the other hand, according to my church, it was among the worst sins a person could engage in. I knew it was a "bad sin" because I had been warned not to tell anyone. So, I knew I must be really, really bad now because I had done something gay.

But this was not the end. Later that Spring, Roy came home one night and said it was time for me to grow up. He said I needed to be honest, and he wasn't going to take no for an answer. He threw me on the bed and told me to be still while he took off all his clothes. It was the first time I saw him totally naked. In fact, it was the first time I saw any man totally naked up close and personal. He was a redhead with a stubble on his face and a body covered in a nice coating of fine red hair. He was a good-looking man. I immediately got aroused. Then he picked me up, took my clothes off roughly as I suppose he thought I liked, and laid on top of me so I could not move. As I struggled, he told me to settle down. He told me what he was going to do. "You can make it easy or hard, it doesn't matter. It is going to happen. You are going to suck my d--k."

"No," I replied.

"Yes," he said. He was determined to make this happen that night.

He tried forcing me, but I refused, just like when Little Billy was beating me up as a child. Back then, all I had to do for Billy to stop was to say uncle. But I wouldn't, no matter how bad the beating.

Roy repeated, "All you have to do to make this easier is open your mouth." I wouldn't open my mouth. He squeezed my nose, closing my nostrils. Still I refused, shaking my head no. I turned blue. He finally gave up, very frustrated and went to sleep. I moved to my bed but stayed awake a long time thinking. Did this make me gay? What part had I played in this? What I knew for sure was that I was a sinner, and I was losing the battle against the Devil and Homosexuality. The next day, I was gone.

We didn't talk when I came back to the house to get my things. In fact, we didn't talk again until the final days of his life, nearly three years later. He asked me to come over to his parents' house where he lived as his cancer progressed. He apologized. He said he had not meant to scare me but to help me overcome my fear of participating in gay sex. I accepted his apology. By then, I knew I was sexually attracted to men and wanted to explore those possibilities, but I wasn't yet ready to permit myself to engage sexually with another man. I now believe Roy was trying to help. But that does not negate the fact that no still means no. He crossed a line and that is not ok.

Punch One, Right Hook; Punch Two, Left Hook

Mercifully, my last semester at MC came to an end before Christmas my sophomore year, and it had been a rough one. Roy was no longer in my life; I was back at Nanny Brill's and more family secrets landed like body punches.

This last semester at Mobile College gave me additional opportunities to stretch my mind. One was speech class, where we had to give a speech and use prompts to help make our point. I chose Death & Dying from a list of approved topics. I thought that was something I knew a great deal about. After all, by this time, I had experienced more death than anybody else in class: Pawpaw Brill, my mother and Debbie's son. The only difficulty I was having was finding a suitable prompt. Finally, it dawned on me that I could use Mom's Death Certificate, a suggestion from Nanny Brill (I think).

Naturally, I asked Nanny for the death certificate, but she referred me to Dad. She said it was his to give if he wanted to. Thinking nothing of this exchange, I asked, and he refused. Sometimes, I'm slow to see the bigger picture, but I didn't think it contained anything but the reason for Mom's death, which was a heart attack.

Dad told me his philosophy of life that day and said there was no reason to dig up the past. He believed in living life one day at a time; when that day was over, it was over. The past is past. After his father, Oscar Brill, died in '66, he never spoke of him again to me. When my mother, Anne Claire Lindsey Brill died in '68, he never mentioned her to me again either.

I told him it was a requirement for the assignment, and to pass I had to have a prompt on death and dying and I couldn't think of anything else to use. He still refused. The more he refused, the angrier I became. Not again, I thought. He never backs me up. I am not sure how or why he changed his mind (I have my suspicions), but he finally gave me a copy of her death certificate a few days later. It contained two MORE very painful, long-held family secrets:

1. Mom had two children before we were born. How had we not known this? Why hadn't this ever been discussed? I was furious. But Nanny Brill interceded on Dad's behalf. The girls, as my family referred to them, were at the funeral. I had just been too distraught to notice, she explained. Additionally, "It wasn't talked about because they had never lived with y'all." I accepted her answer but didn't like it very much.

2. The death certificate also said that Mother had died of a drug overdose and not a heart attack, as Dad told us at the time. It said that it was accidental, which was important for insurance purposes. Why not just tell us that? This didn't ring true to my ears.

Nanny Brill was always the one in my life who helped me make sense of the family and its secrets. This time was no different. We had many conversations that semester about my biological mother and how unhappy she was. Nanny said she had fallen in love with a lounge singer and would be gone for days before Bill would go and bring her back home. Dad had loved her with all his heart, and Mom had broken it. Nanny said she was a broken woman. Mom had apparently found her biological father in Atlanta, the man who gave her away at birth. This information threw her into a crisis. Her solution was to run away to be with the singer. In fact, she seemed to be contemplating leaving the family for good because the day they found her, she had all the family's money in her possession when she took those pills. It was Nanny Brill's theory that Anne killed herself rather than abandoning her four children, as she had her twins years ago. In my heart, I knew Nanny's version of the story was true.

It didn't help when I asked David about it, and he said he knew Mom had two other children. He wasn't surprised about the drugs either. So, it appeared once again that I was the only one not in on the secrets. It was me; it was always me. I was hurt but appreciated learning the truth.

I was so angry that I hadn't been told any of this that I was ready to leave Mobile, Alabama behind, and with it, my messed-up family. Now I knew the rest of the story that Dad had hidden from me for years: I had two sisters I didn't know about, and my mother killed herself. Punch one: right hook, punch two: left hook. I was down and out for the count.

My last semester at Mobile College was difficult in many ways. Betsy was upset with me because she had decided to attend MC to be with me and I had encouraged it. But after arriving, I found dating her difficult. I found kissing her uninteresting. I just wasn't into her physically. I broke it off and stopped dating women altogether for a while. She had a right to be upset. After all, she had given up her beloved Samford for my school. It wasn't fair, she said, and she was right. I had not been fair to her. The last two months were awful. She cried every day. And the more she cried, the harder my heart became. I hadn't done right by her, partly because I thought about Roy, but I couldn't tell her that because I would have to tell her about my attraction to guys, and I couldn't do that for obvious reasons. It felt to me like my life was more uncertain now than at any time since birth.

The Miracle

Not everyone has had a miracle, but they do happen, I can testify to that! By now, I was no longer a new Christian. I had studied Greek. I had preached. I had read the Holy Bible completely through several times and gone on mission trips for years with the youth group. And I had been faithfully dating many women. The only thing I didn't have, up to this point, was a real miracle. But I needed one. I had just come through a rough start to college, and was struggling with this news about my family.

The scriptures say that *When I was a child, I thought like a child, ...but when I became a man, I put away childish things.* (1 Corinthians 13:11, NKJV). I was a man now and it was time to grow up. That is why the truth about my real mother and her twin girls had finally been revealed to me. It was time to move on.

This new information complicated my move to Oklahoma, but it didn't stop it. In fact, it made me more determined than ever to get away from all the Alabama chaos. Dad, already in a foul mood towards me, did not give me a hard time about going out west now that I had broken Betsy's heart by breaking up. Besides, they had promised to let me go if I wanted to transfer after my first year at Mobile College. My parents said I was a man now and I could make my own decisions, good or bad, if I was willing to live with the consequences. I was. So, I applied and was accepted mid-term my sophomore year to Oklahoma Baptist University in Shawnee, Oklahoma, 30 miles east of Oklahoma City.

I had felt for months that I was in the wrong place, not because of Roy or Betsy, but because God was leading me to Oklahoma of all places. Back in the summer of 1975, I had just returned from Shocco Springs Baptist Assembly (camp) when I was asked to participate in their revival in Slidell, Louisiana. I was the preacher for one night of the revival. While there, I saw a poster of OBU and instantly knew this was the place for me. In my heart, I felt the Holy Spirit say, "Mike, this is the school I have chosen for you." It was another "ah ha" moment.

According to the *Blue Book* OBU was a highly rated academic institution. It was also well respected in Baptist circles as a "truly" Christian institution. For me, the deciding factor was John Wesley Raley Chapel, the most imposing building on campus. I thought that any school that would have the Chapel as its centerpiece on campus must have a strong faith-based curriculum, unlike Samford, where Betsy was attending again after transferring back. SU's chapel was a pretty little structure on the quad. At Mobile College, the chapel was located off a wing of the Administration Building.

In high school OBU had been one of my top three choices BEFORE seeing the poster. The poster just confirmed that was where God wanted me. I had no idea how I was going to pay for it. Oklahoma was a long way from Mobile, Alabama. By this time, I knew the truth: we were poor, and even if we weren't, my parents weren't going to help me. But I was confident there would be a way if this was God's will. By faith, I stepped out of the boat (as Peter had in the scriptures), applied and was accepted. As the time to leave approached I still hadn't secured the funding, but OBU had promised to work with me on that issue, which would include working.

Meanwhile, I was still working at WMOO on the weekend shifts and selling ads for the Radio Station. The Station Manager had promised I would make commissions on ads I sold. So, I asked the largest Baptist Church in town to consider sponsoring a weekly radio program, and they accepted. It was the largest ever local sale for the station. Elated, I told the manager, no longer a member of my Baptist Church, as he moved to a better part of town and a more prestigious one. But he was impressed and promised me the commissions. He never dreamed I would or could land such a significant sale and he hadn't thought through how much the commission would be. When he did, he decided that I would only get half of the promised amount since I was leaving. Fifty percent of what they owed me equaled exactly what I needed to completely fund my first semester at OBU, plus 50 dollars extra. God had answered my prayer and confirmed that this was where I needed to be.

I arrived in Shawnee in my 1968 Chevy Malibu in late January, as they had a January Term (J term) that winter before the regular spring semester started in mid-February. Upon arrival, I went to the dorm director's office, but no one was there. Then, I heard the roar of a crowd. I wandered over to the gym, a WWII hanger turned basketball arena, to see the stands packed with students rooting for the OBU Bison against their rival Bethany Nazarene College.

It looked like the whole campus was there. Everybody was standing, and I heard them screaming, "Let's go-Ka Rip," a cheer where the words have no meaning. The spirited cheer was nearly as old as the school itself, and for students, faculty, and alumni alike, it had become an integral part of being a Bison. The cheer went like this:

Bison, let's go with Ka-Rip
Ka-Rip Ka-rap Ka-riplo typlo tap
Oh! Oh! Rincto lincto hio-totimus
Hopula scipula copula gotimus
...Zip Bang, OBU

How exciting! The game was, of course, but also the crowd and that ridiculous cheer. OBU finally won the game in triple overtime! From that moment on I was hooked on Bison Basketball and OBU.

After the game, I went back to the welcome desk and the Dorm Director showed me to my room on the third floor of Brotherhood Dorm. This big old building would be my home away from home for the next two years.

The night was cold with snow on the ground, and I was excited to finally be at OBU. These years would radically change my outlook on life and faith forever. Here, I could start over. I could get straight with God. I had no doubt that I was at a good Christian school. The good Lord above confirmed this was the right place as evidenced by the Baptist Church sale for WMOO. Even being cheated out of half the commissions, God had provided. Life was good.

Why Oklahoma?

I knew next to nothing about Oklahoma before driving halfway across the country to get there. Mother said I would regret it. "Besides," she continued, "who wants to go to Oklahoma anyway?" But I went just the same. I would learn Oklahoma was a wild and wonderful land, best known for prairie landscapes where herds of Bison once thundered free across open plains. In 1830, President Andrew Jackson signed the Indian Removal Act, designating Oklahoma as "Indian Territory." Five tribes from the southeastern United States: Choctaw, Chickasaw, Cherokee, Creek, and Seminole, were forcibly removed from their ancestral homelands to resettle in this new territory. One-third of the Cherokee Nation died on this "Trail of Tears," where all members of the tribes were made to walk, through all kinds of weather, terrain, and unthinkable circumstances, from Georgia to Oklahoma. It is a heartbreaking story, a part of American history of which I am not proud. The play "Trail of Tears" ran at an the *Tsa-La-Gi* 1,800-seat outdoor amphitheater in Tahlequah, Oklahoma from 1969 to 2005. It was a moving blend of music, dance and history, retelling the tragic story of the Cherokee's forced relocation to Oklahoma in the 1830's.

My coming to Oklahoma was a very different "trail of tears" journey, not anything close to what the Cherokee and other First Nations peoples experienced. But it was my time of great sorrow, a time for tears, a time to deal with my personal losses. So many things that needed to happen in my life could not happen if I was in Alabama with my family. I needed to mature and have time to be angry without hurting my family in the process. Neither of these were easy, but they were necessary.

Living in Oklahoma was also my first time living in a place where "the defining moment" wasn't the Civil War. It was the first place where "other history" filled that pivotal moment. Just as Georgia's was Sherman's March to the Sea, and Mobile's was the Battle of the Ironclads and the fall of the Port of Mobile (the last major port to fall in the Civil War), most Oklahomans thought of the dust bowl years of the

Great Depression and many First Nations peoples likely thought of the Trail of Tears.

In Oklahoma I learned that racism isn't confined to Black Americans. First Nations peoples were also suffering from oppression. While attempting to settle in "Indian Country," on their "new" land, they faced extreme hardship, including disease, starvation, a challenging new environment, and constant encroachment and violence from the predominantly white Anglo-Saxon Protestant settlers moving west; not to mention the disruption of their traditional way of life, loss of cultural identity, and tension with tribes who already lived in the areas where they were forced to settle.

This was a new idea to me: racism was broader than a "Southern Black problem." That, of course, is and was a big problem from the '50s, the decade I was born, through to today; actually, beginning when the first black people were shipped to America against their will, becoming enslaved people.

We still have a long way to go before we become the just society we aspire to be. But this awareness that other groups were also being discriminated against was eye opening. African Americans were finally making progress in the '50s, '60s and '70s, thanks to men and women like John Lewis, Rosa Parks, Dr. Martin Luther King, Jr. and many more. New laws were written and passed. On the other hand, First Nations peoples weren't making much headway at all when I arrived in Oklahoma. I learned from this experience that the group being discriminated against must stand up together and take the lead against oppression before potential allies show up in meaningful numbers to help.

After being assigned my room, I learned that John, a freshman from Minnesota, was my roommate. He let me know that he did not respect people from the South. I quickly learned that he had already changed roommates twice in his first semester. "Good luck," the guys snickered as they learned I had been assigned to John's room. Remember I told you I needed to mature? Well, John was lesson #1. He regularly extolled the virtues of his home state of Minnesota and the shortcomings of mine, Alabama. He regularly complained that his high school had more course offerings than OBU. To say we got off to a difficult start is an oversimplification.

Frustration finally set in, and I asked him, "Why in the world did you leave Minnesota if it was so wonderful?" His answer? Because OBU was more conservative and less expensive than the best of the private colleges in his home state. Suddenly, I found myself wondering if I had made yet another mistake. It did not take long to realize that John and I had irreconcilable differences. He said repeatedly that Alabama was inferior to his beloved Minnesota and that any state that would vote for George Wallace was just a stupid state. He was rude and arrogant. He was also very bright and let everyone else know he was smarter than they were. The last time I saw an update on him, he was Dr. John, Ph.D., an administrator for an Institute in a western state. It appears he has had a full career and life. I am glad for him. But after one semester, he moved on to yet another roommate (not his last). I was elated with the change. In hindsight, he was one of the reasons I was at OBU, to grow up. Growing up includes expanding your mind and learning from new experiences, including learning how to deal with difficult people.

Lesson two wasn't far behind. Western Civilization (Civ) at OBU was the most feared class on campus. It was a team taught sixteen credit hour course over two semesters. Because I had transferred, I only had to take part 2, as OBU reluctantly gave me credit for similar classes at Mobile College. The first shock came with books. The professors assigned 16 texts, and I wondered what I had gotten into. I had not read 16 books in my entire life, much less for one semester.

Professors Dr. Don Webster and Robert Scrutchins introduced themselves to the 80 class members, the only large class offered at OBU. They told us their approach to Civ would be from the perspective of "great ideas" that made Western Civilization what it is today. It would not be taught from the standard historical or literary approaches typically used. They also dared to say this would be the hardest class we would have taken to date at this or any college we might have attended.

They expected us to keep up with reading daily, saying, "A couple of hours each night should suffice." Two hours, I thought, they must be kidding! They were not. Then the shocker came: in addition to the 16 books and two hours of reading every night, we had to write not one or two, but FOUR term papers to pass.

I had a sinking feeling that I wasn't going to be able to keep up. In addition to this class, I had three others, plus a 20-hour-per-week job at The Mabee Learning Center (Library). Failing, however, was not an option. It would be a failure I couldn't live with. My parents urged me to reconsider at every opportunity. Mother sent care packages and reminded me that I had "no one to wash my clothes," which always made me chuckle because she hadn't washed my clothes for at least two years. Dad reminded me that Betsy was still in Alabama, and I could make up with her and convince her to reconsider me.

Highly motivated, I dropped almost all the campus activities I had joined early on to concentrate on my studies. Remember, goal number #2 was to mature. Maturity requires one to make hard, necessary decisions. Early on, Western Civ wasn't going well. I immediately fell behind on my reading and got poor grades on "pop" quizzes and the first major test.

The stakes weren't as high for most other students at OBU as they were primarily from upper-middle-class, white, professional families. If they failed, most could just retake the class.

The more conservative students began to question my faith when I stopped attending extra chapel services each day to study. Regular Chapel was required for all students once a week, but the more pious held one each day.

The ideas being presented in Civ were all new to me. I was struggling. The teachers were intent on each student learning the concept of Critical Thinking, which was first introduced to me at MC.

After a deep philosophical discussion in class, one fellow classmate said, "You just don't get it, do you?" I was insulted, but he was right. I was lost in the discussion. Heretofore, I had always taken the word of my elders as truth, be they my pastor or faculty member. Early in the class Professor Scrutchins said that Rousso was a great man, and his ideas were great. A few days later, the great ideas being discussed were Adam Smith's. In the presentation, Professor Scrutchins said that Adam Smith thought Rousso was an idiot and that his ideas were stupid. Scrutchins said that Adam Smith was a great man, and his ideas were great.

Now, I was totally confused. Rousso and Smith couldn't both be great and both of their ideas right, as they disagreed. I couldn't figure out how Rousso could be great one week, only to be replaced by Adam Smith the next. So, I went to the professor and asked which one was right. He thought for a few minutes before asking me to tell him which one I thought made more sense. This perplexed me even more. After all, he was the professor, not me. He was the one with the knowledge, not me. Still, he refused to tell me his opinion until I shared my own. It was the first day I employed critical thinking skills. In hindsight it was probably the most important day in my educational career. Remember the guy who said I didn't get it at the beginning of the semester? Well, as it turned out, we both ended the class with solid B's...a big win for me. I had learned Western Civ. But I had also learned something more important: thinking critically, something I hadn't known I needed to learn. God nudged me away from what I thought I needed to learn, to what I really needed. It was yet another step on the path God had placed before me.

They Really Made Me Think!

I went to OBU to learn, but I hadn't realized that would include Critical Thinking as a skill. Mobile College faculty also taught critical thinking but with a harsher pedagogical approach that was easier to reject. But at Oklahoma Baptist, I liked and respected the faculty a lot. While Dr. Don Webster and Robert Scrutchins taught me to think through ideas, Dr. Dan Holcomb, the Baptist History professor, was the first to introduce me to the differences in scriptural interpretation between the more conservative understanding of scriptures as inerrant in all things, verses Divinely Inspired for Faith and Practice, but not as the only source of truth in other fields such as science or psychology. He also required us to write well. We were expected to write a major term paper on some aspect of Baptist History. I chose the work of Dr. E. Y. Mullins, one of the greatest Baptist Theologians in Southern Baptist life, from an earlier era. That paper was 42 pages long and the best work I had ever written. I was proud of my hard-earned B. He also taught us about the SBC's pro-slavery and segregationist past, which the SBC would not formally apologize for until 1995, fifteen years after I graduated from this university. Dr. Holcomb also taught me about our (SBC's) historical insistence that church and state remain separate for the sake of both institutions.

In addition to the regular Baptist History textbook, he assigned *Churches in Cultural Captivity,* by Dr. John Lee Eighmy, a former OBU professor who passed away a few years before I arrived. This book was monumental in opening my eyes to a confusing reality. So much of the "religion" being espoused in churches has more to do with the culture of the day, than scriptures. I have retained a copy of this book in my personal library ever since.

That first semester, including Western Civ and Baptist History, marked a change in my thinking and both me and my faith grew and matured as a result. I began to not only feel my faith, but also to think about it. I began to question assumptions. This is education at its' best.

OBU taught me how to think, to really think. Whenever I struggled, one professor or another would say, "If your faith can't be examined, maybe your faith isn't worth holding on to."

The forerunner to the Southern Baptist Convention fundamentalist takeover was the *Heresy Paper*, published by an anonymous Oklahoma Baptist pastor attacking our school in 1978. This was yet another time where people who claimed to be "like Christ" didn't act that way toward others. It was still another year before the SBC exploded in rancor over the role of women in ministry. The country was re-examining gay rights, the changing role of women, and the ethical and moral implications of abortion in society. From the tone of the conversations, it was clear the whole country needed better critical thinking skills, not just me.

It was impossible for the OBU community to ignore the role of women in society or in the ministry. For one thing, the University had several women on the faculty, including Dr. Rowena Strickland, the first woman to teach Theology in a co-educational Southern Baptist Higher Educational institution. She was an excellent teacher and outstanding Greek Scholar. And she was feisty, defending her right to be in the classroom against the fundamentalists who claimed to love her, but opposed her teaching because she was a woman.

In 1979, Southern Baptist life began to shift. Fundamentalist faith leaders began attacking moderates in the convention in order to wrest control from those they deemed "too liberal." At the 1979 Convention, Dr. Paige Patterson and other conservatives attacked the SBC in an effort to "return the Southern Baptist Convention to God." Two issues, more than any others, sexual immorality (including homosexuality) and women in ministry, were the focus of this revolt. This effort would lead to 35 years of discord before most moderate churches finally left or were expelled from the SBC.

At the peak of the conflict, more than 45,000 messengers (delegates), including me, attended the SBC annual meeting in New Orleans in 1984. Moderates lost the most critical vote 49%-51%. This was the beginning of the end for moderates as well as direct Baptist affiliation and SBC control over the better educational institutions, at least those with sufficient funds to become independent of the SBC.

I write about this to say that I came to OBU at a time when great men and women of faith stood for critical thinking amid the anti-educational of the SBC. I was fortunate to have faculty who lived what they taught in the classroom. Dr. Timberlake, a theologian and scholar, was "the devil" to the more conservative students because he refused to teach "The Trail of Blood," a theological theory that allegedly traces Baptist roots back to John the Baptist. This theory is widely discredited by religious scholars outside of Baptist Life. But to conservative students this proved he was too liberal. Instead of getting mad, he encouraged his more conservative students to use their critical thinking skills to think through ideas rather than rejecting them outright.

I was also incredibly lucky to have Dr. Oteka Ball teaching Human Sexuality. She was a Methodist and well aware of the dangers of offending the conservatives in the SBC. She carefully allowed discussion on the most contentious issues around sexuality while still managing honest discussions. These included birth control methods, pre-marital sex, abortion and homosexuality, all hot topics of the day. She helped me gain valuable knowledge I had been looking for, in an open and caring way. Dr. Ball, Dr. Holcomb, Dr. Strickland, Dr. Timberlake, Dr. Webster, and a host of other scholars helped me learn, grow and think! For them and OBU, I will always be grateful.

The Conservative Resurgence vs. Bold Mission Thrust

My time at Oklahoma coincided with the Conservative Resurgence by fundamentalists in the denomination against the more moderate Southern Baptist Leaders who had led the SBC to become the largest protestant denomination in America through their efforts to reach everyone with God's love in an effort the SBC named the Bold Mission Thrust.

I bought into this vision of reaching every person with God's Love. I was being challenged in classes, and among classmates for my faith to be broad enough to encompass God's love for the world. This theology, rooted in historical Baptist Faith, especially the understanding that truth is found in many places and the Bible itself is not the sole source of all truth.

This understanding of scriptures, that it was *Divinely Inspired,* but not dictated, was the moment when my own understanding of faith was challenged, and I began to intimately understand two pillars of my journey: Faith and Fundamentalism.

Faith and Fundamentalism are the concepts that, when examined deeply, helped me break free from my Church's teachings on sexuality. When I graduated from OBU, near the beginning of what the initiators called the "conservative resurgence" and its detractors labeled the "fundamentalist takeover," fundamentalism was, and still is, a major part of both Baptist expression and the expression of Evangelical Christianity in America.

The rise of Fundamentalism did not happen in a vacuum. At the same time Dr. Francis Schaffer, the controversial Swiss Theologian and champion of the emerging Christian Right, suggested in 1980 the idea of a "co-belligerent" construct, where people who disagreed theologically, could still work together on policy issues to advance the Kingdom of God. This idea took root among evangelicals seeking more political control. After Heritage Foundation leader Paul Weyrich, said, "There are a moral majority of Americans on our side," proudly fundamentalist

Baptist pastor Jerry Falwell joined him and others in forming the "Moral Majority," the first major evangelical political organization. It was initially formed, ironically, to defeat President Jimmy Carter, "a moderate" Southern Baptist, after the government denied non-profit tax status to Bob Jones University (as it was required by law to do) based on the University's illegal policy prohibiting interracial dating. Falwell, "deploying ever-more apocalyptic rhetoric... pleaded with Christians to resist." He claimed that America in 1980 was "floundering to the brink of death." Falwell's call was answered by fundamentalists looking to take control of the Southern Baptist Convention and later the Republican party.

This seemed to be exactly the same ideology that I had rejected when I became a Republican in 1976, the year I graduated from High School and voted in a presidential election for the first time. I chose to be a Republican because they were for the Equal Rights Amendment and against segregation. Now, five years later, Southern Baptist and other conservative Christian groups had changed political parties and by 1984, I had to also. Additionally this put me at odds with the "conservative resurgence" efforts. Two words became the flash points between the warring sides of the convention that strongly impacted my understanding of God: faith and fundamentalism.

Faith is a strong belief in God or commitments of a religion rather than proof. This means I can't make you believe that Jesus is God's son. I can't make you believe that the Scriptures are divinely inspired. I do believe these things, but it is by faith that you and I accept them to be true or not, as there is no scientific or definitive historical proof one way or the other.

Fundamentalism is often associated with a literal interpretation of religious texts. My home church, where I accepted Christ as my savior, was a fundamentalist Baptist Church, even though the word "fundamentalist" was not used. But because we were a fundamentalist church, our pastors taught us that the scriptures were the "inerrant" Word of God and were true in all things: faith, science, history, psychology, etc.

Early in my faith pilgrimage I began to see things that didn't match up. For instance, there are two creation stories in Genesis. A careful reading reveals differences. Initially, as a teenager and a new Christian, I was unable to deal with this apparent contradiction, so I ignored it. Biblical Scholars taught at both OBU and Southern Baptist Theological Seminary which I later attended. In Old Testament class, these differences were discussed in detail at both schools. Both OBU and SBTS taught scriptures from the view of Divine Inspiration (often understood as God's influence on the writers of Scripture, ensuring the accuracy and truthfulness of the writing), but not from the fundamentalist approach that the scriptures are error-free word for word. These two different understandings of the scriptures would be contested within the Southern Baptist denomination for decades.

I remember the first time I was taught in church that God created the world in six literal days and rested on the seventh. At Rain High we learned about evolution and that the world was billions of years old. This was my first conflict of faith. My church taught one thing; my education taught another. It became harder to believe in the six literal days theology. But in studying the Bible, I eventually read 2nd Peter where the writer told us how to view time from God's perspective: *"But, beloved, do not forget this one thing, that with the Lord one day is as a thousand years, and a thousand years as one day* (2 Peter 3:8 NKJV). *"* This clarified for me that time to God is not the same as our human perspective of time. Conundrum solved! To me, understanding science *increased* my understanding of just how amazing The God of all Creation is. The Bible does not claim a literal six-day creation based on a human's perspective of time on planet Earth – but if God created the Universe, and he created all of the universes and all of the planets with their varying lengths of day based on the speed they rotate on their axis's, etc. ... By forcing God into *our* time, we limit Him – and our understanding of the world He created. At OBU I also learned to study the Bible using context to help me understand what the writer in the first century would have been conveying to his listeners. Examining the Bible through the cultural lens of 21st Century America is dramatically different than a similar examination through the cultural lens of biblical times. This ability to understand and study the Scriptures from multiple contexts will be important later as we look at individual passages regarding sexuality in general, and homosexuality in particular. It also potentially helps one understand why the modern Christian Church disregards so many of the dictates of Leviticus – the "rules" section (don't eat shellfish, certain grains etc.), but still cling to others.

Are there significant differences in understanding the world between our current time and when the Bible was written? Of course. For example, in the first century Roman Empire when Paul was writing, only Roman Citizens had rights, and many people lived as slaves. Today that would be unacceptable, yet the scriptures do not explicitly condemn slavery. In fact, slavery played a key role in the Southern Baptist Convention split from Baptists in the north in 1845, when Baptist leaders in the North refused to appoint slaveholders as missionaries to Africa.

Dr. Holcomb: Southern Baptist History in a Nutshell

Before going to Mobile College and OBU I knew next to nothing about Baptists from a historical perspective. But with my arrival in college, first at MC and then at OBU, that was about to change. Dr. Holcomb, whom I dearly loved and respected was brutal in forcing us to understand our own denominational history. Without this understanding, I would have been lost over the nature of the so called "conservative resurgence" or, as I would characterize it "the fundamentalist takeover." Dr. Holcomb is the first one that made me look, really look, at our racist past. He was the one that asked questions like "should a white slaveholder be allowed to be a missionary in Africa" (at a time when Africans were still being kidnapped and enslaved)? This was a question that the American Mission Board wrestled with in 1845, ultimately deciding it was inconsistent with their belief in God's love for all people to allow current slaveholders to serve as missionaries in Africa. I had to face the fact that we, the SBC had been founded on a racist principle.

Dr. Holcomb also taught us the important concept of covenant relationships as the foundation for the uniqueness of Southern Baptist Life and the strength of our ability to work together. For a long time, Southern Baptists were a denomination with both fundamentalists and conservatives/moderates. The glue that held them together was the principle of *The Priesthood of the Believer*, meaning that you as an individual Christian had the right and the responsibility to struggle with what you learned regarding faith and decide for yourself -- no preacher, priest, Pope, Convention, or Government -- could tell you what or how to believe. It was a matter of faith between you and God. This is why the concept of *Separation of Church and State* was so critical to Baptists when this country was founded. Nobody should tell you what you can or cannot believe. Baptists came to America to be *free* from a parochially dominated society! Our founding fathers understood the danger of blending together Church and the government. Baptists have been a minority religious group for all of its existence, have struggled with persecution for centuries and knew better than most, except perhaps the Mormons, Quakers, and Jews, that a parochial doctrine should never rule government. All these groups have suffered at the hands of the majority, who held different religious views. As a result, Baptists contributed mightily to the *Bill of Rights* freedom of religion clause and were strong proponents of keeping Church and State separate.

When fundamentalists took over the Southern Baptist Convention starting in 1979, it was a complete surprise to most Baptists. Just like individuals had the right to form their own understanding of faith, so too the churches of the SBC had always been autonomous, as were the local associations, state conventions and the National Convention. Yet they were bound to each other through a covenant relationship: a deep binding commitment between them to operate by mutual trust, solemn promises and shared obligations to work together accordingly to meet their shared goal of reaching the entire world with God's Love, as expressed in the 1978-79 Bold Mission Thrust.

About a decade earlier, Southern Baptists surpassed The United Methodist Church as the largest Protestant denomination in the country. After this occurred, some SBC pastors began using their newfound popularity to push politicians to adjust policies they preferred. With 13.4 million members in 1979, they began first by cleaning house. They would eventually succeed in ridding the denomination of those its new leaders considered "too liberal." Moderate and liberal leaders (meaning non-fundamentalists) were systematically removed from office and moderate and liberal presidents, professors and department heads of SBC seminaries and mission groups were replaced with fundamentalists.

Those who gained control of the SBC from moderates in 1984 claimed they wanted to "rid the SBC of liberalism" pledging a new "golden age" for the church, "but the exact opposite happened instead." (Baptist News Global, Jan. 24, 2014). That was the last year a key marker for denominational growth, baptisms, increased. Total SBC membership has been declining since 2006. 2022 saw the largest membership drop in 100 years with a loss of 500,000 members. According to Lifeway Research, the SBC has lost more than 1,000 congregations per year for each of the last three years in which records are currently available (2020, 2021 and 2022).

In fact, Southern Baptist Convention membership has dropped approximately 3 million from slightly over 16 million in 2000 to less than 13 million last year (2024) and it has fewer members now than in 1979. Dr. Albert Mohler, whom I attended Seminary with, later described the takeover as having come at "an incredibly high cost."[1]

In my pilgrimage through Oklahoma Baptist University, I affirmed my faith in Christ and came to understand the Scriptures as divinely inspired for faith and practice, but not inerrant in all things.

At this point in my faith walk at OBU, while I had learned much about my chosen denomination and my personal faith walk, I still had important ideas to learn. My next important lesson dealt with shoes, of all things, yet they were God's next lesson for me.

Note to Readers: More on Michael's Dealing with the Scriptures is found in the Appendix, Page 263.

Shoes

Shoes, of all things, taught me the next lesson I needed on my path to maturity. My new roommate at OBU was named Richard. He was a character from the start, but I liked him, certainly better than John. I soon learned that his mother had killed herself, like mine, but she had abandoned him and his little sister at a parsonage before doing so. As I recall, he told me they came with a note to the pastor saying, "Please raise my son and daughter for me." The pastor and his wife adopted them; now, he was at college. He was a conflicted soul, but deep down a young man, much like me, who had a great deal of work to do to overcome his background. He just wasn't very interested in doing what I knew by then would be a lot of very difficult work. One of the benefits of my counseling (aside from the gay issue) was learning how to work through resentment, anger, and feelings of worthlessness. But Richard was angry and not yet ready to begin that process.

Summer came around and I stayed in Shawnee both because I didn't want to go home, plus there was a Scholarship that gave free tuition to any ministerial student taking summer classes. I took full advantage of this bonus. I remember I took French to meet the foreign language requirements and struggled mightily. In the end I managed to get a C- due to my diligence, more than my ability.

Richard and I agreed to be roommates again in the fall because we got along well. Eventually, he invited me down to his dad's (The Pastor's) church, Bethel Baptist in Norman, Oklahoma. I enjoyed the service but noticed that a couple kept looking at my feet. I tried to cover them up as my shoes were in bad shape. In fact, the top of one shoe had a rip.

A few days later, I received a letter and thirty dollars for new shoes. I was embarrassed that I needed charity. Since coming to OBU, I often wore the oldest coat, the rattiest jeans and had only a few nice shirts. I knew I was not from the same economic class as many of my fellow students and friends, but with a few exceptions, nobody seemed to care. For Spring Break, the Colorado kids went skiing. With special permission, I stayed in the dorm and worked on my studies. A big date for me was going to the A&W and getting a Papa Burger & Fries "on special" for $1.59, but a Coke was extra. Remember, I only had $50 to spend that first semester after room and board, books, fees, and tuition.

So, when I needed shoes there was no money to be found. I hadn't asked God for new shoes, but I needed them. With the unexpected gift, I bought two pairs. In private, I prayed and cried with shame and gratitude. I cried from shame because I needed, desperately needed new shoes. But our family didn't take charity, we earned it. I hadn't earned this money. It seemed to just fall from heaven. I had to pray about this. My first prayer was one of repentance for needing new shoes. If only I had saved more, worked harder, or had an additional job, I wouldn't need any charity. But somewhere in the middle of that prayer, God spoke to me again, saying, "I know what you need. Accept this gift as it was given, with a pure heart and love, as I commanded them to do." I cried again, this time in gratitude. That day, I learned yet another important lesson for living: be grateful for the kindness of others, and in time, you will be the one giving gifts to those in need. God's message to me: "As I bless you, you are to bless others."

My coming to Oklahoma was a life-changing opportunity in many ways. I was no longer under the direct control of my parents. It was a time of self-discovery. It was, in essence, time to either sink or swim in this world. I chose to swim.

Thankful for the plethora of opportunities to grow, I threw myself into as many as I could. One of those opportunities was being a student preacher for OBU Days events at local Baptist Associations across the state.

Adventures with Wild Bill

NO, it is not what you are thinking, but Bill was wild all right, but not in that way. He was married, had a small child, and was the poorest student I knew at OBU, poorer than me. We met at an OBU Day preaching event; more on that in a minute. It was a regular feature of life for ministerial students who wanted to improve their speaking skills to participate in OBU day events. An added benefit for me was that I could earn a little extra cash.

The program director often asked me first to go to these events. I first preached in Ponca City, then another weekend in Bokhome, then in Cooperton, etc. I quickly became a regular on the OBU circuit.

After every OBU Day, the pastor or the Chairman of the Deacons sent a report to the school with a critique of how we had done. Generally, I preached in the morning service for about 20-25 minutes and gave my testimony as part of the sermon in the evening service. The latter, being more personal, usually included Mother's Death, Billy's use of drugs and alcohol, Debbie's child having died, her divorce, and the ensuing custody battle over her daughter. The reports from the churches were all positive, saying they enjoyed me coming to preach and give my testimony. People often cried and said they would pray for me. This support was critical for me to understand that there were people of goodwill everywhere who would "have my back," even knowing the truth about my background. It gave me permission to be honest and to heal. It also allowed me to speak of my childhood without hurting my parents.

Now back to the OBU day event where I was scheduled as backup for Bill. This was not a role I cherished as I preferred to be the preacher. Instead, I led the music and taught Sunday School. I wasn't enthusiastic about going. In addition to being second fiddle, it was a long way from campus, near the Arkansas/Oklahoma line, and it was snowing. I arrived at Bill's small, dilapidated house at 6 am, three hours before Sunday School. I told him that we shouldn't go and should postpone the trip for another Sunday. He disagreed. We debated this for a few minutes, but he prevailed. Bill was a wild man, funny as heck, making it hard to say no. He insisted we were going to have a "great trip," asking, "What is the worst thing that could happen...maybe sliding off the mountain, getting killed, and going to heaven?" It was hard to argue with that logic. I hadn't met Bill until that day we drove to Carter's Landing Baptist Church near Vian, Oklahoma. We laughed all the way until my serious reservations about the weather re-emerged. It was still snowing, and I wasn't sure we were going to make it up the mountain to the church, but we did, crossing a cattle guard into the parking lot.

He preached, I taught Sunday School, and I led the music, which we both laughed about on the way home, as singing was not my strong suit. We enjoyed a good day together...until we had to go back down the mountain in snow and ice. I was truly nervous as we slipped, slid, and glided all the way down the mountain to Interstate 40. But from that day forward, Bill, his wife Penni, and I have remained friends. Bill gave me another much-needed gift that day, he taught me how to laugh again.

OBU Days gave me opportunities to be a part of the SBC's Bold Mission Thrust and I followed that up with being selected for the Youth Evangelism Team that first summer and preached all over Oklahoma. Between French, working at the library and preaching, I was able to stay in Oklahoma until winter break my junior year.

My Broken Heart x3

OBU represented a place to start over with dating, as I had mentioned to my parents at Christmas. I needed to date women I told myself, if I had any chance of overcoming my attraction to men. OBU was a new start with no history. No one except the counselor knew I had a problem with liking guys, and I was more determined than ever to keep it that way.

I didn't go home until Christmas, 1978, a year later. It was January Term (J-Term) and I had an intensive practical learning course in New Orleans, Louisiana, beginning just after the New Year. It was one of the features I liked best about OBU. Learning happened in multiple settings. In New Orleans, I worked with underprivileged kids as part of my psychology and religion major and was assigned to Baptist Friendship House, just off the quarter. The six weeks went quickly, and they requested that I return after my senior year, at least until I had to depart for seminary. The experience was exhilarating as I put my growing knowledge of psychology and ministry together practically and spiritually.

Home for Christmas was another matter. While they were mildly happy that I had come home, I was less so. They asked if I was going to see Roy. I said no. They asked if I was keeping in touch with Betsy. I said not much. I explained that I'd been dating other girls at college. They were disappointed.

I departed for New Orleans and then went back to Oklahoma as soon as possible. I don't think I even stopped back by on the way out to school at the end of J-Term. Mobile is about 100 miles from New Orleans, but I told them it was going the wrong way.

In my junior year I met Ivy, a nursing student. She came from a modest background, like me, and we hit it off as friends first and then started dating. But old problems returned. I found dating her to be uncomfortable. I found kissing her to be uninteresting. I remember thinking it was like kissing my grandmother; something you do, but not because you liked it. I didn't mind being with her but didn't enjoy being physical together. On one date, we ended up at her home, a farmhouse outside of town that she rented with other girls. We were alone, and it was the perfect opportunity to be physical with her. She was ready. I was not. To my great relief, her dog ate my Greek Textbook just as she started making her move. Back to counseling, I went. My new counselor now was Dr. Y., who tried to help students dealing with a variety of issues including same-sex attractions. He advised me to "be happy with myself" and even gave me a copy of his own book on the subject. Like the others, his advice was to date more women, which I did. Nothing much was helpful from his counseling. I tried to continue dating Ivy, but she had other ideas and decided I was not the guy for her and lost interest. I was mildly heartbroken by yet another failed attempt.

Next, I dated the classiest girl I had ever met, Elise, whose parents were missionaries in Africa. She was not beautiful in the classic sense, but she was classy and very attractive to me. She had a warm personality and seemed to understand my struggles better than anyone I had met or dated. Before we started to date, I decided to be honest about my struggles with men. She didn't care, which I thought was unusual and a pleasant surprise. It wasn't long before I felt "in love" with her. She, however, was not in love with me. For a time, I believed I could win her over and tried to accomplish this feat. She did love me, she said, but not in that way. But I wanted, I needed it to work. I did love her in a way that I had never felt about another woman before or since. But she rebuffed my efforts.

We had dated for several months before she decided not to get serious. When I pressed her why she felt that way, she said it was because she would always be second to the Church. I protested that it wasn't true, but she didn't believe me. She gave examples of how that would play out: "If I want to get drunk, would you allow it?" she asked. I said of course not. That was proof positive that my devotion was to the Church over her. On another occasion, she asked if I would be willing to take her to an X-rated movie. Again, my answer was No. Proof positive of my devotion to the Church rather than her again. She wanted a man who would love her unconditionally first. I was not that man in her mind. While I had a hard time separating God from the church, she did not because she had lived as a Missionary's kid and always felt her father put his work ahead of his children. She refused to have a marriage like that.

In her mind, I was more concerned with what others thought, particularly Baptists, than what she thought. In the end she declared, "I will not marry you."

I was truly heartbroken. I did the right thing and dated. I was even honest with her; it still hadn't resulted in a relationship. She finally broke up with me for good my junior year after I returned from J Term.

As Elise and I broke up that spring semester, Betsy reappeared in my life via letter. In it, she said she had prayed to God that he would remove me from her life as a love interest. But after much prayer, she believed it was God's will for us to be together. This came as a shock. So, at Spring Break, I decided I would marry her if this was God's will. While I was learning Critical Thinking, I was still struggling with what to do about what others thought was God's will for my life, especially people I respected. I liked and respected Betsy very much. So, off to Alabama I drove to get her to marry me. The answer to "my girl problem" (not having a wife) was right before me, begging me to marry her. I was determined to do just that.

But the drive was long: Shawnee, Oklahoma, to Mobile, Alabama, then on to Eastaboga where she lived with her family when not at Samford. Mile by mile I debated if I was sure this was the right decision. It had to be correct, right? No, you dated her already and didn't think it would work then, so why now? On and on it went. But this time, I was determined to make it work.

Here is a spiritual principle: "Making it work" is NEVER the movement of the Holy Spirit. As the Spirit moves, doors open, and the next step is revealed. Trying to force it is a clear sign that we are leading and not following the Spirit of the Living God. However, I was determined once and for all to end my woman problem by marrying her. While marrying Betsy wasn't ever mentioned specifically in any of my counseling, getting married and having sex in the sanctity of marriage often was.

When I arrived in north Alabama her parents sat me down. After all, I had hurt Betsy badly after she transferred from Samford to Mobile College just to be with me and then I left for Oklahoma. They had a right to be concerned that I would hurt her again.

Her mother said, "Mike, you had better not hurt my little girl any more than you have already." They planned for me to stay the entire week, with me sleeping off the front porch and Betsy in a separate room near her sisters at the rear of the house.

On the first day we went to the Ave Maria Grotto in Cullman, Alabama, and I asked her to "tie the knot" and to "put on the old ball and chain." She cried and said she had envisioned a much sweeter invitation to marriage. That should have been a warning flag that I wasn't the man of her dreams. But she accepted my proposal anyway. Her parents were less than thrilled.

I am nothing if not prepared. I had picked out rings in Shawnee but hadn't given her the ring yet. I wanted to know if she would like the ones I had chosen. We went ring hunting to a nearby jewelry store. She chose what I thought was an ugly set. I showed her ones like the ones in my pocket, and she proclaimed that she thought that set was ugly. My heart sank because I realized that I really knew very little about Betsy and her tastes, wants, and desires. Now I couldn't give her the ring I had chosen for her, so it remained in my pocket.

By day three, I was bored out of my mind. She wrung a chicken's neck and cooked it for dinner for me and the family. "Wringing the chicken's neck" was one of the most disgusting things I had ever witnessed, and yet she had done it to impress me and show that she would be a good wife.

Her dad took me out on the farm with him the next day. He was kind but questioned me to ensure I was not misleading his little girl. I told him my plans were honorable. That evening, Betsy and I watched the sun go down. Betsy said she was happy as could be and could "sit here and watch the sun go down for the rest of her life." Here? Every night? I knew instantly we did not want the same things. During the next day she mentioned kids, having lots of kids. Her dream come true was being here on the farm watching the sun go down as our big event of the day with a house full of children. However, it was not my dream at all. That night, day four, was miserable because I realized I had made a colossal mistake again with Betsy. I couldn't marry her. It wasn't fair to her. She wanted a simple life with kids. I wasn't sure what I wanted, but I was sure this wasn't it. I struggled with the nagging feeling that I would not be faithful to her if I went through with this. How could I? While I loved her as a person, I was not aroused by the thought of being physical with her. I didn't want to be that kind of husband.

With that revelation, I knew I had to face the music again. At 5 am, I was up on the front porch pondering the mess I had made. I had followed the advice of my last three counselors, who all said I needed to find the right woman. Betsy was as right as any woman would ever be for me. My parents and friends from High School and Mobile College thought she was the one, the right woman. Only my friends from OBU thought this was a mistake since I was more interested in Elise than her. But Betsy had written and told me that God told her she was the right woman, and I was the right man.

At 6 am, she discovered me on the porch by myself and sensed something was wrong. She asked me, "We are not going to get married, are we?" I replied no, we are not. She cried. I cried and told her there was something deeply wrong with me inside. Her parents were mad as hell and asked me to leave immediately. I did. I drove back to Mobile, a defeated man. My parents were in shock and disbelief that I could hurt that "beautiful girl again." I left and drove back to OBU, vowing never to return. I was depressed. Betsy hated me for good reason. Ivy had forgotten me in lieu of another, and Elise refused to love me because I loved God (to her, the Church) too much. My heart broke three times.

My parents were furious. I did not go home for the summer, taking courses and working in the library instead. Once again, even with all my progress, my life looked uncertain.

Misadventure to the Big Apple

What could possibly go wrong with a spur of the moment, cross country trek from Oklahoma to New York City? Nothing my room-mate or I could think of as I worked in the basement of the library.

After the school term ended, including summer school and work cleaning out the basement of the library, with the Betsy debacle behind me and Elise's rejection still stinging, Richard proposed we go on a road trip. He said all college kids go on at least one "stupid and wonderful trip while young." As I cleaned out the basement, he talked about making a grand trip. We could go west to California or east to New York! I dismissed the idea as impossible. I had very little money, and he had even less. But he persisted, saying it would do me good to get away. It would help me get over Elise, for whom I was still pining. She was dating a very nice young man at this time, and they were getting serious. The more serious they got, the more jealous I became. She was the one woman with whom I had been honest about my struggles with sexuality, and she had not rejected me because of them. That I would have understood. Instead, she rejected me because I loved God too much. Ugh!

In the hot, dusty basement of the Mabee Learning Center, I told Richard that if he could figure out a way to keep the trip to $300 per person or less, I would make the journey with him. He was ecstatic. After returning to the room, he was already planning how to make the trip work. He said we had to go east rather than west. By going east, we could stay with more friends along the way. I had a good friend from High School whose girlfriend's parents lived in the Washington, D.C. area. "We could stay with them," he suggested. And "my girlfriend, Lori, we can stay with her on the way back through Illinois."

Convinced, we plotted a masterpiece trip of a lifetime. And it was. A week before classes started back, we loaded the car with $300 each and headed off to Washington, D.C., and New York City. We planned to drive the whole trip and be back before classes started the week before Labor Day. Richard said I should consider this my birthday trip, as I turned 23 that September.

I intentionally didn't tell my parents about the trip until just before we left, so they couldn't stop me. We had thought about everything, or so we thought. In reality, our planning was far from complete. On the first day, we drove as far as Louisville, Kentucky. On the map, Kentucky didn't look that far, but after hours of driving, tired and worn out, we slept in a Baptist Church parking lot. In our planning we thought we could make it all the way to Washington, D.C., before resting.

The trip was an excellent time for Richard and me to share intimate details of our lives. We had much in common. Both our mothers had died while we were young. Unlike many of our fellow students, we struggled with money to be at OBU. Both of us were struggling with sexuality but in different ways.

He had trouble controlling his sexual urges, and I struggled with liking men. We discussed it all as we drove mile after mile through Kentucky, West Virginia, and Virginia.

On the second day, driving through the rugged mountains of West Virginia was amazing. I had never seen such tall wildflowers in my entire life. They were taller than we were. It was a delightful day. On the second night we realized we had miscalculated again as we only made it to the outskirts of D.C., to northern Virginia. We had not planned for a hotel, but we needed to find a cheap one. Richard, who had not washed his clothes before leaving, felt sure we could find a Wash-a-teria along the way. We figured this was as good a night as any to accomplish this task. But we struggled to find one. Surely, people in Virginia needed a place to wash clothes. After several fruitless attempts, someone took pity on us and asked me repeatedly what we were looking for. It took some time before she realized I meant a Laundromat. We washed clothes till late into the night, then crashed in our cheap motel room.

At this point, we were only a little off budget. We planned to spend $50 per day per person, counting food, gas and accommodation. The Motel added an unexpected cost of $35, which we thought was expensive but necessary.

The next day, we met one of my best friends from the youth group at Riverside Baptist, Tracy, also known as Matthew. We graduated the same year and he headed to the University of South Alabama (USA) while I went to Mobile College and then OBU. He met his girlfriend Sue at USA and fell in love. They met us in Washington D.C., and we toured the sites together: The White House, Capitol Hill, Washington Monument, and Lincoln Memorial, the usual ones. Sue, as expected, invited us to her parents' home in suburban Maryland for the night. Watching Sue and Tracy, it was clear they were in love. Tracy confided that they were close to being engaged, and it showed. The next day, Richard and I went back to D.C. on the B&O Railroad and enjoyed a second day in our Nation's Capital.

So far, the trip was going better than expected. We had only spent about $75 apiece and had been on the road for three days. Now came the highlight of the trip.

The drive up from Maryland was not as easy as it looked. First, the interstate was closed in Philadelphia, and we had to detour through very rough neighborhoods around midnight. We were both scared we might be shot and killed. After surviving that adventure, we drove towards New York City. It was spectacular. Aunt Julie would have loved this view of the city. The buildings glowed in the dark night sky in brilliant contrast. But as we approached, I noticed the tall buildings were moving to our south. Richard was driving and I suggested we turn around. He refused. An argument ensued. Finally convinced, he turned around right before we crossed over the Harlem Bridge in the wee hours of the morning.

Back across the river from lower Manhattan on the New Jersey side, we finally found the route into the city via the Holland Tunnel and promptly got stuck in a traffic jam. When traffic finally moved, I stopped the car and asked a cop directing traffic where we could find an inexpensive hotel. He laughed in my face and told us to go back to Jersey City to the Holiday Inn, the only hotel we could possibly afford. We did as directed and found the Holiday Inn. But apparently, NYC's inexpensive was different from Oklahoma's inexpensive. It was $75 per night per person. We debated but had few other options. The parking lot was fenced with barbed wire at the top, and the lot had a guard on duty. I didn't feel safe, but it was a little too late to think about that now. We paid the money and fell into bed fast asleep. At least Richard did. I did not sleep well because I was so keyed up about my car.

The next morning, with permission and at no extra cost, we left our car in the hotel parking lot and took the bus into Manhattan. The bus trip was exciting and a little challenging, but we managed. Everyone taking the bus into Manhattan was dropped off at the Bus Terminal at the Port Authority at Times Square. For the first time since leaving Sue and Tracy, I was pleased to be in New York. Richard and I both had lists of things we wanted to see. I wanted to see the places Aunt Julie had discussed: The United Nations, Times Square, and the Avenue of the Americas. Richard wanted to ride the Staten Island Ferry, see and tour the Statue of Liberty, and go to the top of the World Trade Center.

Both Times Square and The United Nations proved difficult to find. For one thing, Times Square is not a Square, and nobody understood what I meant when I said U.N., as in where is the U.N.? After a while, I finally said United Nations. It was just a few blocks down the street.

My last request was Avenue of the Americas. It was easy to find. Each corner had a circle medallion listing a different country, just as Aunt Julie described years ago. Satisfied with my list, it was time to see Richard's sites.

We were soon on the subway to see the Statue of Liberty, the World Trade Center, and to ride the Staten Island Ferry. Before heading into the city that morning, I made it clear that I wanted to be out before dark. So now, time was of the essence.

We headed south on the subway. Neither of us had ever been on a subway before and didn't know how to read the maps. Three floors below Times Square and five missed trains later a businessman said, "Put that map away, follow the signs to Wall Street and stop looking like such a tourist."

On the ride down, a very friendly African American woman asked if we would like "any favors," and we declined. She then asked if we were a couple. Richard said, "Yes, we are together." Only then did I realize that she meant A COUPLE. Embarrassed, I tried to explain we were just friends. She winked and said, ok. But I could tell she didn't believe me. It was the first time I was mistaken for being gay. While this exchange bothered me, Richard took it in stride.

The Statue of Liberty was the highlight of the trip as we walked all the way to the top and viewed the awesome New York City skyline from Liberty Island. The Staten Island Ferry was also fun, as was the World Trade Center, but I was getting nervous as the sun began to set in the west. Richard didn't want to leave but finally relented.

At 6 pm, I made Richard get back on the subway to the Port Authority, where we located our bus back to Jersey City, New Jersey and my car.

After purchasing our bus tickets and riding for a while, I noticed that nothing looked familiar. I did not see the Holiday Inn. On the trip over it was a short bus ride. This time, it was longer. Concerned, I walked forward and asked the driver where Jersey City was. "Ten stops ago," he said.

"That can't be," I stammered. He explained that the evening bus goes a different route than the morning bus. We got off then at his suggestion and tried to hail a taxi.

It was now sometime after 7:30 pm in nearly deserted downtown Union City, New Jersey. Most of the buildings were boarded up. Hardly anybody was on the streets. I was in a panic. Richard, cooler or immune to danger, never sure which, handled the situation better. He eventually hailed a "homemade" taxi. The driver said he would take us to the Holiday Inn for $10, "which was a steal." We accepted and got in the back of his taxi, which had a wood plank for a seat. On the way, our driver, Hugo, asked if he could smoke pot. Richard agreed.

Picture this: Richard and me inhaling pot fumes, in the back of a homemade taxi with a plank of wood for a seat, taking the backroads and alleyways of Union City enroute to the Holiday Inn in Jersey City. After a U-turn at a five-point intersection I was convinced we were going to die.

Since I am writing this, you know that didn't happen. We made it back to the Holiday Inn at about 8 pm, paid the fare, and started our trek home.

By now we were down to less than $125 per person with half the driving left. I was so stressed by the day's events I demanded to drive for a while. I did not stop the car again, except for gas, until we arrived in Buffalo, New York, on the way to Niagara Falls. We stopped to look at the falls but they were fogged in so we drove on into Canada.

Sometime very late that night I relinquished the wheel to Richard, who had been sleeping in the back seat. He drove the rest of that night and well into the morning as I slept. He drove through Woodstock, London, and Windsor, Canada, hitting Detroit before I woke up. It was a race to get back before we ran out of money. We were on I-75 driving through the flattest land I had ever seen until we hit I-70 north of Dayton, Ohio. Then it was finally on to Illinois, where his girlfriend's parents lived. By the time we arrived in Centralia, we had been on the road for more than 24 hours. We were exhausted.

Richard was happy to be with Lori and I was left to consider my fate. His rendezvous with her left me alone and brought me back to the reality that Elise had rejected me. For all my efforts I was failing to make progress finding the girl of my dreams. Obviously, Richard wasn't having the same problem. Lori was madly in love with him, and he seemed to be smitten with her.

I thought again that maybe I should have married Betsy. Maybe I should try again to make things right with her. But in my heart, I knew I didn't love her like Richard loved Lori or Tracy loved Sue.

Then I considered Elise. That was a different problem. I thought I was in love with her. She seemed to understand me. I believed that with her love, I would be able to overcome any problem, including liking men. I could tell her anything. She listened, cared, and loved me unconditionally. But she knew better than I did that as much as she loved me, we weren't meant to be together as lovers. I could have salvaged that friendship if I had been more mature, but I wasn't.

After resting a day in Centralia, we hit the road again, due back in Shawnee by Saturday before classes started on Monday.

The trip had been Richard's idea, but it was the vehicle for another "ah ha" moment. We arrived back in Shawnee with $2 between us, a world of memories, and I had a new perspective on moving on from Ivy, Elise, and Betsy.

I Finally Did Something Right!

Richard and I moved off campus together for my last (Spring) semester, as only seniors could do at OBU. We had become inseparable except when Lori was around. Then, I had to make way for her. They dated the entire fall semester and things remained good between them. I expected him to desire her time and want to be physical together.

She finally agreed to stay overnight at our off-campus apartment after much hounding by Richard. This pressure from him and her decision to do so was bad for our friendship and was made worse when he broke up with her a couple of weeks later. I couldn't stand that he had treated Lori, a wonderful woman, like that. I left. The day I left, I was so angry that I ran a red light and was smashed by another driver who had the right-of-way. My car was totaled. The adjuster gave me $600 for my Malibu. But he felt sorry for me and let me buy it back for $300. That three hundred dollars allowed me to finish paying for my last semester with enough money left to get home.

When I left our apartment, I didn't know where to go. I couldn't afford the dorm, nor could I have gotten in so late. Upset, I went to Bill and Penni's house for wisdom. They immediately took me in and allowed me to stay until graduation, less than a month and a half away! Amazingly, I still managed to graduate.

Graduation with Dad and Mom

As I walked from University Center to Raley Chapel, all these recent events were playing in my mind, as was the whole of my experience at OBU. It had been transformative. The building that lured me to OBU in the first place was the place of the final momentous event. With the sky slightly overcast and the wind blowing hard as usual, I scurried into the chapel to line up for graduation.

With a flowing robe, I marched onto the stage of John Wesley Raley Chapel and accepted my diploma. For me, the two and half years at OBU had been difficult at times, but great ones. The anger that had consumed me in Mobile largely dissipated as I began to tell my story through testimonies all over Oklahoma. My sense of self-worth was at its highest point to date and being the first member of my immediate family to graduate from college certainly helped.

That day I was thankful for my Nanny Brill who was so instrumental in me going to college and for all her loving support ... and that garage apartment.

Dad and Mother made their one and only trip to see me for graduation, as did Tony, my former high school best friend's brother. I was grateful they all made the trip. My adopted family from First Baptist Church in Tecumseh, Oklahoma was also there for me. It was a glorious day.

The graduation service was nearly perfect. Dean Woodward, head of the Warren M. Angel School of Fine Arts, led the Commencement Chorus in *Lift Up Your Heads, O Ye Gates* (from Psalms 24:7-10 KJV) and it was beautiful. After the commencement address, they first read off the Candidates for Bachelor of Music, Music Education and Humanities degrees.

Finally, Candidates for the Degree of Bachelor of Arts were called to come forward. My name was 18th on the list, one behind John, my former roommate. While still not friends, we were cordial to each other that day. Our class was quite an eclectic group, from conservative student leaders to radical ones who regularly challenged conventions. Perhaps the most inspirational was Peter, whom most of us considered to be the smartest person graduating, the son of the campus maintenance man. With great pride, Peter's father watched him walk across the stage of his beloved school. The saddest graduate that day was my close friend

Gary. His parents gave him an oil well for graduation but didn't attend because they were traveling the world somewhere. During my time at OBU, Gary took me flying several times, but no one was present to see him walk across that stage. Finally, Wild Bill graduated after seven years at Oklahoma Baptist University.

After the ceremony, I was ready for the next challenge in my life. By this time, I believed God loved me unconditionally and was guiding me. I was ready, no longer needing the safe harbor that OBU had been for me. I survived and even thrived. I made friends, proved I could be on my own, earned my own way through, and I graduated!

My last vow was to come back someday as president. Such was the impact this institution had on me. It happened because of many people and events that I now consider to be the work of The Spirit: That high school teacher who made me so mad I researched colleges for academic standing; that poster in Slidell, Louisiana that confirmed OBU was the place; the radio program that paid for my first semester; even the car I wrecked my last semester. All told me that God was watching over and guiding me. I wasn't alone and had never been. I just hadn't fully realized God's presence.

Life looked hopeful, and with gratitude, I looked forward to the next steps of faith before me.

NOTES

1.   https://en.wikipedia.org/wiki/Southern_Baptist_Convention_conservative_resurgence#HeroSection

In Key West

CHAPTER 6

God, Where Now?

"Take the first step in faith. You don't have to see the whole staircase to take the first step."
Rev. Dr. Martin Luther King, Jr.

Where Now?

I was ready for the next chapter in my life. I was excited to return to New Orleans to work at Baptist Friendship House, where I did my J-Term internship earlier. New Orleans is many things to many people. It is a romantic city, a historic city, and a rowdy city. More than 300 years old, New Orleans is a colonial city that more closely resembles Paris than any other U.S. city. It is also a port city with a significant minority population that is largely poor. That is the primary demographic we served at Baptist Friendship House.

Working with latch-key kids that summer was challenging, but the more I worked in this environment, the more I knew I could make a difference. The most memorable moment was when I jumped between two teenage girls fighting each other with broken beer bottles. I haughtily told them they would have to hurt me first. That stopped the fight, but I was severely reprimanded for my stupidity. If I were going to work in Christian Social Ministry, the Director warned me, I would have to use better judgment.

New Orleans was hard in another way. The eastern edge of The Quarter, where the Center was located, was home to a large and growing gay population. Down the street was Charlene's, a tough lesbian bar, but driving home through The Quarter every night, I passed a gay bar where men pawed one another outside the front entrance. It was nearly always packed. I was both offended and aroused. I immediately started counseling at the Ochsner Center.

The next big decision was where to continue my education. I really had no idea. The most likely choices were the 6 SBC seminaries. Still, only two appealed to me: Southern Baptist Theological Seminary in Louisville, Kentucky (SBTS or "Southern") and New Orleans Baptist Theological Seminary (NOBTS).

New Orleans was the easy choice. It was near home, and I already had permanent employment if I stayed in the Crescent City. But being ALL SPIRITUAL, I waited for God to deliver a definitive answer, as God's Spirit had with OBU. I needed a poster or some form of verification, like the radio program sale. I prayed and prayed, but God wasn't answering. I prayed some more. Nothing.

As I waited on God and had time to think, I thought that perhaps my limited understanding of opportunities skewed my interpretation of God's calling. Based on my experience at Baptist Friendship House, I decided to add Christian Social Ministries as an option now. But still, I waited.

Finally, someone suggested that I do research and choose the best program. I discovered that Southern had, by far, the best program. So, I applied to their Carver School of Missions and Social Work, the only seminary-based school of Social Work in the world.

To be admitted, the SBTS Social Work program required the Graduate Record Exam (GRE), a standardized test that top master's degree programs in the nation also require for admission. I decided to take the exam on a whim, just in case I was told to go there. Tulane University, a host location for the GRE, wasn't far away and had an opening for Saturday testing, my day off. I signed up and took the test. Four weeks later, I was notified that my score was below the minimum required for Southern's Social Work program. I have never been a good test taker, which proved true in this case also. This was a clear sign that SBTS was not the place for me. Disappointed but still awaiting direction from God's Spirit, I prepared to attend NOBTS.

While I desired a simplistic approach to faith, the Spirit began to speak in different ways as I matured. While disappointed about SBTS's rejection, I couldn't shake the feeling that Southern, having the best program, was where I should go. I was confused. Why was God's Spirit, the Paraclete, making this so difficult? In Christian Theology, the Paraclete comes from the Koine Greek (the written language used during New Testament times). It is a combination of *Para,* meaning to walk beside or alongside, and *Kalein,* meaning to call. It first appears in John 14:16 and is a name for the Holy Spirit as the Father's representative to the Father.

Just when I concluded I had miscalculated God's will, Southern sent me a letter saying they decided to open the program to 20 additional students with exceptional applications who did not meet the minimum GRE score. Later, I learned from the Dean of the Carver School of Missions and Social Work, who by that time was both a friend and a professor, that I was the last person on the list of 20 newly opened spots. I realized I had unthinkingly walked by faith this time. My "ah ha" moment came after taking a step, not before.

Lou-uh-vul, Here I Come!

Soon it was time to go to Louisville (Lou-uh-vul to locals) in my "fixed up" 1968 Chevy Malibu that I wrecked just before graduation.

The Southern Baptist Theological Seminary was the oldest and most prestigious of the six Southern Baptist Seminaries. Founded in 1859 in Greenville, South Carolina, it was the first national SBC institution of higher education (meaning controlled by the National Convention).

Before I attended SBTS, it was known within the denomination as a bastion of liberalism. But it was also well known as an innovator in theological education. It was one of the first seminaries to offer a Ph.D. (1892), the first to provide a degree in Christian Missions (1902), the first to offer a degree in Religious Education (1925), and the first fully accredited Seminary-based Social Work program that achieved its accreditation the semester after I graduated in 1984. It was important to me that people outside the denomination consider my credentials stellar.

As I walked onto the campus on Lexington Road that first day, I could not help but think of the great Baptist statesmen who had passed through these hallowed halls, including Dr. E. Y. Mullins, whom I wrote about at OBU, the leading Baptist Theologian of the last century by most accounts, and a former president of SBTS.

Classes started soon after I arrived. Sure enough, my gay demons followed me from Alabama to Oklahoma to Louisiana and now to Kentucky. I soon learned that the park across the street from campus was a "cruising place" for gay men. The temptation overcame me twice as I attempted to know how the "pick up" game worked. But I was too chicken to follow through on this impulse.

For this near failure, I started counseling once again, this time with a Baptist Pastoral Counselor who worked with youth at the Kentucky Baptist Home for Children. He advised using a behavioral approach, which included masturbation while cultivating the image of me having sex with women. This was unsuccessful, though I tried it for several years while there. For one, I felt that thinking about sex was still sinning. *"For as he thinketh in his heart so is he,"* the scripture says (Proverbs 23:7, KJV). Secondly, I had a hard time thinking about women in that way (sexually), but I tried faithfully.

On the academic front, classes went well, and I excelled at Southern, too. I was elected to the M.Div. Student Council for two years. After that, I declined to run again because I was a full-time student and a part-time Minister of Education and Children at Second Baptist Church in Greenville, Kentucky. I didn't have time to fulfill student council duties anymore.

Southern was a challenge academically, but not to the degree OBU had been. At OBU, I learned to think, write, and speak well. With those skills now solidly in my toolbelt, the work at Southern, while challenging, was not unbearable.

Not long after I arrived on campus, a fellow student approached me about his struggles with homosexuality. He wanted me to know that he was in love with me. I was shocked someone in the seminary suspected I was gay, much less declared their love for me. In anger, I rebuked him. I told him I was not gay and that "gay people are an abomination unto God."

My homophobia kicked in, and I kicked him out of fear. He did not understand how I could go from such a committed, loving Christian to such a hateful one. He dropped out of Southern the next semester and returned to his native Pennsylvania. It is painful to recall this failure of faith. I knew then, as I know now, that God loves us unconditionally. I didn't extend that love to my brother in Christ, gay or not. I acted out of fear and hate, something I regret to this very day. Seminary, like OBU, had women on the faculty, which infuriated the conservatives in the convention who were now plotting a takeover. Great scholars like Dr. Anne Davis, Dean of the Carver School, religion faculty member Dr. Diana Garland, and fellow OBU alum Dr. Molly Marshall-Green became targets.

Of all the faculty, Dr. Glenn Hinson had the most significant impact on my education at SBTS. His works, including *A Serious Call to A Contemplative Lifestyle* and *Seekers After Mature Faith*, changed my thinking from a student of scripture to that of an earnest seeker and follower of Christ. He taught me to consider other great faith leaders like Dietrich Bonhoeffer, who wrote *The Cost of Discipleship*. Bonhoeffer lived what he preached, leading him to oppose Hitler in WWII. This cost him his life. While other Christians looked the other way, he could not; he would not ignore the plight of Jews, Gypsies, and others persecuted during the Holocaust. My maturing faith was modeled around passages such as *"Since ye have done it unto one of the least of these my brethren, ye have done it unto me."* (Matthew 5:40, KJV). I believed then and now that profound faith is measured by how we love one another, even and especially those vilified by society.

Dr. Hinson also introduced me to two men who led me to deepen my commitment to Christ and his teachings. The first was Thomas Merton, a philosopher, Catholic Theologian, and Monk. After we read Merton's *Conjectures of a Guilty Bystander*, Dr. Hinson took us to the Trappist Abbey of Gethsemane in Bardstown, Kentucky, where Merton had lived. This was one of the most challenging readings of my life. It made me reconsider racial justice, the Cold War, and war in general; it also taught me always to ask, What would Jesus do if he were here today?

Dr. Hinson also exposed us to another profound thinker, Rev. Dr. Will Campbell, an activist for racial justice in the South. We met him at his home near Nashville, Tennessee, and learned that he was no longer a Southern Baptist preacher, but a Baptist who preached in the South. Dr. Campbell stood with John Lewis and other civil rights leaders in Nashville protesting segregation. This action cost him his affiliation with the SBC. He gave us a copy of his autobiographical work, *Brother to a Dragonfly*, a finalist for the National Book Award in 1978. This, too, was a difficult read.

Both of these men, theologians in their own right, challenged my thinking. Through exposure to Dr. Hinson's classes and Bonhoeffer, Merton, Campbell, and others, I learned that true faith requires LOVE in action.

It also highlighted my failure with Mark. I did not respond in love when he told me that he loved me. I was frozen by fear. Later, when I saw him on campus, he wouldn't look me in the eye. Instead, he walked head down as I passed. Even in my guilt, I did not respond in kindness; I did not try to comfort him. I just tried to make sure I didn't fall into sin. But I did fall into sin, just not the sin of homosexuality.

In Old Testament Class I learned that the Hebrew Scriptures say one of the greatest sins is being inhospitable to your neighbors (Ezekiel 16:49). That is the sin of Sodom. Read the whole passage, Genesis 18 and 19, and ask yourself: What town do you know where all the MEN want to have sex with male strangers? None. The townspeople weren't after sex but power and humiliation. That is why the guests (Angels) came back, to give the city one more chance. Lott even offered his virgin daughters, but there were no takers. Before this class, I had never heard a Southern Baptist preacher discuss the context of the story of Sodom, nor the valid message of the story, that being inhospitable to your neighbors is a great sin.

For most men, enduring forced sex by another man is among the most humiliating and vile acts. In fact, through much of history, a man being penetrated was a grave act of defilement. Similarly, raping a woman is seldom about sex; it is also about power and humiliation.

I was inhospitable to Mark. I was anything but what a person of faith should be: Loving...love your neighbor as you love yourself, the scriptures proclaim over and over. When Mark finally left Southern Seminary, I felt relieved.

Ordinary People

I had been going to professional counseling for at least five years by this time; while making no progress in overcoming homosexuality, I was making progress on other vital issues. My current counselor suggested I see *Ordinary People*, the directorial debut of Robert Redford. My counselor said it might be helpful. Not thinking much about it, I went.

The film follows the disintegration of a wealthy family in Lake Forest, Illinois, following the accidental death of one of their two sons and the attempted suicide by the other. I went because it was suggested. I didn't really know or care about the plot before going.

After seeing the movie, I realized this was an ambush by God and my counselor. I came out bawling. I hadn't realized that I needed a strong dose of self-love. In my mind, it was a story about a boy named Conrad who suffers because his brother Buck drowns, but he survives. This is called survivor's guilt. I, like Conrad, felt guilty for living; for surviving when someone else, Mother, didn't. I survived my difficult childhood, but she didn't. I felt guilty. My family, even I, would have gladly put me in her place; it would have saved the rest of my family from the pain of her suicide, and few would have missed me. In the movie, Conrad's mother blamed him for his big brother's death, and in his grief, Conrad tried to kill himself. His mother eventually leaves the family, leaving him and his dad to rebuild their relationship. At that moment, the Spirit of God said, "This movie was made with you in mind. You, too, carry the guilt; you, too, feel unworthy. You, too, have a family who would have preferred it were you. But I am here to give you hope and courage to face life."

Stunned, I cried like I had never cried before about Mother's death. I felt the pain that I hadn't allowed myself to feel when she died. Back then, I became numb and felt nothing. Now, it was time to put her death and those tragic events behind me, starting with grief.

Seeing this movie was another "ah ha" moment. This was a secular movie.

I knew that God, through the Spirit, would use movies like *The Cross and the Switchblade*, but it never occurred to me that God would use a secular film for a spiritual end. My understanding of God was still way too small. What I knew for sure was that God, through the manifestation of the Spirit, was with me the whole time, back then (Mom's Death), through today. I knew the truth that God Loved Me. I also knew from the movie that I didn't love myself. But to love God fully, I needed to do so. I was learning that loving oneself was necessary, not selfish.

We are put on earth to accomplish whatever the Creator God has put us on earth to do. Maybe it is to be a maintenance person like Peter's father at OBU. Then be the best maintenance you can be. He was. God will make that a blessing to others, it was. Maybe it is a missionary overseas, sharing food, medicine, and a message of Good News. Do it out of love, not the number of people "you save." I came away relieved, sad, and determined to forgive myself for living. And I was determined to use my life loving others as I learned to love myself. I was clearly still a "work in progress."

The Grim Reaper Comes Again

My struggles with sexuality did not go away, but did take a short break. During my first semester at the Seminary, I was blessed with a great roommate, Clay, from Sheridan, Wyoming. He was a simple, well-liked man from the Great Plains and eager to learn. He was blond, blue-eyed, and handsome. He was easy to live with, and we often did activities together. He was obviously straight, had a girlfriend he dearly loved, and planned to marry her upon completion of his first year at Southern. This was perfect for me, for it provided no opportunity to "sin," not to say that I didn't have thoughts from time to time.

We were both poor kids who had to work our way through college. We were both serious about our schoolwork, but Clay had a more difficult time with the academic requirements. I helped him as best I could.

We both had jobs to pay for tuition, room & board, and fees. He cut the grass at St. Matthew Baptist Church, and I worked as Associate Pastor of Summit Hills Baptist Church in Hillview, Kentucky. We had no choice but to make money, so we worked and worked hard. Clay was a well-built man of short stature. We went to several job interviews together. I remember he got a job unloading trucks at a warehouse, but I didn't because the foreman feared the "big guys" might take advantage of me. It seems they recently had a gang rape among the men. I admit it interested me way too much. To date, the only sexual encounter I had was with Roy, who had forced himself on me while I was a freshman at Mobile College.

I still had to find other jobs; for example, I sold toys at Christmas Home Parties for a Jewish lady. That was the year that the SBC president made his infamous statement, "God does not hear the prayers of Jews," for which I had a lot of explaining to do. I knew even then that was not true. God hears all and loves all regardless of nationality, religion, background, economic status, sexual orientation, etc.

On weekends, Clay always cut the grass at the church. It would look pretty for Sunday. One late Spring Saturday, I was posting Revival fliers in store windows when the pastor of Summit Hills tracked me down. He explained that I was needed at Southern immediately. "Something has happened to your roommate," he said. Indeed, something had happened: "A 22-year-old student at Southern Baptist Theological Seminary was apparently electrocuted about noon yesterday while cutting grass at St. Matthew Baptist Church..." the notice in the *Louisville Courier-Journal* reported the next day. It was true! I could hardly believe my ears. Clay was as committed to Christ as any student in a seminary. He was so eager to learn and to be used by God. He would have been a fantastic minister because of his heartfelt concern for others. Why was he the one taken??? Clay was to have married Debbie on June 2nd, just a couple of weeks after his death.

When I arrived back at campus, fellow students tried to comfort me. The Dean of Students was there to inform me that he had indeed been killed. I told jokes, made fun of Clay and his hick ways. People were worried that I did not comprehend what had really happened. But I did. Clay was dead. He was yet another significant person in my life to die, leaving me to go it alone. If I were hurting this badly, I knew Debbie, his fiancée, was hurting worse. She was also a great friend.

During the summer, I returned Clay's belongings to his parents in Sheridan, Wyoming. Back in his tiny hometown, he was a hero. The City Fathers named a small park in his honor. I was proud to have known him, even if for just a little while.

On that trip, his family and friends showed me the wonders of God's beautiful creations, including Yellowstone and Grand Teton National Parks. Thus, my lifelong love of nature and nature's creatures, especially those living in the protected environment of the National Parks, began.

A fellow student accompanied me out west so I wouldn't have to do it alone. It was a long and painful trip. I was 24 years old, and the fifth significant person in my life had died: Grandfather (Pawpaw) Brill, my biological mother, my oldest stepsister's child, Aunt Julie, and now

Clay. Southern was proving painful in ways not known at OBU. OBU had been a time of healing and letting go of anger towards my parents. In Louisville, life demanded more growth and maturity. But as I struggled, my maturing faith was giving way to death, and with it, my health suffered.

Something Is Wrong with Me

The semester after Clay's death, I noticed I wasn't feeling well. My new roommate, Mike, was exceptionally bright (Mensa bright, like my brother). He easily got bored with his classes. For instance, he studied 500 years of Russian Orthodox history before writing a paper on just 15 years of that history. Even though he was a month late, he still got an A after the professor deducted points for his tardiness.

That semester didn't start well for me. I was struggling with my sexual orientation, as always, Clay's death, and now my health. Each night, I complained to Mike that my stomach hurt.

On the vocational front, I moved to Second Baptist Church in Greenville, Kentucky. That assignment came about through a little "God Intervention," I'll explain shortly. My stomach pains increased. It soon became clear that something was terribly wrong. Now, on weekends in Muhlenberg County, I was taken to the Medical Center in Madisonville, the nearest big hospital. I was diagnosed with Diverticulitis, a serious but not life-threatening condition. However, I didn't improve with treatment. I was re-admitted to the hospital after my weight had dropped from 130 to 110 lbs. I looked gravely ill. Eventually, the doctors concluded I had been misdiagnosed; I had Crohn's Disease, a condition with the same symptoms as Diverticulitis, but opposite treatments according to the doctors.

Welcome to Lou-uh-vul hell, I thought! It was turning out to be a rude awakening for me: my gay demons were still with me, my roommate was killed, and now I had a life-threatening disease. What had looked so promising the year before was turning into a disaster.

My parents came to visit me when I returned to Southern the next semester, a most unusual event. Dad firmly believed that "children visit parents, parents do not visit children." However, they were so concerned with my mental and physical health (rightly so) that they made an exception, intending to take me home. I refused.

By this time, my roommate was Donnie. With his support and God's help, I was going to graduate from Southern.

Again, my life looked more uncertain than it had in a long, long time.

"Muhlenberg County Down by the Green River Where Paradise Lay" [1]

In the winter of 1981, Second Baptist Church in Greenville, Kentucky, called me to be their Minister of Education and Children in Muhlenberg County. Located in a wealthy, western Kentucky town, the church learned of me through a most serendipitous route. The Church would be a big step in my professional progression.

As mentioned earlier, while I still worked at Summit Hills Baptist, I also held a second job in the psychiatric ward at Humana Hospital in Louisville. This was excellent training, learning to deal with troubled youth. It fit nicely with my request to God to work in places of ministry that few would choose. On the ward, I saw children and teenagers who had tried to kill themselves, others hooked on drugs and/or alcohol, and some came to us after abuse.

I worked the night shift from 11 pm to 7 am before heading off to class at SBTS. This was the toughest shift on the ward because most of the acting out occurred at night. I could relate to all of this. I understood wanting to kill yourself (suicide). I was aware of drug and alcohol abuse through my brother Billy, and while I had not experienced physical abuse, I understood it. (But I really chose the shift for the pay differential.)

The nurse I worked with on the night shift was a stunningly beautiful woman. She realized I was gay when I did not hit on her. She said all men hit on her, but I hadn't. She talked with me about this, and I denied being gay. She wasn't convinced. She suggested I accept this as the way it is, "Nothing to do about it but accept it," she said. She contended that being gay was an unchangeable part of life, and the healthiest response would be to accept it. I liked her very much, but I didn't like this conversation or her opinions on it.

A young man was admitted to the ward due to alcoholism and drug addiction. He also happened to be exceptionally good-looking. His Grandparents, not knowing what else to do, sent him to us for help. He had lost his parents in a tragic automobile accident the summer before and, in his grief, lost himself in chemicals to relieve his pain. I found that I could relate well to him and his struggles. But I also found myself very attracted to him.

I was discreet, of course, but the nurse observed my interest in him and lack of interest in her, which she used as proof that she was right. When she provocatively asked if I thought his butt was cute or his legs were nice, I'd blush in response.

He was big, strong, extremely handsome, and from Greenville, Kentucky. I met his Grandparents when they drove up to see him in Louisville; Second Baptist Church learned of me through them. When I received the invitation to apply, I really, really didn't want to go, afraid that I would fall into sin. I assumed he would be a "great temptation" because eventually, he would be released back into the world, most likely to Greenville. I prayed that God would not put me in that position. I decided not to go unless God's Spirit gave me a clear signal, like the guy himself asking me to. He wasn't very religious, so I felt safe making this deal with God. His Grandparents told him of their church's interest in me, so he asked me about it. I told him I would consider it, but probably would not go. Hearing this, he asked me to reconsider, telling me I had been the one person on the ward who understood his struggles and that the Church could use someone like that.

To keep my promise to God, I interviewed and was hired. From then on, I drove down to Greenville every weekend, about three hours, which meant giving up my job in the hospital.

Muhlenberg County is in the heart of the western coalfields of Kentucky between Bowling Green and Hopkinsville. Paradise, mentioned in the song at the beginning of this chapter, describes the paradox of strip-mining beautiful Muhlenberg County (paradise!) by the Pride Coal Mine and others. Pride, the last operating coal mine in the county, finally closed in 2024. Scattered throughout Muhlenberg County, there are dangerous "coal" ponds 50 feet deep or more, where youth go skinny-dipping during the hot summer months; in some years, kids drown in these hazardous ponds.

My time at Second Baptist was my most enjoyable since entering the ministry. They helped me through my diagnosis of Crohn's Disease, demonstrating what the love of Christ is all about, to me, a young Baptist preacher. It was a very mission-minded church, and they let me lead them on numerous mission trips from the Cherokee Indians in eastern Oklahoma to the Haitians (Liberty City area) of Miami and the Mountain Folk of eastern Kentucky. So many church members were extraordinarily kind to me that I do them an injustice by not naming them here individually.

My position as Minister of Education and Children meant I worked with the Sunday School and Vacation Bible School (VBS). I was affectionately referred to as the ABC Minister: Announcements, Bulletin Boards, and Children. The church is very progressive, encouraging me to help children from public housing attend VBS. I proposed, and they agreed, that I also work with the "Boys of the Job Corp," mostly troubled teens.

A funny thing happened at VBS the year our theme was "Jesus is Our Friend." We had the largest VBS in Church history that year and were one of the three largest in the county. We bought every child a helium-filled balloon for the commencement ceremony with their name and the church address printed on it. As we concluded, we marched out of the sanctuary with 400 children and balloons. We were going to let all of our balloons go for the finale and wait for responses from our new friends through them. En masse, the younger children screamed and cried as I made them release their balloons, a terribly difficult ending to a great VBS.

While in Muhlenberg County, the issue of homosexuality was ever-present. While I had decided to come to Second Baptist in part because of the young man on the ward in Louisville, I was still adamant that I was going to overcome my attraction to men. By the way, the good-looking hunk never came back to live in Greenville. After I left working in the psychiatric ward, I lost contact with him. He only returned to town once to tell me how much he appreciated my help and care while on the ward. He also saw his grandparents and heard from them that I was doing well at the church. It was fulfilling that he appreciated my efforts in his time of need, but it was a bittersweet reunion of sorts. For while I tried not to think of him in sexual terms, I did...a lot. I never acted on them, and I do not believe he had even the slightest idea of my interest, which was just as well.

For a small town, Greenville had a serious "homosexual problem," at least as explained by a member of the church I adored. She said Greenville had a vicious gay community. Apparently, they had humiliated a man in town.

It became apparent in counseling youth, another requirement of my position, that there was a man in the church who was picking up young teenage boys for sexual purposes. Many in the leadership knew this was happening, but preferred to keep it a secret to prevent a scandal from emerging. They were apparently hoping it would "just go away." I asked the pastor about it, but he refused to "make an issue of it."

Nothing happened, and the abuse continued. Finally, I spoke with some of our male youth (individually) who I knew were taking gifts from this older man in exchange for "favors." I told them that if I found out that any of our youth had taken any gift in exchange for going to this man's house or meeting him in other, less desirable places again, I would be forced to talk with their parents. One of the youth took me up on this challenge, and I met with him and his parents. All hell broke loose:

(Prayer Journal: Dec. 30, 1982) Dear Jesus,

I feel I have messed up, but I am trying hard to develop into the type of sexual being that is good and wholesome, and yet the pressure of Second Baptist is beginning to get to me in this area. You see, in the Church, we have a practicing homosexual who has been seeing some of the teenage boys in the Church. After a series of meetings, the relationships have broken off! But J.W. (intentionally abbreviated) is angry with me, and now I have to defend my actions to the deacons without Bro Jack's (The Pastor's) support. All this sexual dealing has put pressure on me internally. I have not practiced any of my homosexual feelings in the past seven years and only once in my whole life, but the fact is, I have felt some homosexual feelings, which makes me wonder about my actions. Am I opposed to J.W.'s actions because he is a threat to me? Am I opposed because of the pressure his lifestyle is putting on me? God, help me do the right thing in this situation. Help me follow you...

    Your Son,

    Mike

Looking back, I know I did the right thing, the hard thing. It is both unhealthy and illegal for gay men to seek out underage youth for sexual purposes. In fact, it is immoral and unlawful for any adult to engage in sexual activity of any kind with underage youth, gay or straight. I would have the same response if I were confronted with the same situation again.

Eventually, with pressure from church leadership, the abuser resigned and accepted a position in a nearby county. He wrote me a letter before I left Greenville telling me that in his "new place," he had found a new boyfriend, a 15-year-old. I should have informed the police about his activities, but regrettably, I was young, overwhelmed, and gave in to my fear of repercussions, deciding it wasn't my problem any longer.

Back then, these discussions of "homosexuality" interfered with my ability to accept myself. From my viewpoint, it affirmed the stereotype that all gay men are sexual predators, and I bought into this big lie. I became even more determined to "live the straight and narrow path."

But my sexual yearnings were getting harder to control. I would drive across the border into Tennessee and buy gay male pornography. Once, the Chairman of Deacons from whom I was renting dropped by my house and may have noticed the magazines in the trash. He never said anything, but I am convinced he saw them.

Overall, my relationship with the Church flourished throughout my tenure at Second Baptist. When I arrived at the church, it was the fourth largest in the county. By the time I left, it had moved into the #2 slot behind Mount Pisgah Baptist.

While there, my struggles with homosexuality intensified, but other than looking at magazines, I did not act on these thoughts. I continued counseling once a week in Louisville, along with my classes, and prayed about it a lot.

Remember the church member who told me the local gays were mean? Well, after the man resigned, this saintly woman told me how he had been the victim of humiliation by "these vicious gays," who made him walk home naked. Back then, I had no reason to doubt the word of this beloved church member. Today, however, I am pretty sure it wasn't "the gays" who had humiliated him. Shortly after I came out in Mobile, Alabama, a friend was jumped by a small group of young men outside the gay bar where he had been. They called him names and jeered at him as they made him strip naked and walk home from the bar, all the while having a great laugh at his expense. This was the ultimate humiliation to my gay friend and a cheap laugh for the cruel straight boys.

Many prayers are written in my journals. The journal idea came as a way to review the good things God had done in my life. Another benefit was being able to go back and read my conversations with God and understand what I was thinking at the time.

(Prayer Journal: Jan 1, 1983) Dear God,

I am so lonely and depressed as I have been for a long time. I feel guilty and abnormal. I feel like true love will never come my way. Your influence in my life is weakening, and your church is being questioned in my mind!

Please help me.

Your Son,

Mike

I wrote that entry when I was back home in Mobile for the New Year's Holiday. While there, I became reacquainted with Diana, an early girlfriend from High School. It seemed she was God's answer to my plea. I was soon pursuing her to be my "significant other." The Greenville situation paralyzed me so severely that I felt an overwhelming need to find and marry "the right girl" again.

Diana met all the criteria, and we were now 10 years older than when we dated back at Rain High School. We were both ready for some-body significant in our lives. She wrote me letters, and I wrote back and called from Kentucky, returning during spring break to see her. It looked promising until the relationship got serious. Not even aware I was doing so, I began to undermine it. While I had great hope for Diana, we were never physical, and it seemed a repeat of Betsy, Ivy, and Elise.

Diana and I continued to date throughout the remainder of my time at Southern, which was convenient because I didn't have to date women in Greenville anymore. But it also meant denying the obvious: my at-traction to men.

As my time at Southern and Greenville was coming to a close, I was forever grateful for my opportunity to serve the church and to learn more deeply about God's love, as demonstrated by so many members.

Donnie, my last roommate, knew I was struggling in my relationship with Diana and decided to help. He had been so good in helping me through the grief of Clay; his suggestion that a little "adult growing up" would help me along my journey sounded good. Idea: Since I was still a virgin, he suggested I go to an X-rated movie to get more acquainted with sex. I wouldn't go alone, so we watched an X-rated movie on a snowy night. I was so paranoid that I thought people would recognize my footprints in the snow. After reviewing the experience with Don-nie, he concluded I had picked the wrong movie. I remember that I paid more attention to the guys than the girls. Go figure.

I graduated from Southern Baptist Theological Seminary in May 1984. It was my second "first" within the family, as none of my brothers or sisters had graduated with a master's degree. Graduation ended a period of controlled growth and ushered in the next phase: a decade of travel.

In the spring, with money raised from students and faculty, I was selected to be a Missionary at Rhein Valley Baptist Church in West Germany. It was a big honor. A week later, Pat Patillo, the VP for Development, for whom I worked my last semester, offered me a full-time job working with him. But it had come too late. I had already agreed to go overseas. I grieved the lost opportunity but felt obligated to follow through on my "already made" commitment.

When Diana learned I had accepted the position in West Germany, she was upset I took the assignment without considering her feelings. But having made the decision, I left anyway. I decided I would work on her feelings once there. Maybe she can come over and visit? Or I could bring her gifts from Europe? But on the flight over, she, Southern, and Second Baptist all became distant memories. I was headed to the world stage: West Germany!

NOTES

[1] Prine, John. "Paradise." *John Prine*. Atlantic Records, 1971.

CHAPTER 7

Just a Traveling Man

"Not all those who wander are lost."
J.R.R. Tolkien

Rhein Valley Rendezvous!

With Diana mad at me for going to West Germany without consulting her first and Pat Patillo disappointed I didn't take his job offer, I was ready to get out of town. West Germany, the free side of the still-divided country, was the leading economy in Europe in the summer of 1984 as I arrived at my new assignment. Rhein Valley Baptist Church (RVBC) was located in Waldorf of Hessen, just south of Frankfurt, near Rhein-Main Air Base, our target for prospective new members.

I had never traveled outside of the United States, and I found West Germany beautiful. This was an amazing opportunity, and I took full advantage. I visited many historical sites during my time off, including Castles along the Rhein River. During one visit, I heard a familiar voice from the past. "Mike Brill? Is that you? Mike Brill, is that you?" I turned around, amazed that anyone would know me in Germany, and in a confused voice said, "Yes." It was Dr. Slayden Yarbrough from OBU. Of all the people, he was the last I would have expected to remember me.

We had a "history" together back in college. Dr. Yarbrough came to OBU towards the end of my career there. He had previously been a somewhat controversial professor of Religion at Southwest Baptist University in Bolivar, Missouri. He held a Ph.D. from Baylor University, and his area of expertise was church history. He had replaced one of my best professors, Dr. Dan Holcomb who left to teach at New Orleans Baptist Theological Seminary. So, when Dr. Holcomb left, I took it out on his replacement, Dr. Yarbrough. He was an accomplished Baptist historian, having written extensively, including *Southern Baptists: History of a Confessional People* about the conflicting traditions that led us to our current state of internal strife and conflict.

At my graduation five years before, he shared gracious words about me to my parents: "Mike is not the very brightest student that I have taught, but he was one of the most enthusiastic and committed to learning. He has a love for learning, which I appreciate." But now, five years removed, I realized he had remembered me better than I thought at the time.

It was but the first of several rendezvous while in Germany. I arrived at Frankfurt International Airport with an invitation to learn a whole new culture and world far beyond what I had ever known: Baptist, The South, OBU, and Southern Seminary.

Pastor Neal Schooley and his lovely wife, Shirley, met me at the airport and brought me to the town of Waldorf where the church was located. The church was situated at the back door of the air base. RVBC had been founded by the European Baptist Convention (EBC) to "provide a place for U.S. Servicemen and their families to worship while stationed overseas." At the height of the Cold War, the United States deployed more than 100,000 servicemen and women to West Germany alone. My title was Associate Pastor in charge of singles. The church was one of the strongest in the EBC. This was quite a good assignment.

My first roommate did not last very long, quickly moving out of the apartment the Church had rented on my behalf. This meant I had to find a new roommate for cost-sharing purposes. The first person I convinced to come to the Singles Meetings at the church, Tom, an airman, mentioned when he showed up at the event that he was looking to live off base. And that's how I found my new roommate. He was a red-headed, extremely masculine man who liked to earn the most difficult patches from military training, including swamps, survival, and the like. We got along well and became friends.

My primary job was getting single military men and women to attend the church. This proved a challenge at first. As a group, single military personnel are not generally very church oriented. I was learning on the job and needed to find something that would interest them. I soon learned that every soldier had physical training (PT) every week. If they did some physical activity during the weekend, they didn't have to do PT the next week. BINGO, that was the inside information I needed. I learned about an activity called Volksmarches, which were designed to get Germans and Americans to socialize together. People could walk, run, or swim together on these Volksmarches each week and earn a medal. It benefited the Air Force through improved relations with the local Germans and helped the soldiers by eliminating PT duty. It was a win-win. At our peak, we had 12-16 singles coming every Saturday for Volksmarches and about the same number coming on Sunday for Sunday School & Church, which was considered wildly successful. As for my assignment, it was the easiest one I ever had.

Soon, though, I had an unwelcome Rhein Valley Rendezvous. While the assignment was going well, the Demons that followed me from Mobile to Shawnee and on to Louisville arrived for a visit in West Germany.

I'm fairly certain my first roommate was gay and left because "I was so conservative." I am also sure, if truth be told, he left because I was too homophobic and anti-gay. He only stayed a few days before deciding "to get out of here." Tom, on the other hand, was an All-American Male, which was a great deal more tempting for me. He was big, strong, and masculine...did I mention that before? Well, he was. He had all the qualities I find attractive in a man. My fantasies took off when he became my roommate, not that I acted out or he suspected my interest. My problem wasn't with him. It was within me, an internal battle to "control and overcome" these impulses. Welcome to Rhein Valley I thought. Even here, these feelings put my career in jeopardy.

Without Diana to give me a flicker of hope, my feelings intensified. It was not that I loved Diana in a physical sense, but she gave me hope that I could overcome these feelings. But I was in Germany, and she was upset with me. I justified my actions by telling myself she should understand because I am doing God's work in the world. I was so pious and inconsiderate. Feeling guilty, I tried to make amends. She wrote me while in Germany and I promised to make things better between us. I knew what I was going to do. Before I left, I was going to go to Paris, France, and buy her something romantic like a necklace and expensive perfume...girls like that, don't they? I did just that. I used my pent-up energy towards guys to win her back. That helped keep me from acting out, but it didn't do one darn thing to stop my attraction to men. By this time, I was getting good at camouflaging my real self.

Outside of church activities, I decided to do a spiritual pilgrimage to historical sites of the Protestant Reformation (1517-1648) and follow in the footsteps of Martin Luther. My first visit was to Marburg Castle on a Volksmarch. It was where Huldreich Zwingli (1484-1531), a Swiss Theologian, John Calvin (1509-1564), a French Protestant Theologian, and Martin Luther (1483-1546), a German Catholic Theologian, met to form an alliance seeking to break away from or reform Catholicism.

From there, I visited Worms, Germany, where Luther stood before the Diet of Worms (leaders of the Catholic Church) on April 17, 1521, and consciously chose to defend his belief in a personal faith-based relationship with Christ (a far less formal and less rigid approach than traditional Catholicism). Later, I visited Coburg, where he translated the Old Testament into German in 1518 while the Diet of Augsburg met to expel him from the church. The trouble with these trips was that I did them alone. While the pilgrimages were wonderful, they made me more aware of how alone I was in the world without a "significant other" in my life.

One day, Pastor Neal raised this topic with me while confiding that he did not believe his oldest son would ever marry. He didn't specify why he thought this, and I was afraid to ask, but he said it was a shame to live without a loving, caring person to share it with. He said he had been blessed with a wonderful person in Shirley, his wife. He was right. She was wonderful, and life certainly seemed better with someone special to share it with.

The breaking point between me and Diana came when I decided it was impractical not to date for a whole year should the opportunity arise. She objected, but I held firm. I later discovered this worked far better for her than for me.

Eventually, I did date a woman from another German city, but she eventually decided she wasn't interested in me. I learned before my arrival that by a strict policy, women in the RVBC singles group were off-limits. This is a policy I followed all my years in ministry to avoid even the appearance of a conflict of interest. I did, however, make some female friends there, including Vanessa, an army recruiter who started coming to the Singles group from Frankfurt. We became friends and agreed after my tour was over to keep in touch.

I learned a lot that year. Most importantly, I learned how different Germany was from America, especially how they saw the world in terms of a moral code. I met beautiful people, including a German couple who were living together and were bothered by smoking but not for-nication. I didn't understand, so I asked about it. The handsome man said, "How do I know I want to marry her if I don't know how she is in bed?" He was sincere and had no guilt or doubt about the beauty of sex. He was also a committed Christian. This, of course, confused me about morality. This strappingly handsome, blue-eyed, dark-haired man did nothing to help me otherwise! Of course, his girlfriend was beautiful, but I didn't pay much attention to her.

As the year ended, Shirley encouraged me to return and earn my doctoral degree if I wanted to pursue a career in Baptist Higher Education. She suggested I consider her alma mater, Oklahoma State University. Another school worthy of consideration was North Texas State. I wrote to both and set up appointments upon my return.

The year afforded me three big trips unrelated to work: Paris, France, Austria, and communist East Germany. My final trip was to East Germany with fellow SBTS alumni and missionaries Jane and David, who drew a very different assignment from mine. Their year was difficult from the start. While I don't know the details, it was clearly a tough assignment. To end our year, we went over the border into East Germany together to see Martin Luther sites, including Erfurt (where he repented all winter naked in the monastery); Wittenberg (where he nailed 95 theses' against the practices of Catholicism on the door of the Church); and Leipzig, not a Martin Luther site, but we went to the bar, Auerbach's Cellar, where Johann Georg Faust (1480-1540) frequented, and of course visited East and West Berlin.

German social customs were very different from Americans. For instance, on a retreat, we told the youth (high schoolers) that they could not order from the Baptist Retreat Center's bar. We (Baptist Americans) thought the bar was inappropriate at a Baptist Retreat Center, but the Germans felt that coffee, which is addictive, was a bigger sin than alcohol. I was struggling to figure out right from wrong. It had been clear all my life, but my old assumptions were being challenged with these new perspectives. Who was right? How was I to live a Holy Life if what's right and wrong varies according to geography?

I departed Germany a couple of weeks early for my college appointments. On the flight back, I thought about the year. It had been a good one. The highlights included teaching at the retreat center in Belgium, seeing Coburg, Wittenberg, and Berlin on the trip to the east, learning to ski in Austria (with Tom's help), and seeing the Baptist Seminary in Lucerne, Switzerland. Vanessa accepting God's Love through Christ also made the year abroad special.

On the flight, I had a lot of time to think. I made an action list: 1) a plan to win Diana back, 2) interviews for the doctoral programs, and/or 3) finding God's next place of ministry.

Life was still uncertain, but I was brimming with optimism.

I'll Go Where Nobody Else Wants to Go - NOT REALLY!

Remember I told you earlier that I promised God to go where nobody else wanted to go? Well, don't make a promise to God, or anybody else for that matter, if you aren't willing to keep it. God's Spirit took me up on my offer.

I arrived back in Mobile, Alabama after a year abroad in May 1985, and it felt strangely foreign. My childhood friends had always talked about living abroad but never did. I had just returned to the States from this great adventure with no more direction than a lost sheep.

With the adventure over, it was time to decide what I was going to do with the rest of my life. The first action item was getting Diana back. When we first reunited, she was different and cool towards me, as expected. I surprised her with my thoughtful gifts, expensive perfume from Paris and a beautiful and expensive necklace. I was sure that would do it. Not so much. Beautiful gifts are wonderful when wanted. Diana didn't want them and told me, "I'll understand if you want them back." That wasn't the response I expected. She went on to say, "I think we should just be friends." Ouch. That hurt. My grand plan failed miserably. I was disappointed, but it gave me a license to seek opportunities beyond Mobile. I didn't tell her I had already made travel arrangements to go to Oklahoma and Texas for my doctorate interviews.

I met with Oklahoma State University (OSU) first, visiting the head of the Department of Higher Education Administration. I liked him and OSU, and they seemed to like me, but I couldn't shake the feeling that it was not where I was supposed to be.

Next, I ventured down to North Texas State University and met with faculty there. The meeting went well, and I liked it better than OSU. But neither school offered a stipend to help defray the costs, and I was totally broke. While the year abroad had been a great experience, it was hard on the pocketbook. So, with regret, I left the opportunity to obtain my doctoral degree behind.

The logical next step was to seek employment. My first idea was to "find a job." But that didn't seem right. After all, I was called into the ministry. I did the most logical thing: I decided to see what opportunities the Placement Office at SBTS had on file. It took me a couple of weeks to go from Oklahoma to Texas to Kentucky, but I saw no other way to investigate the opportunities. Plus, it allowed me to see old friends and faculty at Southern.

In the first meeting with the Placement Director at Southern, he said, "I have just the place for you: East 7th Street Baptist Ministry in New York City. It is perfect for a person of your skill set and experience." I was flattered but declined immediately (#1). I looked for other opportunities that caught my eye, but nothing did.

On that same trip, I made an appointment to see the Dean of the Carver School, Dr. Anne Davis, who was very excited to see me. She said she was so looking forward to it because she had the ideal place for me to continue serving: East 7th Street Baptist Mission, NYC. I graciously declined on the spot (#2).

Next, I went to see Pat Patillo in the Development Office to see if he had an opening. He was very sorry but said he couldn't wait a whole year to fill the position. It was already filled.

Upon completing the 600-mile drive home and a month on the road, almost entirely on I-65, I still had no place of service and no idea where God wanted me to be. I prayed each morning for God to answer where I was supposed to be.

I visited Diana upon my return, and we went out a few times, but it was clear she had moved on without me.

A week after returning to Mobile, the SBTS placement director called to see if I had found a place of service. I told him that I had not. He suggested I reconsider the offer in New York. I said no again (#3). Each morning, I prayed and received no offers for ministry service. In fact, I was praying the morning Dr. Anne Davis called me again to make sure I didn't want to "at least think about New York." I thanked her, but said, "no thanks" (#4).

That same day, Ray Gilliland, the Associate Director of Missions for the New York Baptist Association, called and asked me if I would at least come and look before deciding. I said "yes" (#5). In fact, I didn't say I would come and look. I said I would come. After all, this had been my fifth request. I had prayed and prayed and prayed for a place. And God answered the first time. I just didn't like the answer.

Ray, a wise older man, was surprised when he picked me up from the airport and found me with all my bags. "I thought you were coming to look," he offered. I said. "No, there's no reason to look when obviously God wants me to be in New York." I explained that his call had been my fifth invitation to come to New York and East 7th Street Baptist Mission. After a night with Ray and his wife Anne, I toured the mission and association offices, where I filled out the required paperwork for employment, met the staff, and was introduced as the official Interim Director of the Center.

East 7th Street Baptist Mission was known colloquially as Graffiti Baptist Center because the building was painted so often that they gave up trying to keep it clean. The drive down took much longer than expected. My arrival at the Center was met with distrust the minute I set foot on the property. The previous Associate Director had an ongoing war with the previous Director. The previous associate director was now attending The Church of the Unbroken Chain, a fringe Charismatic Church in town. The previous Director, while loving and smart, held a Unitarian Theology. Together, it was a very bad mix. As a result, the Center lost its way. The Association searched the globe for a suitable replacement. Soon to be Dr. Taylor Field was set to become the new director once he completed his doctorate at Golden Gate Baptist Theological Seminary in California the following year. So, here I was, the fill-in for a year until he graduated.

On the first day, the children acted out badly. The girls, for example, refused to leave the Center when it was time for the boys' club. The groups began to fight, and Ray threatened to close the Center for a day if order wasn't restored. The girls didn't like me initially because, they said, the prior Associate Director told them I was the "mean new Director" who had taken her place. That was day one.

On Day Two, a guy living on 7th Street got into a brawl with another 7th Street parishioner and said, "If you don't like me, just shoot me." So, he did. Well, that shocked me: a murder on the block on day two. To further complicate matters, the adult members of Graffiti Baptist asked me to lead a service for the victim so he wouldn't be stuck in purgatory. We gathered at a stolen church pew which was chained to a 10-foot-high chain-link fence and held a memorial service. I left the matter of purgatory to our Creator God, and all seemed satisfied with my first service.

Eventually the children began to see I wasn't an ogre and relaxed. The clubs worked well, and the boys and girls enjoyed the Center. This is not to say there were no more fights or disruptions, but generally, the sessions were peaceful, chaotic, and full of boys and girls.

On the first Saturday of the month, we held FLIP: Free Lunch in the Park at Tompkins Square Park, diagonally across from the Center. With no support beyond the center (one staff person, two volunteers from the block, and me), we made 250 sandwiches and coffee for more than 200 guests. Over the course of the year, we built a strong support network of volunteers for FLIP, from one Church to two dozen Churches committed to providing volunteers, each assisting for one week and then getting a six-month break before their next volunteer commitment to FLIP. This allowed us to expand the program. The result was a shared load and stronger community support for a critical ministry (not to mention long-term burnout prevention).

The biggest shock was when Ray came down to tell me that my job now included cooking the Wednesday night adult meal. I told him he had to be kidding as I had never cooked in my entire life. He decided to send help to teach me how to cook. From the time I started at the center until I left, I participated in all meals, but not as the cook if I could help it! After my first try, we all agreed it wasn't the best use of my talents. But my coffee, now that became legendary... legendarily awful!

They joked about my terrible coffee for a very long time even after I left Graffiti Baptist Center.

One Wednesday evening (adult meal night), we had hamburgers, which was a rarity since most meals were notoriously light on meat. This evening, each person in the group got one hamburger. But one of our regulars, a colorful character, decided she was going to have two. We knew she had a temper and often struggled to follow the rules. After snagging a second hamburger and attempting to slip away, the biggest and toughest man in the crowd challenged her. In typical fashion, she flung her hamburger across the room, like a Frisbee, hitting him in the chest. He lurched towards her, giving chase, but thankfully, she was at the other end of the room. Like in New Orleans, I moved between them and told them they could not fight here. The tough guy told me I had better get out of his way or I might just become collateral damage. Seeing the writing on the wall (literally and figuratively), the staff had already called the police who arrived within minutes. Both were arrested for disturbing the peace. Though I remained calm throughout, realizing I could have become one of the casualties raised my internal scare-o-meter from moderately scared to a hair-raising experience!

Graffiti Center worked with and welcomed all kinds of disenfranchised people, from homeless men and women, gays, substance abusers, troubled youth, and single mothers to hippy youth from prominent families. The Center was a unique community of people whose lives were hard, all attempting to help one another in the spirit of Christ.

One group I didn't mention was the local gang, the "Ball Busters." Their leader took me aside early in my tenure at Graffiti, explained who they were, and told me, "Because you are helping the children," if I needed any help, I could let them know and "We will snuff out anybody that gives you trouble." I can tell you that was a most interesting conversation, but I never took them up on their gracious invitation.

That winter was unusually brutal, even by New York standards. Mayor Ed Koch issued an order forcing all homeless people into shelters whenever the temperature dropped below 32 degrees. On the first night of enforcement, shelters filled up in an hour. Typically, homeless people avoided shelters if possible because they had a reputation as dangerous places. The New York Times reported that 8,239 individuals were placed in shelters under Mayor Koch's mandate, with another 4,000 families staying in hotels, for a total of approximately 25,000 homeless in the city. Estimates by homeless advocates were much higher.

This was a significant increase in the homeless population following a change in government policy from President Carter to President Reagan. This was my first time observing the real-life impact of President Reagan's "trickle-down economics" in action. I was anxious about this because I had voted for him. In 1980, President Carter signed into law a mental health reform act that included a patient's bill of rights and moved many mental health services from institutions to local communities, along with increased funding for community care programs.

When Reagan defeated Carter, one of his first acts was to repeal the Patient's Bill of Rights and close most government-run mental institutions while simultaneously dramatically underfunding community mental health programs. In doing so, President Reagan's administration said these people would be better off if they were cared for by their own families. But most families, for financial, emotional, or reasons related to their own physical or mental health (especially poor families whose loved ones were most likely to wind up in government-run rather than private mental health facilities) were wholly unprepared to handle bipolar, schizophrenic or other seriously mentally ill people. We had all of these types of folks as our parishioners.

Seeing the effects of Reagan's policy firsthand helped me better understand the real-world consequences of our choices as a Nation and a society. While it sounds wonderful to re-home the mentally ill and/or infirm with their families, without training, financial support, and/or a network of trained professionals to assist was an unmitigated disaster – recent experience with dementia patients demonstrates that a combination of the three based on the family's needs, is the key to success. I was unimpressed with Reagan's "economic conservativism" and became a stronger advocate for the poor and homeless.

One young man named Joel came to us by way of an elderly couple who had taken pity on him. They were already struggling themselves, living well below the poverty line, but they couldn't let Joel die on the streets so they took him in. They lived south of the center on Houston Street, an even worse neighborhood than where the Center was located. I don't remember exactly where he was from anymore, but somewhere rural. His parents were Pentecostal Holiness and had performed an exorcism on him to rid him of his demons. He had at least two, according to them: Homosexuality and Bipolar Disorder. The exorcism scared him so badly he fled to New York. In response, his parents disowned him.

Gay people were my biggest challenge. I knew they needed to be loved, like Joel. Many were here because their families discarded them, like Joel. We would not do that. But I didn't know how to minister to them and still not be overcome by "their sin." To make matters worse, a summer volunteer decided to stay, and I inherited a new roommate, John, though I didn't know he was gay until *after* I agreed to let him live with me.

John's decision to stay was great news at first and I welcomed and encouraged his participation, even being my roommate. The entire staff was pleased. He was a good worker and was willing to work for free rent. After moving in, however, he informed me he was gay and seemed very content about it. I wrote in my journal that he was "one of the deviants." I beseeched Ray to move me from the apartment without telling him that John was gay and that I was struggling with being gay. Without that information, he could see no reason why I should be accommodated. John and I got along well that summer except when we discussed whether you could be gay and Christian. I told him there was no such thing.

Fall turned into winter, and I was in for a surprise. The winter was extremely cold, and so was the apartment. That was good on the gay front, as we were always bundled up in clothes and blankets. But winter became a time of death in NYC, as temperatures took their toll on our regulars. Three people froze to death in the park, and two were killed sleeping on a grate, which turned out to be a hot air vent for a building's A/C system. They burned to death.

As spring thawed and summer approached, John asked me if I would like to "play around a little." I told him that I was not gay, and even if I was, it wasn't pleasing to God. He was persistent. I'll give him that. That spring, he encouraged me to accept his invitation to play around. Still, I refused. He made every effort to encourage me. For instance, I slept under my covers while he slept on top of his, wearing little or nothing. Eventually, he made an overt offer to engage in sex. I was stunned and went to the Associational Office the next day and again requested a new place to live. Ray refused. For the remainder of my tenure, John continued to sleep on top of his covers in his sexiest briefs while I remained primly under mine. I also did what I do, I found a new counselor to give me the strength to not give in to John's invitations. Like always, I found little relief from the sessions and was still attracted to men.

Having a gay roommate made matters worse because it kept in the front of my mind how badly I wanted to be sexual and how much difficulty I had controlling these urges. So, I sometimes walked the 16 blocks to Greenwich Village just to observe gay people living freely. They did not seem so bad. They typically laughed, held hands, and acted like "ordinary people." I occasionally wandered into a bookstore or newsstand and considered buying something on the subject, but I never did. On a few occasions, I bought magazines of nude men, looked, and cried as I walked back to the Graffiti Center, only to throw them away before I got back. Once or twice, I thought about going to a gay play or movie but never did. Well, except once by accident.

We often got free tickets to on- and off-Broadway shows that weren't sold out and we were encouraged to go if we didn't have any pressing duties. John and I were invited to an off-Broadway production of *Pirates of Penzance.* I greatly enjoyed the show, and the cast members invited *me* backstage to visit. I did and had a good time. They also appeared to enjoy my company, and everybody signed my playbill. As I was about to leave, a cast member asked me to join him for an after-party. This was a big honor, and I was flattered. But I begged off as I had duties at the Graffiti Center. John, who was not invited backstage, waited for a while but eventually left as I was taking too long. When I got home, I told him what had happened, showed him the playbill, and told him about the invitation to the after-party. I think John was a little jealous and informed me with a smirk that "the nice cast member" was hitting on me, and that was the reason for the invitation backstage and to the after-party. This was the first time, other than Roy, I had ever been hit on, to my knowledge. With my duties at the Center, I thought God had saved me again.

At Christmas time, we gave the homeless gifts of cloth bags with personal items like toothpaste, brushes, combs, and razors, etc. This way, when they had the chance to take a shower and shave they had the necessary items to accomplish the task. Youth often dared me to go into Tompkins Square Park at night, calling me chicken for not doing so. After we gave out the toiletry bags, friends from the park (our homeless clients) came banging on my door for help. It seems one person from our community couldn't get his bag open and was getting overly agitated. I went in after dark because a client needed me. I approached as he was still trying to untie the knot. I attempted to help when he announced, "What the hell, I'll take care of this." He pulled out his 7-inch knife and slashed the drawstring. This verified for me the wisdom of not venturing into Tompkins Square Park at night unless I was needed for something REALLY important.

While West Germany had been my easiest assignment, this was the hardest. For one thing, I was too sensitive to live in a world where people were always in dire need. I often gave away my own clothes to a homeless person in greater need. I was not wealthy, the opposite actually. My salary was only $600 per month with free rent plus $300 in subway tokens. But when someone asks, "Do you have a shirt I can have," I couldn't say no. On multiple occasions, Ray scolded me for giving away my possessions.

The medical treatment available for the poor was deplorable, which led to frequent problems for our constituents. We took one woman to the hospital dehydrated with two broken ribs and a bleeding ulcer. She wasn't seen for over six hours. When she was, they sent her home as "not sick." While in the hospital, I met a cab driver who brought in a man with gangrene in his leg. This man did not even get to see a doctor. Instead, after waiting to be seen for eight hours, he was referred to another hospital.

During the winter, it was clear I was going to have to figure out where I was going next, as my permanent replacement was scheduled to arrive that summer of '86. I did not want a replay of the previous year, so I interviewed for the open position of Community Center Director in Barre, Vermont, and visited in the dead of winter. It was cold. Very cold. I complained about NYC's winter, which had been the coldest in memory; it did not get above 15 degrees the entire month of January. They laughed and informed me that the city had a "heat wave" compared to what they were experiencing. Regardless, I accepted the position starting that summer with ONE reservation. If I received an offer in Higher Education Development (fundraising), I would rescind my acceptance in Barre and accept the offer in Higher Ed. They agreed.

The rest of the spring and early summer passed quickly with only one additional death, a stabbing the last month I was there. During my 11 months as Director of Graffiti Baptist Center, we experienced a total of 11 deaths.

God blessed the Center by allowing us to rebuild the relationship between the Churches of the Association and the Center. By the time I left, we had more than six months of volunteering calendared for FLIP, 10 Churches participating in Wednesday night suppers and supporting the worship experience, and a successful ongoing mentoring program between youth and professionals. In addition, the youth groups enjoyed several camping trips and a youth retreat on Long Island hosted by churches there.

I/we did have one huge failure. In the past, I had always believed that people could work if they wanted to. But that view was put to the test when I launched a job training program, which included resume building, and teaching interview skills to our homeless parishioners. Sadly, we did not place a single trainee in a real job despite our best efforts.

The week I was leaving for Vermont, the offer I had been hoping for came through: Cargill Associates, the fundraising firm whose mission was to raise money for church-related Colleges and Universities, offered me a research position. Therefore, I was off to Texas rather than Vermont. I thought of this not as leaving the ministry but as fulfilling God's call to acquire the knowledge and skills necessary to succeed in Christian Higher Education.

As I was driving across the country once again, God began to speak to me in my heart about my experiences in New York, reminding me what I was told years before that one day I would work in inner-city New York with poor youth. Then I remembered seeing the movie *The Cross and The Switchblade* as a teenager, shortly after I accepted Christ. The Holy Spirit told me then, "One day, you will work there." I remember being afraid of that message and not mentioning it to anyone. But as I drove to Texas, I remembered. God had kept His word. He reminded me that I had declined the invitation to come to New York four times before accepting. Trust me, The Spirit can convince His/Her children to take the next step, reluctantly or not.

I drove away, both relieved and utterly amazed at God's work in my life. I also left just in time as my Crohn's Disease had begun acting up under the constant stress of the city.

The Texas Two-Step

At this point in my life's journey, I had already lived and worked in West Germany and New York City. But this traveling man wasn't finished yet as I packed my 1975 Toyota Tercel, loaded with all my belongings, and pulled away from the curb of East 7th Street and Avenue B for a world none of my parishioners knew anything about. For many residents of the Lower East Side of Manhattan, the world began and ended with the Hudson and East Rivers. The world beyond the five boroughs of New York was unfathomable.

For me, Texas was a return to a kinder, gentler world, where facing death, disease, and overt discrimination were not everyday events. I was relieved and happy to be going back to familiar territory.

By the time I left NY, Diana was a distant memory of yet another failed female relationship. I tried to make it work, but she grew less and less interested all the time. But another woman had appeared on the horizon. Vanessa from Germany, who was now stationed at Fort Polk, Louisiana, wrote to say that she had thought a lot about me since I left Germany. With a world of opportunities, possibilities, and youthful optimism, I looked forward to Fort Worth, Texas. Dallas and Fort Worth are the biggest cities in the Texas Metroplex. Fort Worth is less glamorous, more cowboy, western and conservative, and home to both Billy Bob's Honky-Tonk and Southwestern Baptist Theological Seminary.

OBU alum Robert Cargill founded Cargill Associates to raise money to help transform small Church-related non-profit colleges and universities into viable institutions of Higher Education. The firm was a significant player in the field. After reading my resume, they hired me, and I was proud to be chosen. My only concern was that my Crohn's disease was not currently under control. The interviewer had not asked about that, and I had not volunteered any additional information.

Readjusting to the Southwest was more difficult than I expected, as I was now considerably more liberal than most of the people around me. After attending many of the larger Baptist Churches, I finally settled on

Broadway Baptist because it shared more of my views, such as Women in Ministry and the Priesthood of the Believer. But it was more formal and less socioeconomically diverse than I would have liked, not a particularly good match, but at least it wasn't a fundamentalist church.

I was highly praised at work for my research on two institutions, one Baptist and one Pentecostal. However, I was missing a lot of work going to the doctor for my Crohn's Disease, which was getting out of control. I wasn't feeling well and was losing weight. I'd never been heavy, but I was already on the thin side after New York from all the stress (or so I assumed). As summer rolled into fall, my weight continued to drop from 140 to 125.

My health plan doctor, whose office was 40 minutes away in Dallas, was concerned. He ordered test after test, trying to find out why I was not getting better. After months of searching, he located the cause: a cyst the size of a grapefruit. He ordered me to the hospital immediately. I protested because I had already lost a lot of time at work, and he reluctantly conceded. However, before leaving the room, he pressed on the location of the cyst. He came back about five minutes later and saw me crying in pain. He immediately reversed course and ordered me to Methodist Hospital in Dallas (an adjoining building). As I rolled across the brick floor in the foyer of Methodist Hospital in a wheelchair, all I could think was, "Who was foolish enough to pave a hospital entrance with bricks?" Each little bump sent pain shooting through my abdomen. I thought, "Just a few minutes ago, I talked the doctor into letting me postpone this surgery because I was too busy at work to take time off. Now I'm in so much pain I'm trying to remember what was so important at Cargill. If only my doctor had discovered the cyst months ago."

After my doctor pushed on the cyst, a dark mass appeared, moving towards the surface. The doctor was extremely concerned it might rupture. He prepared me for emergency surgery, soberly explaining that if we didn't get to surgery right away and the cyst ruptured, the poison inside the cyst could get into my bloodstream, and I would probably die.

He made me sign paperwork promising not to hold him or the hospital responsible for various outcomes, including my death. I remember thinking that was funny. How could I bring a lawsuit if I was dead?

None of this was welcome news to a bright, energetic, though very sick 29-year-old! I felt like Cargill Associates was my last chance to transition to a career in Christian Higher Education. My experience in New York confirmed that the most effective way to significantly impact people's lives was to provide them with the tools/education needed to compete in our highly competitive society. This revelation came as a result of our ambitious but unsuccessful effort to help NYC homeless people join the workforce.

As I was wheeled into surgery, I didn't understand how God could have given me this opportunity, brought me through so many difficult times, just to "take me home" now. I didn't understand.

The surgery was successful. The skilled doctor cut out the cyst, for which I was thankful. But with recovery starting, it meant more missed work. I was initially sent home to my apartment in Fort Worth, Texas with a home health nurse visiting daily. For two weeks, the vile fluid drained and drained from my body.

After surgery, the doctor prepared me for the possibility of a second, more invasive surgery to remove the "damaged intestines" caused by my Crohn's Disease, which is what caused the cyst in the first place. At first, the healing went better than expected and it looked like I wasn't going to have a second surgery. Then, all heck broke loose, and the vile, black, smelly fluid was back. I was rushed to Methodist Hospital and again signed papers not to sue in case of death. This time, my doctor explained that I would likely wake up with an Ileostomy bag where my body waste would drain. This was the most frightening news. I was once again blessed with successful surgery, but this time I was ordered back to Mobile to fully recover instead of going to my Fort Worth apartment. I knew that this was another nudge from the Spirit. I knew God had a purpose in sending me home with this not-so-pleasant recovery before me.

Cargill Associates terminated my employment, but I wouldn't know it for a few weeks. My doctor said he would go to court to fight this discrimination, but I was too sick to worry about that now. On the flight home, now 110 lbs., people were nice, but I was too sick to care. I looked and felt like "walking death." Texas had indeed been a two-step: two serious surgeries, then getting the boot. Surely, the next place would be a waltz in comparison, but first, I was headed home for Mother and much-needed rest and recuperation.

Auntie's Death

The week I arrived home from Texas, Auntie Finley, Ruby's (my stepmother's) sister whom we all just called "Auntie," was taken to the hospital's ICU. She was dying. I knew this before I came home. I haven't talked about Auntie yet, but she was the one to whom many of us kids in the youth group turned when we couldn't talk to our own parents about things. She was a wonderful Christian who had a great deal of influence on my life during my tension-filled growing-up years. She offered me a place away from stress and was a friend in times of pain. Her daughter Gina was one of my best friends.

During a quick trip home the summer before my hospitalization that fall, I visited my old home church where everyone was praying for Auntie to be healed. During the service, a dear friend testified that God was going to heal Auntie. "But" she said, "If you do not believe that, DO NOT pray for her because your lack of faith will cause God not to answer our prayers."

Shocked, I found Dad, now a deacon, and expressed my deep concern about demanding God to take a specific action. When God didn't heal her, what was going to happen? It was one of the rare occasions where Dad and I saw eye to eye. He too was very worried that Auntie wasn't going to make it, prayers or not.

In my heart, I knew I had been sent home from Texas to be there when Auntie died. Otherwise, it didn't make sense. I had endured the removal of a grapefruit-sized cyst and was sent home alone to my small Fort Worth apartment for two weeks while poisonous fluid drained from my body. But after I had a section of my intestines removed and while still very sick, I was directed to fly home alone, across the country, to convalesce with my family. I arrived home on Tuesday. Two days later, Auntie's doctors called Mother, Auntie's husband Uncle Jerry, and their children to the hospital. I was much too weak to go. Auntie died in the early morning hours. When Mother arrived back at the house she was as angry as I had ever seen her. I was up awaiting what

I knew would be dreadful news. She immediately asked me one question at 3 a.m. "The Bible says to ask believing and God will answer. Why didn't God answer? We prayed believing, but God did not do what he said he would. As far as I'm concerned there is no need to pray because God is not trustworthy."

Mother's pain was real. It was an agonizing moment in Mother's faith walk and in my life. I did not confront or challenge her. I just listened to her grief. But God had answered, just not the way Riverside Baptist and my mother wanted. But at least God had allowed me to be there for her in this particularly difficult moment.

Tennessee Waltz

After I felt better, I flew back to Texas to pack up my apartment and drive my car home. On the trip home I decided that if I wanted to work in Baptist Higher Education, I had to look there first. I had been certain of one thing for a long time: my heart sang when I thought about working in Baptist Higher Education. I was sure this was the right area. After all, OBU started me on this path. Dr. Neal and Dr. Shirley Schooley in West Germany had affirmed it. I had seen firsthand in NYC and in my own life that education was often key to whether one survived, thrived, or perished in our capitalist society. And finally, Cargill, while not a happy experience, taught me HOW to fundraise, an important silver lining in an otherwise unpleasant experience.

So, I wrote to all the Baptist schools, Colleges, and Universities that had openings that December. Gone were the days of "God, I want to go where nobody else wants to go." I did that in NYC and it nearly killed me. Now, I was going to follow my passion and use the talents and skills I had acquired to really help people. I know I made a real difference at East 7th Street Baptist Mission in NYC, but we didn't succeed in the area that could have made the biggest difference, economics. And though I had not yet pieced together my future, I knew the tie between education and economics was critical!

That Christmas I was home for the first time in a long time. Mother was not herself, still grieving Auntie deeply. Getting on with my life seemed like a good idea. The letters and resumes to SBC schools, colleges and universities were mailed.

One, Harrison Chilhowee Baptist Academy (HCBA), called and wanted to interview me. I arranged to go to the mountains of East Tennessee to visit the beautiful little campus nestled in the woods of the Great Smoky Mountains, in the same county as Gatlinburg and 20 miles outside of Knoxville. Harrison Chilhowee was founded before there were public schools and was part of the Mountain Missions Schools of Appalachia. Most other religious schools closed after public schools came to the mountains, but a few remained as part of the SBC educational program offered to the world.

Another school close to Harrison Chilhowee, Oneida Baptist Institute in Kentucky, specialized in "troubled children who needed a structured environment." While working at Second Baptist Church, we helped place several students there. It was a very conservative and stern place. It also had the distinction of never turning away any student who applied, regardless of his or her parents' ability to pay. However, parents were not permitted to interfere with any discipline administered by the staff. Oneida Baptist was located on a farm and all students were required to work. For some it was a life-saving institution. For others it was hell on earth. Many of these students ran away repeatedly, even at great personal risk. Oneida was 12 miles from the nearest city which was so small most people wouldn't even consider it a city.

In contrast, Harrison Chilhowee's niche was attracting good kids who needed a more structured environment, but without turning it into a prison camp. I preferred this approach and could more easily see how I could make a difference here. Harrison Chilhowee once took a path similar to Oneida but ultimately chose a different mission. Troubled kids were and are tough work. Besides, the administration did not want to send their own children to a school where troubled teens were the primary population and parental input was unwelcome. Thus, HCBA settled into its' mission of attracting good kids in need of structure. However, Harrison Chilhowee's enrollment had been in decline for the last ten years.

When the HCBA Director of Admissions, Russell Bridges, hired me my purpose was clear: help him recruit more students. The Board of Directors met in late January 1987, and I was hired with a start date in late February. My new employment did not come a moment too soon. Living at home with my parents was very tough and something I prided myself on never doing. Mother had not recovered from Auntie's death, and we were both relieved when I accepted the position and left.

The first year's work was already in progress at Harrison Chilhowee. With my help, we managed to break even for the first time in ten years. The next year Mr. Bridges and I increased enrollment by nearly 20% from 105 to 125 and increased the number of boarders over recent years. We were thrilled.

I was given residence in the Boy's dormitory reserved for RA's (Resident Assistants). Soon I regained my health, and my weight improved from 110 in December to 145 by April. An added benefit was that meals were provided in the cafeteria with students. I liked this arrangement because I could keep track of the recruits and didn't have to cook my own meals. We were off to an excellent start, but all was not well under the surface.

The president of Harrison Chilhowee, Dr. William Palmer, took a hands-off approach to discipline and allowed his staff to administer it in all but the most severe cases. The rules were brutal. If you were caught with alcohol, you were expelled. Drugs: Expelled. Smoking (3 times): Expelled. Any sexual activity: expelled. It was an unforgiving place for the students who lived there. We preached and taught "the loving forgiveness of Christ" the whole time but practiced little.

During the second year, nepotism reared its ugly head. Someone on the Board of Trustees managed to get his son, William D., hired as principal, the second-highest position, behind only the president. Rumors swirled about why William left California to return to East Tennessee; I don't know if any of them were true, but I can tell you that from day one, Mr. D. had his sights set on becoming president and eliminating anyone loyal to Dr. Palmer.

A number of issues surfaced over the course of the first year. HCBA prided itself on being a conservative Christian School and, as such, did not tolerate drinking, drugs, tobacco, and especially sexuality of any kind outside of marriage, not that we were actually able to control young men and women during puberty. Some students were exploring their new sexual feelings which is normal at this age. But when they were caught, we expelled them. One girl gave the football star a blowjob on the game bus. She was expelled, and he was disciplined but not expelled (you can't lose a star football player, after all).

Dr. Palmer sometimes made "special exception" admissions, meaning a student's rejection by our Admissions office was "overruled" and the student was accepted. One student accepted in this way was the child of a friend or donor, I don't remember which. He was an older student, perhaps 19 or 20 when he came to us. His parents were desperate for him to graduate. That year, he disappointed everyone. He was caught in the Knoxville Mall, a favorite outing for students, having sex with an underage girl. The police arrested him, and we expelled him.

Controlling "non-Christian" sexual activity became a priority after that. Near that same time, a Resident Assistant was caught kissing his date late one night on campus. That would have been acceptable. But he was kissing a guy, which was not. Students delighted in telling Dr. Palmer. However, he was terrified it might get out that we had "a homosexual" on campus. He lectured the friendly RA who then resigned before the end of the semester, probably by agreement with Dr. Palmer. All single members of the staff were then called into the President's office and asked directly if we were gay. All denied it, including me. I was terrified I'd be caught. Even thinking about guys that way was sinning in my mind. I was on alert.

Terrified I would be terminated, I restarted counseling, this time in Knoxville, for the fifth time in 10 years. I had now gone through counseling in every place I had lived since High School except Germany! But nothing seemed to help me "get over the hump." But I wasn't giving up.

I really loved Harrison Chilhowee. I loved its mission to help students receive a quality education when it was not otherwise possible due to family circumstances, failures of their local school system, or students who struggled "growing up," like I did before I found Christ. This was a worthy mission.

Sam was a case in point. I had not recruited Sam, but he came to HCBA as an eighth grader who failed every class the year before. He was not dumb, but he was a truly angry young man with an inability to control his hyperactivity. Mr. D. immediately disliked him and determined to get rid of him as soon as possible. But Sam, with my help, managed to stay out of trouble and remain at HCBA. In the 1989 yearbook The *Chilhowean,* he wrote:

Mr. Brill,

I can't believe this year is almost over. It's hard to believe I've been here 2 years. Thanks for everything you have done for me. There is too much to list. I never thought I could pass, but because of you pushing me, I did, thanks to you. Well, I hope you have a really great summer. Don't work too hard. Hope to see you next year.

Love in Christ,

Sam

I significantly impacted several students at HCBA. Ray, Martin, Jose, and Dennis, all of whom I recruited out of New York, would most likely not have graduated had they stayed up there. All did and went on to do well in life. There were also Becky and Sandy, two others whose lives would have been vastly different had they not come to Harrison Chilhowee. These kids are the success stories Harrison Chilhowee Baptist Academy should have celebrated, but these were not the stories William D. liked. These were students from rough places or with tough family backgrounds or kids with personal problems. They did not come to HCBA as "good Christian students" like his children. These were great but ordinary kids who needed a structured environment and to be loved. When that happened, they thrived. We failed in our mission many times, but when we succeeded, we succeeded big.

Mr. Bridges resigned after my second year to take a position at Blue Mountain College in Virginia, leaving me no cover from Mr. D's assault. As principal, Mr. D. had the authority to expel students. He expelled the most in recent history during my second year: 25! In my annual review, he told me he considered my work to be "crap." He also took aim at other faculty, especially those who were favorites among the students.

At no time did I use my position on campus to act out with adults or students. In fact, just the opposite, I lived in terror of being thought gay, especially after the RA's fiasco. I went to counseling faithfully but told no one on campus lest my secret get out. I knew if William D. found out I was even in counseling, regardless of the reason, that alone would be enough to oust me from the school.

While in Tennessee, I continued to date several women, with more pressure than ever following the fiasco with the gay RA.

Vanessa, the Army Sergeant I met in Germany now stationed in Fort Polk, Louisiana and I made several trips to visit one another, and I decided maybe "she was the one." She arrived at the perfect moment, right after the Male RA was caught kissing his male date. I had briefly dated a female RA (dated with permission by HCBA) who told me early on that her biological clock was ticking, so we needed to move this along. I pulled the plug on that one quickly. She soon left our school, got married and became pregnant shortly thereafter. I also dated women from various Baptist Churches. None lasted more than a date or two. Still, I was trying.

This set Vanessa up as God's answer to my need for a woman. Vanessa was a different kind of woman, and I hoped she was the one. I traveled to Fort Polk, Louisiana and she came to Seymour, Tennessee. On her first visit, everybody encouraged me to consider her as my wife-to-be except my assistant, Janice M. She did not like her from the beginning. According to Janice, Vanessa was too butch.

That July '88, I ventured to Fort Polk to see her. It was a miserable trip, I must say. The base and town are in the middle of nowhere. The weather was hot and humid and when we went to see the 4th of July Fireworks at the base, the Army caught the forest on fire. It took hours to put out the fire and get everyone, including us, safely away from the threat. To top it all off, Vanessa confronted me about our relationship. She was concerned that I had never "tried anything," and she asked, "Are you normal?" I explained that I was a Christian and that we should wait until marriage before getting physical. She told me that she had dated a lot of guys, including Christians, and I was the only one to never try anything. Then she said, "I must ask, are you willing to come live at Fort Polk with me?" I refused. I told her it was her place to come live with me, "her man," not the other way around. After the trip, she wrote me a very searing, angry letter. I, too, was angry and told her in response that our relationship was off for good. She concurred.

In my third year, Mr. D. decided to personally approve or deny all admission candidates completely bypassing the Admissions Committee. He warned me in a one-on-one conversation that he would make my life as difficult as possible. He succeeded! Buck Donaldson, a beloved faculty member and another of Mr. D.'s targets, took me aside one day and suggested I consider looking for another position. I respected Buck and took his advice. During spring break, I interviewed for a position at Hargrave Military School in Virginia but did not get the position.

Later that spring, Russel Bridges whom I worked with for two years at HCBA had done well and was now Vice President of Blue Mountain College. He invited me to work with him again. I went and looked over the college. It was quaint and I seriously considered it but worried it might be too isolated. Mobile College and Blue Mountain College both called at nearly the same time to invite me for an interview.

Before accepting Mr. Bridges' offer, I wanted to interview for Mobile College's Associate Director of Development position. Being offered this job at MC would be a dream come true. I would be back working in the area of higher education from which most private school presidents came. However, it was in my hometown of Mobile, Alabama. I had not anticipated ever working in Mobile again. I went for the interview, was offered the position, and resigned shortly after the students left for the summer in June 1989. I took the job with a $25,000 starting salary, a $7,000 increase from HCBA, with the promise that if I was successful after two years, I would be promoted to Director of Development. I was ecstatic!

I told a few students at HCBA that I would not be back the following year. They were not happy. Sam took it hard. Sandy, Piti, and Jose did not like it either and felt I was abandoning them. Without me, they had no adult to talk to who would listen, they said. They also had no one to defend them against Mr. D.

A number expressed their appreciation for me in the *1989 Chilhowean*. I'll only bore you with one accolade, from a student whom I impacted significantly.

From Martin: Mr. Brill, I have a lot of things to be thankful for, and you are one of them. Thanks for the help in my coming (to HCBA). Also, thanks for listening to me, Martin."

Many students were disappointed when they arrived back in the fall and found out I was gone. But I went back to HCBA in the fall to see a football game and check up on "my students." Later that year, I returned again following the tragic death of a recent alumnus, Matt King, who was killed as a freshman in college. This was an especially difficult return to campus. Matt was exceptionally bright, well-liked, and well-behaved. He was a deeply committed Christian, and his death ripped the heart out of his mother, one of the school's best faculty members, and many of us who thought of Matt as a bright and shining star.

During that return trip, I noticed several students enrolled at HCBA who Mr. D. had personally rejected while I was there. According to my former assistant, Mr. D. "reconsidered" them once I resigned. Of course, he took credit for the largest enrollment in recent memory. But what the heck, I wasn't there anymore. I was in Higher Ed. That year, Mr. D. began executing a plan to convert HCBA from its founding mission as primarily a boarding school to a Christian Day School. He also changed the name to "King's Academy" in order to sound more appealing. I lost touch after a few years, but before I did, I lived to see Mr. D. succeed Dr. Palmer as president. What a surprise! It was neither the first nor last time I witnessed the impact of the growing rift within the convention or the empowerment of incompetent but well-connected bosses. The year Mr. D. was promoted, the school barely survived a motion at the Tennessee Baptist Convention to close it.

Soon, I was at Mobile College as Associate Director of Development. Sam and I stayed in contact, and he decided against graduating from Chilhowee. I was concerned he would not graduate from high school, but he promised he would now, having grown more confident. He kept his promise, graduating three years later and on time, something no one thought possible when he first came to Harrison Chilhowee Baptist Academy.

Finally, several student relationships lasted into their college days: Piti sought my help getting into Samford's dual engineering program with Georgia Tech. He was accepted and received both degrees. Martin likewise reached out when he applied to a university in Florida, and he, too, was successful. I kept up with him for a number of years. The last time I saw him, he was married with children and was doing extremely well in business.

Sam is probably the one who exceeded everyone's expectations! He graduated from High School, then Mobile College. He is married, has two successful children and a wonderful wife. Today he is a national executive of a major company.

My two and a half years at HCBA were fruitful for me, the school, and the students. Our college admission acceptance rate, a critical metric for boarding school enrollment purposes, increased significantly, rebounding from the low 60th percentile to nearly 80%. I realized upon arrival that without improvement in this area, we would never be able to attract enough students. I did my best to improve our college acceptance rate and professionalize the recruitment process, and both numbers (College Acceptance rate and New Recruits) improved dramatically, despite active resistance from Mr. D. Most importantly, though, breaking the decade's long decline in enrollment through aggressive admissions, recruitment and acceptances was the metric by which my success should be judged. The Admissions Office was very successful, and we made it happen despite Mr. D's shenanigans. Kids' lives improved as a result, and it felt great!

By the summer of '89, I was back in Mobile, optimistic that God had brought me full circle to my hometown to finally accomplish "his" will. Amazed at how God was working in my life, I felt, then and now, overwhelmingly blessed.

The process of following God's will, led by the Spirit, had been a Waltz, slow and deliberate in Tennessee. I remember thinking, "I love my life," ... big change from when I left Mobile in January '78.

Sweet Home Alabama: I'm coming home!

With my hire by Mobile College, I headed back to my Sweet Home Alabama! By this time, I thought of myself as very progressive. I believed in "women in ministry" but had not yet made a similar connection to the role of women in relationships. I still held a residual belief that the man "ruled" the family. I had just said that to Vanessa the year before and what a mess I'd made of that!

Back in Mobile, Alabama one would have thought that treating women as equals was here to stay, or treating African Americans as equal citizens was a reality. But neither was true in the South or in the larger society. But it was especially not true in Alabama, and this quintessential Southern Town. Mobile had long prided itself on its "Southern-ness," while other places were becoming the "New South." It had been twelve years since I lived and worked here full-time, and I was struck by how little had changed.

One of my first fundraising trips was to The Club in Birmingham, Alabama, overlooking our state's largest city. Mr. F., the Interim Director of Development, and I were there to meet a top prospective donor. We were seated in the dining room and getting ready to eat when the prospect called and canceled. Thank God he wasn't present because all of a sudden, Mr. F. slammed down his fork and said, "I can't believe it, I can't believe it." Looking around I saw nothing out of the ordinary and asked, "What can't you believe?" He told me he realized that in today's world, you had to work with blacks (but he used the "N" word), "But we sure as hell don't have to eat with them." I was shocked and at first thought he was joking. He wasn't. The couple he was referencing was a well-dressed, elderly, African American couple seated directly behind me. He was so upset he could barely eat his dinner. This shocked me because my impression of him had been so different. I thought he was caring and very Christian in every way. I was wrong, at least on this subject. I soon learned he was not alone. In fact, I found it to be the prevailing attitude in Mobile at the time.

At the College, a second issue resurfaced: the role of women in society. This issue more than any other, had united the conservative faction within the SBC to bring the convention back to its' "historical roots." But a clear understanding of Baptist History showed that, although a minority position, women had always been an active part of the church and had been ordained as far back as the 1700s. As we were closing out the 20th century in preparation for the 21st, much of the country had accepted the premise (or at least the appearance) that women should be treated as equals. Not so in Mobile, Alabama. No woman had ever held office as a commissioner (The City had a three-commissioner council form of government). Many around Mobile felt a woman's place was still in the home, and the College largely reflected this opinion in 1989. At MC, men dominated the cabinet. (Note: This view is still being espoused in some quarters today. Read *Project 2025*, being promoted by The Heritage Foundation and the current administration!)

To my dismay, the churches were worse than the College. Only three out of 120 Baptist Churches were considered "liberal" in the Mobile Baptist Association. I chose to attend the most liberal, Hillcrest Baptist Church.

These first few months were proving difficult in transition. Shortly after arriving, a racist hoax occurred in Boston that led to a racist manhunt, enflaming and re-exposing Boston's racist history. A white man who killed his pregnant wife and unborn baby called 911 falsely claiming a black man forced him to drive to the mixed-race Mission Hill neighborhood where the Black man allegedly shot them both. It was the talk of the town and racial tensions flared. Discouraging discussions swirled around campus that northern cities were racist too, so why is the South getting such a bad rap? To me it doesn't matter where prejudice is found. I firmly believe that as followers of Christ we have an obligation to treat all people with respect and that justice and equality are for all. But that was far from the dominant view in Mobile, Alabama in 1989.

I have always wondered why Mobile is so different than other places. Mobile fashions itself as the "Mother of Mystics," home to the original

Mardi Gras (that most people know nothing about). It sounds so pagan for such a Christian community, but I always loved Mardi Gras with all the parades. Walking down from my house in the Oakleigh Garden District, it finally dawned on me. The whole Mardi Gras Society concept relies on being invited to join. This concept allowed the Societies to keep all the "right" people in and all the "wrong" people out. The Societies not only required an invitation, but they were also ranked - and the older the Society, the better... the more powerful, the more privileged, the more restricted. This rigid structure served its desired purpose by locking in the status quo almost in perpetuity. You (blacks, women, gays, and others) may be able to form your own Societies, but you can't join ours, and yours will never be as highly respected as ours. This structure permeates not only Mardi Gras Societies, but nearly every facet of life in Mobile.

Upon my arrival, Dr. Michael Magnoli allowed me to stay in his garage apartment behind The President's Home on Government Street. That street is one of the most beautiful in the world, in my opinion. It is lined with gorgeous 200+ year-old oaks and turn-of-the-century-before-last mansions. There is a spectacular canopy of Oaks all the way from downtown to Memorial Park, where the trolley used to turn and loop back downtown. The city definitely has "Old South Charm."

Living in the Garden District with Dr. Magnoli's permission until I got settled was fine, but it was another matter when I bought my first home, an 18th-century Victorian home there. Friends were "concerned" for my safety. The Oakleigh Garden District was my intellectual oasis amid a cerebral desert in Mobile. Young professionals came into the district from across the country, finding architecturally appealing homes in a wonderful setting. The diversity was amazing for Mobile: Episcopalians, Baptists, Evangelicals, Catholics and Jews, all got along together. Also, African Americans, Whites, and Hispanics all lived within this area and worked together to build a better neighborhood. What a relief and how refreshing this realization was for me. Who would have thought this to be true? Not me, but I was sure glad it was the case!

All was not lost in my move to Mobile after all. But it didn't take long before I knew I wasn't in Kansas anymore. I wasn't at Southern Seminary where they made a conscious effort to improve race relations. I wasn't in NYC, where diversity was celebrated and appreciated. My Southern Baptist Church there had a wide array of worship experiences celebrating diversity: one week, a Ukrainian singer, next a Ballet Dancer from Japan studying at Julliard, followed by a country singer from Texas the next. Nor was I in Germany, where I learned that Baptists have an order of Deaconess's who, like Catholic Nuns, are recognized as leaders in the Church, though still not recognized as equal to Pastors, who were all male. I wasn't even in Texas or Tennessee either, where most churches had integrated, at least a little. Alas, I was in Mobile, Alabama, where the "N" word was still in use, though not as often in public, and lack of tolerance the rule of the day.

My welcoming attitude toward outsiders was a cause for suspicion, and my acceptance of black people as equals and women as leaders was downright unchristian to many. I felt like I was frozen in time. I had explored our changing world but back in my hometown, nothing much had changed. But I came to Mobile to do a job, and that is what I was going to do.

Dr. Michael Magnoli, who hired me in 1989, was only the second president of the College. As the former Director of Development, he had been president long enough to reverse course on several decisions made by founding president Dr. William K. Weaver that led to declining enrollment (there were currently fewer than 1,000 students at Mobile College). He first reversed Weaver's ban on sports teams, starting with men's and women's basketball. A few years later, Magnoli added men's tennis, baseball, and soccer; for women's teams, he added tennis, softball, and soccer.

The sports program, while costly, brought the college much needed publicity. When archrival Spring Hill College, our local Catholic College, squared off against Mobile College in basketball it was front page sports section news. Slowly, enrollment started to climb.

But new funds were slow in coming. The endowment was less than 4 million at the time I started (with generous accounting). Before hiring me, Magnoli had gone through several Directors of Development, but none were successful. He had a particularly difficult time letting go of this, his former administrative area, before becoming President in 1984.

At nearly the same time as I started, Dr. Magnoli hired Mr. F. as his acting director, and I became the new Assistant Director of Development and Alumni Affairs. While living in Mobile was a challenge, the College was good for me, and I was immensely happy. I had the opportunity to talk with people who had the means to support the school and who could provide the money necessary to fund scholarships, thereby making it easier for students to attend. I saw my New York revelation becoming real. The first year was very successful and I raised a good deal of money.

However, the relationship between Mr. F. and Dr. Magnoli deteriorated, largely because he could not open doors to his many contacts, thereby failing to bring in new, much-needed development dollars. Soon after, Mr. F. resigned, and Dr. Magnoli, who didn't think I was ready to be the director, hired Mr. W., a former IBM executive. I had my concerns, as he had never worked for a college or non-profit organization before and, more importantly, had never done fundraising. But he supposedly was a "good salesperson" who convinced Magnoli of his ability. He immediately began working on a computer system upgrade with a friend of his and set up new procedures and accountability measures. Meanwhile, I went out and raised money.

Soon, my duties expanded to include Estate Planning, Alumni Affairs, and the Annual Fund. Estate Planning and Alumni Affairs grew wildly. My record speaks for itself. In a little less than five years, I raised over four million dollars. The most productive area was Estate Planning. I even outraised Magnoli one year, with three of the top five gifts coming from my solicitations. Alumni giving also increased significantly during my tenure. When I started, alumni gave at a rate of less than one-half of one percent. It increased each year and rose to just over 5%

during my five years. Homecoming attendance, a good marker of on-going alumni interest in and commitment to the school, also improved from 75 people attending the year before I arrived to almost 500 in my last year. Even the Annual Fund, which was eventually given to another staff member, grew significantly. But ultimately, my estate planning work provided the college with the most dollars.

My employment coincided with the Southern Association of Colleges and Schools accreditation process, where Mobile College was cited for not upgrading its library. Ironically, library fundraising was the first project I assisted with and the first project I completed. Dr. Hazel Petersen, by this time Dean Emeritus, was called back into service to help correct the erroneous report. Working with her in the Development office gave me the opportunity to get to know her and learn from her expertise and wisdom. Her best advice was to get certified as an Estate Planning Specialist, a key element of my professional development plan. Dr. Petersen and I presented the idea to Magnoli, but he declined, concluding it was unnecessary as I had already proven I could raise funds.

With this kind of success, you would have thought I was a shoo-in for the directorship when Mr. W. resigned. Instead, someone else on staff was promoted. The writing was on the wall; I was never going to be promoted here, success or not.

Mobile, like all my other stops, proved successful in business but not so much in my personal life. I dated, and dated, and dated. I even switched Churches to one of the largest because it had an active Singles Ministry with many more prospects, to no avail. By now, my "women-dated total" was pretty significant. After all, I had been at this since age 13, and I was now 36 years old.

CHAPTER 8

Leaving Ministry?

"There are far better things ahead than we ever leave behind."
C.S. Lewis

Reconsider

Conservatives/fundamentalists in the denomination launched an attack on the Southern Baptist Convention in 1979. By 1993, it finally found me at The University of Mobile, formerly Mobile College. By '93, the denominational landscape had shifted significantly. The first institution to fall under conservative/fundamentalist control was Southeastern Baptist Theological Seminary in North Carolina. Its fall marked the beginning of an effort by the strongest and most respected institutions in SBC life to separate themselves from direct denominational control. The first and wealthiest, the University of Richmond, successfully seceded from the Virginia Baptist Convention. Next, Wake Forest, the second richest, followed suit by terminating its relationship with the North Carolina Baptist Convention. Most of the other Baptist universities with high academic standing and sufficient economic resources followed suit.

The Alabama Baptist Convention had been relatively calm compared to the ongoing controversies at the national level and other state conventions. But with Dr. S.'s promotion to the University of Mobile's Board of Trustees, that was about to change. He was a former Baptist pastor, and as a trustee, he promoted and won approval for a "Board of Regents," a pseudo-trustee board, to be the conservative voice in the University's affairs. The Board of Regents began to attack Samford, our sister Baptist institution in the state. Dr. S. also convinced University of Mobile President Dr. Michael Magnoli to replace our more moderate members on the *REAL* Board of Trustees with conservatives.

I, among others, expressed our concern to Dr. Magnoli on several occasions about the need to keep a balance on the Board of Trustees, but these suggestions were rebuffed. He said while he had no respect for these preachers, he had a philosophy of "keeping your friends close and your enemies closer." I attended several Board of Regents meetings. During one, I overheard a private conversation in which members of the Board of Regents openly discussed taking control of The Alabama Bap-

tist Convention and Samford University, and replacing Michael Magnoli with a "true conservative." Upset, I found Dr. Magnoli and told
him what I had heard. He said I was overreacting to a bunch of Baptist
preachers. I had already witnessed what I considered the academic
demise of my seminary, Southern Baptist Theological Seminary, shortly
after Southeastern in North Carolina fell, so I wasn't so sure I was overreacting. SBTS was a much stronger institution when it fell than Magnoli's University of Mobile was in 1993.

At about the same time, the University, through the pioneering work
of Dr. Hazel Petersen, opened the San Marcos, Nicaragua campus of the
University of Mobile. It was the first fully accredited English language
college or University in all of Central America. Unfortunately, it did not
survive the ongoing controversy between moderates and conservatives,
and the state convention forced its sale.

Dr. Petersen and I were working together at this time in the Development Office. As mentioned earlier, her special assignment was working on the Southern Association of Colleges and Schools Accreditation
Report to correct its cited deficiencies. She was frustrated that UM had
not reported this error promptly to the accreditation team.

As the point person in the Development Office, I was to have our report to her by a specific date. I informed her that the Development Director said we would be late. She said, "What a shame. I thought that
you were serious about being an administrator." Stung by her criticism
because I respected her greatly, I took action by urging my boss to provide the required documentation so I could submit it to her on time.
Others were late, but not our department. This information was critical
in removing the citation from our accreditation report.

By 1994, with the storm brewing within the Alabama Baptist Convention, I was approached by New York Life to become an agent. I
had never considered working in the secular world, except for my short
tenure at Cargill Associates, where I learned how to raise funds —a critical skill required for anyone seeking to become President of a private
College or University. I had been called into ministry and faithfully fol-

lowed that call for 13 years. I declined the opportunity. When Bill Coley heard about my refusal, he called me in for a consultation. He was an administrator with excellent skills and integrity, someone I deeply respected. He said, "Michael, you are a young man. You can't afford to get caught up in this mess with the Convention. I sincerely ask you to reconsider the offer from New York Life." Ok, I thought, maybe I should, but I didn't.

Shortly after, Dr. Petersen asked me to visit with her. That was rarely a good thing, I thought. But I went and had coffee with her in the Canteen, where years ago she caught me dancing as a freshman. "Young man," she started, "You know I love and respect you, right?"

"Yes, ma'am," I replied.

"And you know I would never tell you what to do, right?"

"Yes, ma'am."

"But Bill tells me that you have a good job offer, and you won't consider it."

"Yes, ma'am."

"Do you want me to tell you what I would do?"

"Yes, ma'am," I replied. But really, I didn't.

"Reconsider," she said.

She left quickly to allow me to ponder my decision. I didn't want to leave the University. I considered it a stepping stone to becoming President of OBU, my life's goal. But God's plan for us is seldom the one we imagine for ourselves. God, who sees the beginning and end of our lives, knew this was not my path. Reluctantly, I tendered my resignation just as my former incompetent boss resigned and his replacement was announced, and that person wasn't me.

In hindsight, C.S. Lewis was right: "There are far better things ahead than we ever leave behind." But in 1994, it sure didn't feel that way.

Secular Life

My career at New York Life started rough, very rough. A week after I joined them, the manager, a woman whom I respected, was promoted to a bigger office in Roanoke, Virginia. She told me I was going to be ok, but I was scared to death. I had come to work *for her* because of her stellar reputation and skills.

But I did ok. Bradley A. was appointed her replacement, and I was sent to the American Airlines Training Center at DFW, Texas, for the national NY Life recruits training. I excelled in training and was selected as one of the top three leaders by my classmates.

Back in Mobile, Bradley was old school, cold calling to get new accounts — a challenging task that few accomplish. He also employed punitive measures. Every night, Monday through Thursday, we made cold calls from 6 pm to 9 pm or until we had three appointments for the next day. The least productive recruit was required to wear a Dunce Hat the following day while in the office. It proved to be an effective motivator for me, as I neither wanted to wear that stupid hat nor ever had to.

Highly motivated by fear of failure and the need for money, I soon rose to the top of our class of 8 recruits. Fear and hard work are a good combination. I was on my way to a successful career as an agent. That's when I made a career mistake. Bradley approached me about becoming an Assistant Manager (i.e., a recruiter). He told me it was a big promotion, but, as I learned later, he omitted important information that was critical to making a wise choice.

One last comment, the NYL office in Mobile was very homophobic, and "gay jokes" were often told. I laughed along as one of the guys. It reminded me that it wasn't just Baptists who were anti-gay; it was many people!

Time to Be Who God Created Me to Be

The years between 1995 and 1999 were among my life's most joyous, yet they were also challenging. I had survived the Dark Night of My Soul, left the University, and essentially the Baptist Church, remaining a member but not attending. I was also estranged from my parents. And yet, life was better than at any time in recent memory. I wasn't burdened with guilt for being gay anymore. I could see a guy and think, "he's cute." Or I really think so and so is hot, without shame. It was invigorating. Of course, I knew little about what I wanted in a man. I just knew my jets were going, and I didn't have to hide my feelings about that anymore. What a relief!

Dr. Baker continued to see me, and all was going well. He employed the Family Systems Theory method of counseling. This period of my life proved pivotal in understanding my family dynamics and our fusion. Fusion is where one person starts and the other ends without a clear distinction. Family is good, but one must be their own person, or they can lose themselves in the family, as I had done. This was going well, but my coming out to others was not.

Soon, I began meeting guys, all as dates, and some became friends. One of those was Thomas, a guy who rented a garage apartment from me. He was OBVIOUSLY gay, and when he smiled, I would blush. His gaydar quickly picked up that I was, too. While we dated once, I was never interested in him as he was "way too gay." I still had much to learn about what I liked and didn't like in a guy. But I knew I wasn't comfortable with very gay acting men. With Thomas, it was hard for anyone NOT TO KNOW he was gay. He was out and proud. Still, we became friends. He guided me through as if he were my professor on gay life. He taught me about bar etiquette, for example. One of the most significant problems in gay life, then and now, is that there are few places to meet guys other than bars. Bars, of course, are how many straight people meet, but it isn't necessarily the healthiest option.

He learned about my horrific early dates (from others) and helped me navigate the gay dating sites, steering me away from the gay pickup apps. Who knew there were different kinds of gay profile sites? He also helped me eliminate poor choices, those unlikely to lead to a relationship. While new to Mobile, he also had an extensive network of friends from elsewhere. These friends would be instrumental in helping me overcome depression after my first serious boyfriend dumped me.

No Turning Back

1995 was a big year for me: near suicide and then coming out! I continued to work through the ramifications of being gay. This passage came back into my mind, *"...You shall know the truth, and the truth will set you free."* (John 8:32, NIV) It was true. I began feeling freer and lighter than ever in my life. The burden of hiding was over, and the cloud of darkness that covered my life was turning into light. Coming out was hard, but not as hard as hiding in the closet, which surprised me.

Dr. Baker encouraged me to start telling my friends, family, and others that I was gay. I knew no gay people at the time I finally came out of the closet. After coming out to my counselor, I began telling people on a very selective basis and slowly started meeting other gay people.

This did not go well initially. I told Dr. Petersen first, and she rebuked me. She said, "I've never asked about your sexuality before. Why in the world would you think I want to know it now?" Ouch, that hurt. She wasn't mad about me being gay, just about me talking about it; another example of the code of silence.

Next, I slipped off to the Cornerstone Metropolitan Community Church, a gay-affirming denomination and the only faith-based place I knew where fellow gays were welcome. It was scary as hell, but I survived. This was a good step.

Next, I went to a bar for the first time (other than to get Billy out of one), and it was a gay bar. This was challenging. I didn't drink and didn't want to get picked up for a rendezvous. I did, however, feel a rush of excitement when a guy shook my hand upon entering the bar. It was like an electric shock went through me. Unfortunately, the bouncer wasn't interested in me.

Clearly, I was out of my element. After that first night at the bar, I frequented them more often, as Dr. Baker had suggested, as this was the only place outside of Church to meet gay men. To make matters worse, after a few months of going with Thomas to gay bars (Mobile had eight at this time), a member of Mom & Dad's church was at the bar and threatened to tell my parents. I decided to tell them first.

Remember, my parents believe parents don't visit their kids; the kids see the parents. But I asked them to please come to my house after Sunday Service, I had an important announcement to make. Very worried, they came. I told them that after 15 years of professional counseling, I had accepted the fact that I was gay. They knew, liked, and respected Dr. Baker very much. But they weren't happy with this news.

Dad's first response was, "Well, don't get AIDS." I assured him that wasn't my goal either. Both wanted me to try harder to be straight. I said, "Dad, Mom, that is what I've done all this time. It doesn't work."

They weren't convinced. They said Dr. Laura Schlessinger, a conservative radio psychologist, said it was possible, so why not try? I refused. Once out, I was NOT going back.

Then the most painful moment in my relationship with my father occurred. He told me it would be better for the family if I moved away because it would be less embarrassing for them. Wow, that's cold, even by my family's standards. There was no unconditional love, as Christ commanded. When people say they love you but do not treat you with respect, that is not love. If they say they love you and intentionally discriminate against you, that is not New Testament love either. That is not what the scriptures mean when they say to love your neighbor as yourself. In the good Samaritan story, the one who truly loved the person who had been robbed and beaten was the one who showed him kindness and took care of him (Luke 10:25-37): no judgment, just compassion.

I told Dr. Baker how my parents reacted, and he agreed with my parents that I needed to move; they were right, but for the wrong reasons. He said I knew too many people, too many Baptists who, like my family, were never going to accept me. In a new place, I could start fresh and make new friends who weren't homophobic. It made sense, but I didn't want to move. I was doing so well at NY Life. I stayed another two years against his advice. It was a mistake, but I was out for good, and there was no turning back now.

First Love - First Heart Break

While at NYL, I came out to myself. And with that, my whole existence changed. I kept my Baptist Church membership but often left during the service to go to Cornerstone MCC, the gay-friendly church, where services started a half hour later. This was scary at first, as I hadn't previously allowed myself to associate with known homosexuals. I quickly discovered they are just people, like any other, except they are oppressed. Oppression over a long period of time is detrimental to a person's health and sense of well-being. Dr. Evelyn Hooker was the one who demonstrated that homosexuality wasn't a mental illness, but rather, behavior associated with this group was the result of long-term oppression.

In 1991, the American Psychological Association presented Dr. Evelyn Hooker with the Award for Distinguished Contribution to Psychology in the Public Interest. The citation read:

When homosexuals had a mental illness, were forced out of government jobs, and were arrested in police raids, Evelyn Hooker courageously sought and obtained research support from the National Institute of Mental Health (NIMH) to compare a matched sample of homosexual and heterosexual men. Her pioneering study, published in 1957, challenged the widespread belief that homosexuality is a pathology by demonstrating that experienced clinicians using psychological tests widely believed at the time to be appropriate could not identify the nonclinical homosexual group. This revolutionary study provided empirical evidence that normal homosexuals existed and supported the radical idea then emerging that homosexuality is within the normal range of human behavior.... Her research, leadership, mentorship, and tireless advocacy for an accurate scientific view of homosexuality for more than three decades have been an outstanding contribution to psychology in the public interest.

Before long, the people I met at Cornerstone or through Thomas became "my friends," though not anyone I introduced to my Baptist friends or family. One day, while at Cornerstone, a very nice-looking man came to the church for worship. I greeted him in a friendly manner, but it was clear he wasn't comfortable at this church.

Nothing happened between us. But one weekend, while I was on yet another of my many early dates after coming out, he saw my date and me in downtown Mobile. He followed us around the whole evening. This angered my date, who asked me, "Who is this fellow?" I told him he came to my church a few times, that's all. My date terminated our dating relationship that night. But Brad, the guy who went to the church and followed us around, seemed interested in me. I'm no longer sure of the sequence of events, but we started dating shortly after this experience for six weeks, the longest I had dated a gay person at that time. He started coming over to see me.

This happened to be right when I was working hard as an agent to earn my benefits for the next year after being sent back into the field by my manager, Bradley A.

After a month of dating, we were together every weekend, going out to eat, movies, biking, and even looking at investment property to possibly buy together. At the six-week mark, he came over with presents, nice ones, and told me he loved me. My heart broke open with happiness. We got more physical than we had before, heavy petting. Then we went to dinner together in the Garden District, where I lived, and Brad noticed people noticing us. He said, "I think people think we are a couple." I said, "They should; we've been together for six straight weeks." Wow, that seemed to shock him. The next day was Sunday, and he asked if he could come over after church. He didn't attend Cornerstone MCC, but an open and affirming Presbyterian Church instead. After church, he came in visibly upset. He said, "I do not know what you think we are, but we are not a couple."

I replied: "Yesterday, you said you loved me."

"Just to be straight with you, I don't," he said.

Devastated, I tried for weeks to get him to talk to me. What had I done? I fell into a depression. I had finally been REALLY in love, and he rejected me after telling me he loved me. I was hurt, angry, sad, and confused all in one...just like most teenagers are when their first boyfriend or girlfriend dumps them.

He remained in my life for the next ten years, sabotaging all my more promising relationship prospects. He didn't really want me, but he wouldn't let me go either. Sound familiar? It should, because I now feel just like Sheila did that night, the night I almost killed myself.

In 1999, I moved to Tampa. In 2001, Brad left Mobile and moved to North Carolina. We kept in touch, as he had a sixth sense about me and dating. Whenever a relationship started to develop, he would drop me a line or call me, and I would end the new budding relationship. Then, in short order, he would lose interest and stop interacting with me.

When he unexpectedly moved to Tampa in 2006, I was suspicious. It was time to sink or swim. With much advice from friends to just "let this guy go," I decided I would only do as much as he did, nothing more and nothing less. His move was a surprise because I had not been consulted on it. But there he was. We started doing things as friends. That Christmas, he invited me over to his house and started hinting at it being "something more." I made up my mind that I would stick to my "one for one" strategy. This continued for a little while until his cold feet returned. Soon, without notice, he returned to North Carolina. I saw him only one more time after that, on a business trip to NC, but I had moved on. The fire I had for him was finally extinguished.

I learned from my experience with Brad that there were other guys like me, from similar backgrounds, who, like me, were struggling with being gay and Christian. His parents were even stricter than mine. When they moved from Mobile, Alabama, to Virginia, they moved to Lynchburg, home of Liberty University. Once there, they joined Falwell's church only to find it too liberal. Eventually, they moved their membership to a "truly Christian Baptist Church." The rest of that story is for Brad to tell.

One last detail about my breakup. Thomas, my renter, was worried about me. I was in a deep depression, and nothing he or anyone else did seemed to help me get back on my feet. Thomas told me there were other guys out there. I just needed to find one—the right one. Still, I didn't respond. That Thanksgiving of 1998, Thomas had friends from all over coming to Destin, Florida, and asked me to go with him. I refused. He persisted. He told me his car wouldn't make it, but mine would. He pleaded. Finally, after enough badgering, I drove him to Florida. There, for the first time, I met a group of professionals who were also gay, happy, and healthy. It was a joy to meet them. I finally came back out of my funk and returned to life. I finished the year with enough commissions to earn my benefits before the bomb went off at work.

Only if You Come Out for Good!

In 1998, New York Life turned from a dream job to agony. After three years as an agent, I was promoted to assistant manager in 1997. I was the fastest person to ever move from agent to management in NYL's Mobile Office, which meant I was a recruiter. But by '98, the company changed its policy and compensation for senior managers, deciding that offices had too many recruiters and not enough agents. This prompted Bradley A. to send me back into the field. He "forgot" to tell me I had only six months to fulfill the average monthly requirements to keep my health benefits, and it was already late August when he did. This prompted a swift response from me. I told him that if I didn't have health insurance, I wouldn't stay at NYL.

Now that the race was on, I worked very hard to meet the numbers. By the end of December, I had met the stated goal when Bradley dropped the bomb, "I forgot to tell you," he said. "The home office informed me that it isn't the monthly average but the total amount an agent needs for the entire year." That meant instead of doing what was required for the last six months, I had to do what was needed for the entire 12 months in just six months. When you are an agent, it takes a while to get up and running. The first goal was challenging enough, but the change was unfair. I had made up a massive shortfall and was ahead of the monthly average number, running about 67% of the total for the year, but with less than a month remaining in the fiscal year (Jan 31), it looked doubtful that I could make up the last third. I reiterated to Bradley that I would not stay at NYL without health benefits.

In the meantime, I was diagnosed with sleep apnea and had started seriously dating a man for the first time, as mentioned earlier. I also started reconsidering Dr. Baker's suggestion to move from Mobile.

First, I worked within the company to get reassigned as a trainer, as some offices had learned of my success. I heard that St. Louis, Houston, and Miami wanted me, but nothing happened. Finally, the manager from St. Louis called me directly and told me that my manager was blocking me because I was a good producer. She said, "As long as he is your manager and getting compensation for your sales, you are not going to be able to move within the company."

I was crushed. I had been his rising star. Now, he was using me for his own financial gain. Welcome to the secular world of work, I thought.

That left me little choice but to start seriously looking elsewhere. With this development and Dr. Baker strongly suggesting I move to "a more accepting" location, the question became, where? Over the remaining few months, I narrowed my choices to six cities close enough to Mobile where I could get back quickly if my parents needed me: Houston, Dallas, New Orleans, Atlanta, Orlando, and Tampa. I visited them all. The first trip was to Orlando and Tampa, where I met friends of friends from the area. It went poorly. I didn't like Orlando at all, and in Tampa Bay, there was a massive split between the Tampa and St. Pete sides of the bay. I thought this community was too small for such petty considerations.

Next were Dallas and Houston, but the economy wasn't good there. Texas is a boom-bust state. At that time, oil, the driver of Texas' economy, was in a bust cycle. Eliminated. I had lived in New Orleans, and after a quick trip since it was the closest, I crossed it off my list. The gay scene there was much too gritty for me.

After visiting all six, Atlanta looked like the best choice. I started going up regularly on weekends. After the five-and-a-half-hour drive, I started exploring the Atlanta scene, from open and affirming churches and bars to the gay bookstore and The Gay & Lesbian Center. The problem with Atlanta was that, like Dallas, it was an expensive city to live in. Both had thriving gay communities, but to live near those areas of town required resources I didn't have. And to live outside the Beltway was like living in Alabama, not gay affirming. Reluctantly, I dropped Atlanta down the list as a second option. The list was now down to two: Tampa/St. Pete or Atlanta.

An acquaintance I met on the Thanksgiving Day trip to Destin, who was living in St. Petersburg, suggested I give the area another chance. Dr. Van offered to let me stay at his house in Bel Air Bluffs, Clearwater, to help make the trip more economically feasible. I took him up on the generous offer. My trip to the Tampa Bay area was fruitful. The unemployment rate was very low, and the area seemed to need more workers than it currently had. I got several job offers to apply for, the most appealing from Lucent Technologies. I came home thinking I was going to work for them, but I wasn't excited about making another career change. While driving around the Bay Area, I passed Raymond James's Home Office. When I got back to Mobile, I applied online for a position and heard nothing.

The NY Life fiscal year ends on the last day of January, so I had less than a month to go before I lost benefits, which looked increasingly likely. I repeated to Bradley that I wasn't going to stay without medical benefits. He said he would do what he could but made no promises.

Meanwhile, Lucent Technologies was very interested and requested that I return for a second interview. Two weeks later, in late January, I returned. Still impressed, they began pressing me to accept their offer. I told them I needed two more weeks to think through the move and to take their offer. They agreed, and I flew home.

On the way to the airport I picked up *The Gazette*, the local gay newspaper. On the back was a full-page ad for the Tampa Bay Business Guild's (The LGBTQ Chamber of Commerce) Job Fair the following weekend. I knew God's Spirit was at work. I made plans to go back the following weekend, knowing God had a job for me if *I made the effort to come out all the way.*

I came back and sure enough, Raymond James had a recruiter at the Job Fair who offered me an interview. I met with him first and was then interviewed by seven different members of RJ's management. First, I met with Erwin Katz, the manager of the Tampa Office, and then it was off to the home office, where I interviewed all the way up to the President of Raymond James & Associates, Denis Zank. The most complex and best question came from Tom Hudson, who asked me what I would do if I invested a client's money in a stock and it lost 20% the next day. I thought about it. "Well," I said, "if I bought it because I thought it was a good stock and it was appropriate for my client, I would tell the client to hold on. It couldn't go from a good stock to a bad stock in so short a time unless there were information that had not previously been disclosed."

It was the correct answer, and my toughest interviewer approved my hire. I flew back home and waited. It would be another few days before I knew if Raymond James was going to hire me.

During the week, Lucent Technologies pressured me to give them a final yes. On Lucent's ultimatum date, Raymond James called, and I accepted a position in Raymond James's downtown Tampa office. Lucent Technologies called within minutes of that conversation, and I turned them down. The Lucent recruiters were not happy.

CHAPTER 9

Next Twenty-Five Years

"Therefore, since we are surrounded by such a great cloud of witnesses, let us throw off everything that hinders and the sin that so easily entangles. And let us run with perseverance the race marked out for us."
Hebrews 12:1, New International Version

Fools Rush in Where Angels Fear to Tread

After accepting Raymond James & Associates (RJ)'s offer, I started planning my transition for the end of March 1999. Bradley had succeeded in getting NYL to reinstate my insurance, but it was another too-late scenario, as it had been with Pat Patillo at SBTS years ago. I didn't tell Bradley that I was leaving immediately, giving me time to wrap up my duties, collect commissions owed, and avoid his distress that I was leaving (costing him my commissions). Two weeks before my departure, I tendered my resignation.

I moved down to Florida and settled into a small apartment in the Hyde Park area near downtown Tampa. On April 1st, 1999, I officially joined Raymond James. Mr. Katz asked me if I wanted a different start date, but I declined. I thought April Fool's Day was perfect for my state of mind, *Fools Rush in Where Angel's Fear to Tread*. What had I done? But it was too late to turn back. I was in Tampa now, starting at RJ, my employer for the next twenty-five years. My new life in Tampa felt uncertain at first.

I'm going to Make It, Just to Spite Them!

Over the next twenty-five years, my life settled down into an easy, healthy rhythm. I came fully out of the closet at Raymond James & Associates during training because I had to describe to the fourth recruitment class of 1998/99 what my three target prospects groups were and how I was going to reach them. First was Alabama residents whom I had worked with at NYL. Second was seniors; after all, I was in Florida, and there was an abundance of them. Third was the LGBT community. I assumed when I announced my third group that the class would know I was gay. Several classmates expressed their condolences now that they "knew" I wouldn't make it as a Financial Advisor. Before my announcement, Amanda M., a fellow recruit to the Tampa office, defended me as "A Baptist Preacher" to the guys who suspected I was gay. She was probably the most shocked of the group. No matter, I had come to Tampa to be fully out, as my promise to God if He granted my request to work for Raymond James.

At this point in my life, I loved a challenge. Whenever someone told me I couldn't do something, it made me work harder and smarter to prove I could. No longer hiding, I now had far more energy to put towards more important matters like productivity.

It helped that I was in a very supportive office. The manager, Erwin Katz, upon learning my three target groups, called me into his office for a chat. He first asked me if what he had heard was true, that Alabama, Seniors and Gays were my targets. Yes, I confirmed. He then launched into a speech on tolerance and acceptance. Upon reading my resume, which basically said Baptist, Baptist, Baptist, and New York Life, he suggested I choose a group of people that I respected, not one I hoped to change. That's when I realized he didn't know I was gay. It was a great moment in my career. Here was a man who was worried I was going to try to convert gays to be straight! I assured him I was not and explained I just wanted to work with a group of people who didn't have anybody working on their behalf in Tampa Bay at Raymond James.

The class was ranked against itself each month for the first three years. I decided I would be at the head of the class. I started as the least likely to succeed because I accepted the lowest job offer while in training, 50% less than the most promising candidates. I didn't care; I was going to show them all.

With no family money (most recruits came from upper-income families) and no natural market (friends and family where you live), the outlook for my success looked doubtful. I was again in a place of uncertainty. But month by month I knocked off the person in front of me on the class list. During the first six months, the weaker candidates typically self-select out. Our class started with 24 people and by the six-month mark we had lost at least six. After that, the real competition began, as these were the candidates serious about making a career in financial advisement.

Soon I was moving on up, as George Jefferson used to say on the 70's TV sitcom. Of the two recruits still ahead of me, both had worked in the business before RJ and brought books of business with them. The leader started on day one with a $4-million book of business. Most of us thought that was unfair, but RJ's leadership did not, as it was "new money" to the company. I never caught the two who started with existing books of business. Still, third overall and first among "true rookies" was an accomplishment.

Something BAD Happened: 911

Al-Qaeda was clever when they chose 9-11 as the day to attack the United States of America; 911 is our universal number for emergencies. On September 11, 2001, the world shook. It was an awful day in my life and for our nation!

I was still in my three-year training period, doing well. All of the TVs in the office were on CNBC market news when an announcer broke in to say a plane had crashed into one of the World Trade Center buildings in NYC, the same one Richard and I had gone to the top of during our 'misguided' cross-country adventure back in college.

At first we thought it was a tragic accident. But soon another plane appeared; it looked like it was heading for the other World Trade Center Tower. How could this be? Who in the world would dare to attack the strongest country in the world? And why? The second plane hit the other tower. The Trade Center towers were on fire, and we watched in horror as people jumped to their deaths rather than burning alive. What an awful choice to have to make. It was the most heart-wrenching thing I had ever witnessed as people dropped like bombs from the 110-story Twin Towers.

We quickly realized we were under attack. Two additional planes hijacked out of Boston Logan International Airport were in the air, destinations unknown, but speculation had begun.

Not long after, the Twin Towers were totally engulfed in flames. Commentators wondered if the structures could withstand this kind of damage. They could not. New Yorkers were told to stay away from Wall Street as the buildings began to fail. It is estimated that nearly 3,000 people were killed that day in the deadliest terrorist attack in U.S. history.

As if the Twin Tower horror wasn't enough, we learned two other hijacked planes appeared to be heading toward the Pentagon and/or the U.S. Capital. On one of those planes, a group of courageous passengers that included at least one gay man overtook the hijackers and it crashed in Shanksville, Pennsylvania, killing all onboard. The other plane crashed into the southwest corner of the Pentagon, killing 184 people, all those aboard the plane and more inside the building.

Al-Qaeda's Osama bin Laden was considered the mastermind, though Khalid Sheikh Mohammed was the operational planner and the attacks were carried out by 19 terrorists. They hailed from four countries: 15 from Saudi Arabia, 2 from the United Arab Emirates, 1 from Egypt, and 1 from Lebanon.

That day, something broke in America. We no longer saw ourselves as invincible. We no longer saw ourselves as "especially blessed and protected by God." This reminds me of Mother after her sister died when she declared that God wasn't trustworthy anymore. It seems the whole country felt that way after 9-11.

The U.S. vowed revenge, and President George W. Bush reacted by attacking not Saudi Arabia, not the United Arab Emirates, not Egypt, nor Lebanon, but Afghanistan, where the planning took place, and Iraq, which had nothing to do with the attack. The end result was we destabilized the entire Middle East, removing the delicate balance of power between Sunni and Shia Muslims. Ultimately, the United States' response emboldened and gave new life to Islamic Fundamentalists, who grew and blossomed into ever more terror organizations.

But the event did something else. It changed the hearts of many Evangelicals who had previously been reluctant to get overly involved in politics. From this moment on, the mission of Southern Baptists and other Evangelical groups seemed to switch from preaching primarily about Christ as savior. The new imperative became to bring the country "back to God."

"If my people, which are called by my name, shall humble themselves and pray, and seek my face, and turn from their wicked ways, then I will hear from heaven and forgive their sin and will heal their land." (1Chronicles 7:14, KJV)

Ironically, this was the scripture passage I used for my Alabama Baptist Speech contest where I finished third in the State with *Where Now*

America? In the speech, I said something like: "If good people do nothing, then bad things are going to happen." My speech was about turning from immorality (wicked ways meaning sexual sins), and with prayer God would heal our land.

Indeed, many previously non-political Evangelicals, including Southern Baptists, started promoting political activism at a new, more intense level.

The front runner for the Evangelical's political activism was Pat Robertson, who in June 1998, launched vitriolic attacks against Orlando, Florida for allowing Gay Pride Events and at Walt Disney World for allowing an event called Gay Days. At this time, Florida was experiencing terrible wildfires. Robertson said that God was punishing Florida for its wickedness. Ironically, at the time, I remember thinking that God must have gotten his geography confused because the wildfires were in Volusia County (an ultra-conservative part of Florida) while the greater Orlando/Disney area remained unharmed. "God must have missed," I mused.

Three years after the World Trade Center attacks, many conservative/fundamentalist Christians interpreted the attacks as God's punishment on America for our wickedness: abortion and homosexuality! Many in the SBC decided now was the time to put 1 Chronicles 7:14 into action. Sadly, many directed their actions outward, blaming others, rather than searching their own souls.

Thriving Not Surviving

While in Tampa, I continued going to Counseling, but now I used it primarily to continue growing as a person. Being Gay was no longer the primary issue I struggled with, though I still had "residual stuff" to work through. I had several different counselors while in Tampa, but none were as impactful as Dr. Will Baker, who first introduced me to Family Systems Theory, a type of psychotherapy that treats the family as a unit based on the idea that what affects one family member affects the entire family. I was eventually referred to Renee Gillombardo, who practiced this type of therapy. She became my counselor for the next 20+ years, but less frequently as life continues. But even now, from time to time, I check in to make sure I am still on the right, healthy path.

We had worked on my attitude towards my biological mother for some time until I finally reached a place of both acceptance and forgiveness. My real Mother was dealt a bad hand in life for sure. She didn't have the skills to cope and gave up that day (July 12, 1968). While her suicide hurt me, it was now time to forgive her. I did. With that came relief. Carrying a burden like that is hard work. I was glad to let it go.

Next was Dad, my forever "You're not a good enough son" father. I loved him, and he was a kind and gracious man to most. But that was not my experience with him. I am an adult now, and it is time to take responsibility for my own mental and physical health. "Holding a grudge isn't good for him or for you," Renee reminded me repeatedly. I made amends and forgave him.

A person is only responsible for their own actions, I learned. I needed to apologize to Dad for my role in our broken relationship. I did. He did not apologize back. It took more sessions before I came to another truth: A person can only do their part in rebuilding a relationship. The other person also has free will and can choose to engage or not. But regardless of whether they choose to engage or not, "fixing them" is not your responsibility.

My relationship with Dad started to improve. He still didn't approve of me being gay, but he did admit that apparently, Tampa was where I needed to be. I was doing better.

In approximately 2007, Dad started exhibiting symptoms of memory loss. I noticed it when I drove him to the airport to pick up my sister, Carol. He didn't want me to leave him alone anywhere. I knew something was wrong, as Dad had never been like this before. He was eventually diagnosed with Alzheimer's Disease. I came home again the year of the diagnosis, 2009, to be with family around Thanksgiving. Dad, who was in a memory loop by then, told all kinds of inappropriate stories about DiAnne and Mother, both of whom he adored when in his right mind. But now, with Alzheimer's, he spent a lot of time as a teenage boy in his mind. But when the loop returned him to his old self, he was so serious that he did not want to be a burden on Mother or any of us. On another loop back to himself, he said, "Mike, I know you are gay. I want you to know that I am not against you. I love you, and I just want you to be happy." Soon, though, he was back in yesteryear, but that one affirmation was terrific. He died that December between Christmas and New Year's. Dad had given me his final blessing.

I returned home to work and counseling. When I told Renee about the experience with my father, she suggested it might be time to shift my mantra from "Surviving" to "Thriving." She pointed out that *surviving* was appropriate when, as a child, I was being battered by early death experiences in the family, poor support for my emotional health, and bullying. But, she said, "It has been a long time since you were surviving. It is time you were thriving," she

pointed out. I had heard something similar in sermons, from friends, and even in counseling. Why it struck a chord this time I do not know. But I do know that after 11 years in Tampa with Raymond James, I was definitely thriving.

Two years earlier, in 2007, Michael Ragsdale and I formed a professional partnership to become M2 Financial Advisors of RJ. It was the first year I made President's Club, reserved for the top 10% of brokers in Raymond James & Associates. I remained in the President's Club for the next 13 years with the exception of one year in the Leader's Club (Top 20%) and one year in the Chairman's Council (Top 5%). I began my retirement process at RJ with Michael Ragsdale taking over as the team leader in 2020, just as COVID hit. Jesus said he came to give life and give it abundantly (John 10:10, paraphrased), and abundance has shown up in my life since I accepted my authentic self.

There are, of course, many more stories I could tell about my time at Raymond James, but for the purpose of this book, I was then and am now thriving, even in the midst of difficult times like the Tech Crash of

2001-2003, the Financial Crisis of 2008-2009 and the 9 surgeries and/
or hospitalizations that my husband Rick or I had from 2018-2022.
Through all this, I have realized that God's Spirit, the embodiment of
God's love, has, is, and will always be with me, as promised the day my
13-year-old self said yes, I want to be in a relationship with God.

A Four Standard Deviation Year: 2008

After nine tough but glorious years at Raymond James, I was doing well, having made President's Club for the first time in 2007 and partnering with Michael Ragsdale to form M2 Financial Advisors. Then, we hit an abrupt stop. 2008 was labeled a four-standard deviation year because the financial markets were so out of the norm and unusual. In the financial markets a four standard deviation happens approximately once every 100 years. It had been a very long time since so many things went wrong at the same time. Banks crashed, and houses that were selling for $450K last year were down to $250K this year. People just walked away from their debt. Though President George W. Bush's administration claimed to have contained the crisis, "too big to fail" institutions, including Bear Stearns and Washington Mutual Bank, started failing. Soon, there were runs on banks, and many became insolvent and closed or were forced into mergers. The market experienced the worst decline since the Great Depression, but more closely paralleled the Panic of 1907.

While the financial markets were running amok, my non-market-related year began with a Frozen Shoulder, which required physical therapy. After that was completed, my Crohn's Disease broke loose, requiring Prednisone to get it back under control for the first time in twelve years.

With the market in decline, family and friends' incomes were severely cut, leaving many in serious jeopardy. This led to my extended family moving into my Tampa home. Billy's oldest daughter, Christy, and her son, Kaynen, came to live with me. Travails ensued, with burglary and alcohol playing a role in making it such a very difficult year. In addition, Billy's other children, Daniel and Jacob, were experiencing economic difficulties in addition to other serious challenges.

Grounded in the knowledge that God really is walking with us, the Spirit helped me see that all was not lost. As with any serious event, I was able to see opportunities where others see only despair.

The Financial Crash would not end until March the following year. Only at the very end did Michael Ragsdale panic a little. "What are we going to do if we don't make it?" He asked, knowing my faith background. I replied honestly but not piously, "We will have to do something else with God's help." Literally the next day, March 9, 2009, the market started rebounding. My financial net worth took a hit. My challenging relationship with Christy and Kaynen eventually ended badly for all concerned several years later, and Jacob and Daniel eventually ended their relationships with their spouse (Jacob), and significant other-common law wife (Daniel).

While I do not regret my efforts to help Billy (I got him into treatment centers several times) or support for Billy's kids, as he was by then an absentee father living on the streets, the efforts were only marginally successful. In hindsight, though turbulent and unpredictable, I was still thriving throughout the financial panic year.

You Are an Abomination unto God

A final note about RJ: When I made Chairman's Club in 2015, my husband Rick and I went on the Raymond James and Associates congratulatory trip that year in Canada. Rick and I were sitting together with another broker friend, Janet N. I left to get my plate of food for dinner. They remained sitting at a table when a woman asked Rick if he was married to Janet. Janet, a leading female financial advisor with RJ and nationally, replied that Rick was married to Michael. I was just returning to the table with my plate when I heard the woman say, "You are not married in the eyes of God. You are an abomination unto God." As I sat down, Rick and Janet got up and left. At first, I did not fully grasp what had just transpired. After a few awkward minutes attempting to eat, I said, I guess I should go too and got up and left.

The statement stung. It was mean-spirited and discriminatory. She, in her self-righteousness, had acted like a legalist, not a follower. Then it dawned on me that she had said and done exactly what I had said and done to Mark at SBTS years ago. "You reap what you sow," or as others might say, "That's Karma." I now know without a doubt how badly I had hurt Mark because this lady had caused us similar pain. The leadership at RJ was not pleased when they learned what the woman had said and were terrific in dealing with it. But it still hurt all of us Janet, Rick and me. For me, it was another opportunity to grow, feeling even more strongly the impact of my past mistakes. But we all survived, and yes, even thrived.

Finally, Somebody Wanted ME!

Actually, this is not a good title. A lot of people wanted me: Betsy, Sheila, Vanessa, Diana, Mark, and even Harry had wanted me. But I wasn't interested in or ready for any of them. A better title for this chapter might be: Finally, Somebody Wanted Me, and I was ready!

After 15 years of dating men, someone who I wanted to be in a relationship with finally wanted to be in a relationship with me. It happened in another of those "ah ha" moments. By this time, I had dated a lot of men, probably in the couple of hundred range, though some suspect I exaggerate these numbers too. But once out, I was ready for a relationship, or so I thought. Of course, I wasn't! I felt it was way past time to get going on having that significant other. I dated very interesting characters at first. I was unable to decipher *BEFORE* dating them which ones were or weren't candidates for a real relationship, so I went on a lot of dates. Some of these dates were funny, and some were not. But unlike women, who I started dating at 13, I had never dated a man before.

Then I fell very hard for the first guy I liked before leaving Mobile, as mentioned earlier. Before him, I had dated maybe 50 guys in Mobile, Alabama my first few years after coming out. I even dated a Muslim, which was a big step for me. I met up with a bisexual guy who, unbeknownst to me, was married. If I had asked the right questions, I would have known he was an unlikely match. I was horrified when, after meeting at Subway (always my choice with someone I didn't know), he said, "Now that I've met you, we need to get on with the sex before my son's birthday party." Stunned and mortified, I turned him down, of course, which did not go over well.

In Tampa, I continued to date as often as I could in search of the "ideal man." This looks ridiculous now, especially in light of how I dated women – the same way, looking for the "ideal wife." I was in such a hurry I wasn't thoughtful about the process. And because I wasn't, I kissed a lot of frogs along the way. It always made the guys I dated feel as though I was desperate to get into a relationship. I was, but I wasn't. I mean, I wanted a relationship to start, but I was in no hurry for it to turn serious. But my approach attracted all the wrong guys.

After many failed dates and miserable experiences, I finally started dating Harry Knox, a preacher turned activist. We dated for a year, around 2002 or 2003, before I realized I cared about Harry but wasn't in love with him. He was in love with me, he said, but with far more experience than I, he realized the relationship wasn't going anywhere. He received a job offer to work for *Freedom to Marry* in NYC and told me to get my reaction. I told him, "I would not stay on account of me." That statement confirmed what he already knew in his heart. He accepted the offer and left, and we have remained friends since.

So now, still lonely, I resigned myself to being single. Maybe my struggle to find a significant other was just not meant to be. I was happier with myself than in the past, though I still wanted someone in my life as "that person."

In late January 2011, attending King of Peace MCC for the express purpose of meeting a spiritual gay man, the associate pastor asked me to please welcome Richard McDonald when he arrived. She explained he had attended the grief support group after having just lost his partner. She also told me what he looked like. To most, he looks like a George Clooney clone. So, I looked for him. Sure enough, he walked through the front doors. I made an effort to say hello. He was a handsome, nice-looking man but seemed reluctant to engage in conversation. That was ok, as I knew he was in a tough place. Loss is difficult. Sometimes, when people try to help, they don't really. "Maybe he just needed a sanctuary of peace and tranquility," I thought.

After that initial greeting, I continued over the months to say hello. He was wary of me for a long time. But what would it hurt if I kept saying hello? I heard through the grapevine that Bob Pope, a leader in the church and the gay community, knew him. I asked Bob and his partner Lawrence if they did. They said yes, adding, "And his partner who died." They thought he was a Republican. Oh well, I thought, as I am pretty progressive in my politics.

One Sunday in October 2011, Floss and Kay, clients and friends who always saved me a seat at MCC (I taught a Scripture Class before the service and often came in late), didn't. This Sunday, they not only didn't save me a seat, they weren't sitting in their regular row. I wondered what was up. They told me they didn't have a seat in their row, but I could sit in the row behind them. Richard was sitting in that row with an open seat by the aisle. I took it. I noticed that Richard was holding the hand of the guy sitting next to him. Oh well I thought, maybe he has found somebody. Over the months, I had become more interested in getting to know him but didn't want to push as he was still grieving the death of his partner. I had decided months before that I would do nothing to encourage or discourage a relationship. I would just wait for him to make a move or not. So that Sunday, I guessed I had my answer. He had made a move, holding hands with the guy next to him.

Richard leaned over and whispered to me during the service, "I need to tell you something at the end of the service, don't leave." After service he said, "That guy was holding my hand, but I don't like the guy that way." Ok, I thought, that's strange. But the more I thought about it, the only conclusion I could draw was that he must like me a little, or there wouldn't have been a reason to tell me that.

The next Sunday, I invited him out to lunch after church for the following week. He agreed. I was encouraged, but only a little. That Sunday he brought a friend to church who bolted once the service was over. He apologized, but said he couldn't go. Rain check? I said "sure." For the next couple of weeks, I was out of town on business. When I returned it was now November, and I sat with him. At the end of the service, I asked if we might try again for lunch after church next week. He said "sure" but didn't seem very excited by the idea. From his point of view, he thought the invitation was a "get to know the Church meeting." I thought it was a get-to-know-him-better meeting. He stood me up again. Now it was the week before Thanksgiving and I was concerned for him. Holidays are the hardest the first year after a death. I asked and got permission, though it was against policy, for his telephone number. I told the associate pastor I thought something was wrong and just needed to make sure he was ok. I called him. He was surprised and pleased that I had. He explained that he hadn't come to church because the guy who was holding his hand was driving him nuts to the point where he didn't want to be around him. Richard tried to be helpful to him in his grief (they met in the grief support group) and was clear he wasn't interested in a romantic relationship with him. The man, however, wasn't giving up. He bought Richard presents, unwelcome gifts. He called sometimes nicely, sometimes hostile. By Thanksgiving, it had turned ugly. The guy wasn't happy that Richard wasn't responding appropriately.

Relieved that he was ok, I asked him if we might have a dinner date to try something different than after church. He said sure. Because it was Thanksgiving week, we decided it would be best if we waited till afterward. So, on the first Friday, December 3rd, 2011, Richard and I went on our first date, but neither of us knew what it was. I brought my travel book from my recent trip to Alaska, ready to help keep the conversation light. I was dressed in a nice coat and tie. Richard came more casual. We sat in "outside seating" at Seasons 52 in Tampa, talking, laughing, and eating dinner for three hours. Afterward, I walked him to his car, where I kissed him on the cheek. Appropriate for a first date I thought and checked his car for political bumper stickers. I was happy to learn he wasn't a Republican after all.

I had first registered as a Republican when George Wallace, a Democrat, was my governor. Segregation wasn't a value I held, then or now. Back then, the GOP seemed to reflect my values more than the Southern Democrats. But soon, those Southern Democrats started leaving their party and joining the GOP. Having seen firsthand the impact of Reagan's "trickle-down economics" and not being impressed, I switched to the Democratic Party.

Richard, not sure what to expect, thought maybe he should dress down because at Church I typically "dressed down" to avoid bringing attention to any difference in economic status. The church had a significant income gap among parishioners. As for the kiss, he thought, "What was that? Was it a kiss your grandmother kiss? Was it a first-date kiss? What was this guy, twelve?"

A day or two later, he called me. The call almost killed our budding new relationship. He called at about 9 pm and said, "I just want you to know that I really, really, really, really, really like you!" I said Ok. But in my head, red flags went off. He didn't really, really, really, really, really know me. So how could he really like me?

The next week, I went on a business trip to Atlanta. One of my appointments canceled and I dropped by the Outwrite Book Store in midtown Atlanta, the gay bookstore, and picked up a novel. I read the book that night having nothing else I wanted to do. In the book, the main character falls for the team's Quarterback, but at some point, the Quarterback does something, and the other guy breaks up. The QB tries his best to say he is sorry, but the guy won't listen. In the end, he loses the relationship only to find out that the QB really did love him. I was pondering this when The Spirit of the Lord said in my heart, "You are that guy; you are throwing away this man I have set before you." I came home and Richard and I arranged our first real date.

That night, we *kissed* as the date was winding down. I thought my body was going to explode because there was so much energy. I had never felt like this before: not Roy, Brad, Harry, not anyone. We started dating in earnest then. We've never stopped. That was 13 years ago, going on 14 as of this writing. We were married in 2013 and celebrated our 12th wedding anniversary earlier this year.

In these years, there have been uncertain times. There have been challenges, but it has never felt hopeless. Life is better with Richard in it, and he tells me his life is better with me in it.

At our Wedding in Maryland, my former boyfriend, Rev. Harry Knox, officiated. We each chose "our song" to be played. This is mine to Richard:

> *You gave me hope*
> *When I was at the end*
> *And turned my lies*
> *Back to truth again.*
> *I can't believe it's you, I can't believe it true!*
> *I needed you*
> *And you were there,*
> *I'll never leave, why should I leave? I'd*
> *Be a fool 'cause I finally found someone who cares.*

You Needed Me is a song written by Randy Goodrum and sung by Canadian Artist Anne Murray, winning a Grammy Award in 1978. It is a song the writer describes as being about "unconditional undeserved love." That's how I felt when God, through Spirit, sent Richard to me. It summed up how I felt about him that day we were married in Chevy Chase, Maryland. It still does.

Life with Richard & Raymond

I met Richard, Rick to friends, when I was 54. We got serious quickly and married before I turned 56. We asked God to give us just five good years. We said if we had that, we would be eternally grateful and would have lived a good life. That was granted. Those five years were the least stressful and most enjoyable of my life to date. We traveled everywhere from Iceland to see the Aurora Borealis to the Pantanal in Argentina, where we slept in a 1600's Jesuit Ranch house and later saw Iguazu Falls, the largest complex of waterfalls in the world.

We have enjoyed each other's company very much. Rick, much more experienced than I, took the lead in helping me enjoy physical contact (sex). This has remained a trouble spot for me, but he has always been gracious about it. But you can't go from thinking it's the worst sin one could commit to suddenly being ok and enjoying it now. It doesn't work that way, at least for me. It has taken me a long time to relax, and I still have residual guilt over it. Rick, who is in his third long-term gay relationship, likes to say his first and last were Virgos with "Catholic and Baptist guilt." (Both of his earlier partners passed away, and he was there with his love and support through their passings from difficult diseases).

We have thought a lot about what comes after Raymond for us, Raymond James & Associates, that is.

First, we decided to buy a place in St. Petersburg because he loves St. Pete and hates Tampa. He moved into my house in Tampa around the time we got married. Because he prefers the St. Pete side of the Bay, we bought a weekend place in Skyview in February 2017. We spent the year gutting it and renovating it into a showplace. But once it was finished Rick never came home to North B. Street, my house on the other side of the bay. Eventually, we sold the Tampa house and moved to St. Pete full-time. As the next five-year clock started, my gradual retirement plans loomed large. We talked about if we could have a house anywhere, where might that be? The Canadian Rockies came to mind. In late

September 2018, we made our first trip to check it out. No luck. In '19, we came back and found Kicking Horse Mountain Resort near Golden, British Columbia, the perfect getaway spot, where we bought a little condo on the mountain.

We continued to do well on other fronts during those first years. Then, as if by magic, life became more difficult with a series of health-related issues. From 2018 to 2022, we had 9 different hospitalizations and/or surgeries. I had three intestinal surgeries (two minor, one serious) due to Crohn's Disease, and Rick had glaucoma, Prostate Cancer, and a Sudden Cardiac Arrest. By this time, our relationship was strong enough to withstand these difficult winds that were blowing.

Meanwhile, life with RJ was progressing nicely. We had a growing book of business, and we added Sharon Dunaway-Alt as an assistant. The future was bright. In the next five years my business continued to grow, and I was selected to join the Diversity and Inclusion Advisory Council to the Board of Directors. We worked on diversity and re-designing the affinity groups to be more business-minded. We also had the first-ever Gay Flag Raising at RJ headquarters. I left the committee only after beginning my retirement transition because I no longer held a title that entitled me to be on that committee.

Michael Ragsdale moved to the lead position on our team, and Sharon Dunaway-Alt, our assistant, agreed to start training to take my place as the junior member. Maggie Broom was hired to take her place as our assistant.

Coincidences

Do you believe in coincidences? We don't because we laugh all the time about the unlikely pair we are. You know how we came to be a couple, but it didn't happen by accident and didn't happen because we made it happen. Of course, we were participants. Coincidences, by definition, are a remarkable concurrence of events or circumstances without apparent causal connection. This describes our unlikely pairing from a secular viewpoint.

First, the most obvious is that the associate pastor only asked me one time to specifically greet someone coming to church. I had known her at that time for over 12 years, and we went to the same church for most of that time. The Sunday she requested that I greet Richard was the only time she ever asked me to greet a specific person. A coincidence? Maybe.

Another coincidence was we both are from blended, somewhat dysfunctional families. We are both one of nine children, though neither of us lived with all nine siblings at the same time. And in order of birth, we are both next to last. Coincidences? Getting harder to think all these could be.

Both of us had experienced the death of our biological parents before getting together in our 50s. While this isn't wildly out of the norm, it is young for that to be the case.

We both moved to Florida to be in a more gay-friendly place than our home states. While mine was a more direct route, it was still the impetus in both cases.

Last, we are total opposites. He was an out gay man since his twenties, and I was a virgin until 40. He wasn't particularly churched, and I was a regular churchgoer. He was a partier, and I was a prayer warrior. We seem, then and now, a most unlikely "perfect couple." But here we are 14 years later, growing and becoming more than we were when we first met. It is hard to deny that God, through the Spirit, didn't have a hand in this, he certainly has a sense of humor. It is too improbable that we would date, much less marry. But we did. The Spirit knew what each needed and that we were a match regardless of what others thought. His friends thought I would reject him as "too wild" or that he wouldn't be himself because of my religious leanings. But he is who he is, and I am who I am. Neither of us asked the other to change. That honesty became the bedrock of our relationship.

One of our trips was to France and Spain. I tried for three months to get tickets to go up the Eiffel Tower for New Year's Eve 2012. I tried every day. No luck. He tried as well but gave up. I checked the whole time we would be in Paris, the day before, New Year's Eve, even the day after, New Year's Day. No luck. It looked doubtful I could make this happen. I prayed, asking The Paraclete (Spirit, our advocate to The Father) to help. I continued to look. Suddenly, about a week out, I couldn't believe my eyes; there were two tickets for 5:30 pm, right at sundown. These were the only tickets available, exactly what we needed. We were there as the sun set and the lights of the city glowed. Maybe coincidence, maybe not.

That night in Montmartre, an artsy neighborhood of Paris, Rick proposed to me at midnight. Who does this ever really happen to? In the movies, maybe. But for most, this is too unreal to believe. But it happened. I remember being stunned. He had brought the rings up with him on The Eiffel Tower, unbeknownst to me, where he thought he would propose. But once up there with 500 hundred of our closest friends and "be wary of pickpocket" signs all about, he waited. Then we went to the restaurant for a five-course, four-hour meal. Then, out of the blue, he popped the question. I had no idea it was coming (I had previously proposed making our relationship more serious and had been nicely rebuffed). But here in Paris, on New Year's Eve he asked, and I said yes. We were both stunned. He asked again, "What did you say?" I said yes. I SAID YES! Then, just after midnight, we walked to the Metro, hand in hand, and then, in a very Paris-like drizzle, back to our hotel. It was a magical night.

Our relationship didn't happen because we made it happen, not a chance. Our relationship happened because of "a remarkable concurrence of events or circumstances without apparent causal connection." Maybe. But I believe it happened because of the work of God's Love through The Spirit, who capped off a most unlikely relationship with affirmation in Paris, France at Midnight as the year turned from 2012 to 2013.

He Should Have Died

Another "ah ha" moment happened when we decided to move from Skyview to Garden Terrace, down the street. We found it by accident if you believe in that sort of thing. We do not. We believe things happen for a reason. We had been looking for some time when we went to a party and someone mentioned there was a condo for sale down Sunny Lane. We looked and bought it. We bought it in February 2020, just before COVID hit.

Rick's theory that God loved and protected me more than others was put to the test in March 2022, not that this was the first challenging time we'd had. I had already had another intestinal surgery and he had already had prostate surgery where he nearly bled-out. But this was different.

Rick was home alone when Eva, the Polish lady who lives above us, felt the need to tell Rick something important. She always had suggestions about how to make our condo community better. She felt compelled to make this important suggestion to Rick right away.

She knocked on the back door, no answer. She knocked on the front door, no answer. She went around to the sliding door on the Tampa Bay Side overlooking the bay. He didn't answer that one either. So, she opened the sliding door and came in anyway. That's bold, but she was the right person in the right place at the right time. She saw Rick clutching his necklace in one hand with his phone in the other, turning blue. She immediately found a woman in our complex who keeps up with everybody's whereabouts. That Angel soon found one of only two people certified in CPR at the condo complex. Tony and his wife only came down to their condo a few weeks a year. He was outside that day and rushed over.

Rick only had 12 minutes to get his heart restarted before brain damage set in, the doctors told us later. Within that window of time, three angels were sent: two helpful friends and a doctor certified in CPR. If we still lived in our previous high-rise condo where we lived on the top floor, even if someone came looking for Rick, there is no way anyone would have been able to get in to see if he was ok or not.

EMS was called, and he was rushed to the hospital. My other up-stairs neighbor, from Mobile, Alabama ironically, called me. I was in the middle of a client appointment and sent a message back that I wasn't available. She called again. I refused to take it again. When she called a third time, I knew something bad had happened.

When I answered, she told me Rick had a heart attack and to get to the hospital immediately. But he didn't have a heart attack. He had something more deadly: a sudden cardiac arrest (SCA). Rick was taken to the trauma emergency room at about 3:30 pm. For hours, we (friends from Garden Terrace and his best friend Dee and I) waited. By 9 pm, they had all gone home and I was finally allowed to see him. As I got to his room, he was thrashing about and had pulled all the tubes out of his arm. I was again sent back to the waiting room. Around 11 pm I was finally allowed back in. I learned that the nurse on duty was the Code Blue Nurse. The Code Blue Nurse is assigned to the sickest person in the hospital. I asked him if Rick was going to be ok. He said if he was in the emergency trauma ICU, then no, he wasn't going to be ok for a long time. He wasn't even out of the woods as far as making it through the night.

Reality hit like a ton of bricks. I prayed and cried. I stayed until they needed me to bring medical records from home. I left and returned with the requested records. At about 2 am they told me to go home, rest and I could come back later, and he would still be here. I went home and crashed for a few hours, returning at 5 am. When I got back, Rick wasn't in the emergency trauma ICU anymore. He was now in the Trauma ICU ward, and I couldn't see him until 9 am.

I went home, slept a few more hours, then headed back. At the worst point, he had 13 different medications going in at the same time. They asked if they could put a port in because he was getting so many medications. I said yes. Becky, Rick's sister, flew in from Ohio, unsure if he would survive. Becky, Dee, and I stayed with him as much as the hospital allowed.

Then, the waiting game was on. He wasn't breathing on his own. During the day, they took him off medication to see if he could breathe unassisted. Day 1 in the ICU was a no-go; he could not. Day 2 was still a no-go. By day 3, the Doctors were worried. The longer you stay on the breathing machine, the less likely you are to get off it successfully. Still not much luck. In the meantime, I learned that SCA's typically happen for one of two reasons: heart blockage or stroke. That was sobering news.

On day 4, the doctors did MRIs of his brain but couldn't find any damage from a stroke. They did a Heart Catheterization to find a blockage. He had one artery with a very small blockage, but the doctors said that couldn't have been it. He finally got off the breathing machine later that day, which was good news. To get him off the machine, the doctors reduced the machine's output to force his body to work harder and start breathing again. As he started breathing on his own, he was in a medication fog and began asking every nurse and doctor who came by if he was dying. A nurse said, "Honey, you know you just asked me that, right?" He didn't.

Reality struck. Rick might live, something that looked very unlikely just three days before. But he might not survive this intact. I went to Church that Sunday morning and broke down during the worship service, weeping.

I put on my game face for Richard at the hospital that afternoon. He still wasn't remembering much, so he went back to the MRI lab for more brain testing. The neurologist was convinced he'd had a stroke. However, upon returning to the ICU ward, they still had not determined the cause.

In all, he was in the Hospital for ten days, mostly in the Trauma ICU. The doctors concluded he was in the "we don't know why this happened" category for SCA. The best thinking was that two electrical signals went to his brain at exactly the same time. Confused, his heart shut down, not knowing which signal to obey.

In the end, everyone concurred that a miracle had happened, even Rick's neurologist who is not a person of faith. A few weeks later, his neurologist told us, "I think organized religion is a crock of S---t, just to get your money. But in your case, since your chances of survival were less than one-tenth of one percent, I would say you had a real miracle."

Rick's memory did return. After the trauma was over, I told him that he had a "front-row seat" to a miracle. I reminded him that he could no longer say that God loved and protected me more.

Checkers vs. Chess

Do you play checkers? As a child, I loved this game; one of the few games I was good at. In checkers, the rules are set before the game starts. The objective is to capture all of the other players' pieces. I liked black best and generally won by taking all the red ones. This is a simple, one-dimensional game.

Chess, on the other hand, is multi-dimensional. Different pieces make different moves. One has to be aware of the implication each move may have on all the other pieces on the board before moving his or her piece. One must think ahead about the consequences. This game is harder and takes more skill.

Such is the difference between simple faith with simple answers and mature faith, which is multi-dimensional.

All my life I desired to grow in faith but wanted simple answers. I liked it when The Spirit showed me a clear path, like the OBU poster in Slidell, Louisiana, and the radio program sale that provided the money to pay for that first semester. I liked it when God, through Spirit, showed me a clear path, like going to Texas instead of Vermont.

I didn't like it when I had to make a choice based on the best-known facts BEFORE I had confirmation. Those times were scarier. I often resisted those choices. But, if we are to grow, we must take those "Leaps of Faith" and step out of the boat, as Peter (in scripture) had done. If we look down at the water, we sink. If we stay focused, we walk. This multi-dimensional understanding of how The Spirit works is important for growth. We can't stay forever in the "show and tell" mode of walking by faith. At some point, our faith and understanding must grow. People like easy answers to difficult questions. However, those easy answers rarely lead to good results. Good results require good work.

I remember a lesbian couple coming into my office, wanting to retire early. They saved a couple hundred thousand dollars and had a mountain of debt. They made 160K in annual income. The easy answer would have been to accept them as clients and tell them they could retire because that was what they wanted to hear. But it wasn't true. In one of my career's toughest meetings, I had to tell them that their chances of success were just 28%. They fought with one another and me because they wanted to retire. Needless to say, they did not become my clients. I couldn't deploy Checkers thinking to a Chess problem.

Five years later, they came back. While the day of the initial appointment had been tough, very tough, they had heard what they needed to do. They needed to get their debt under control. They needed to fund their employer retirement plans fully. They needed to live on a budget. They did all of this. Now, five years later, the higher wage earner was disabled. Now they needed to, had to retire. They sought me out again to see what it would look like. With fear and trepidation, I took the meeting. To all of our surprise, they were now in a radically different place. While they made more than $160K this last year, they brought their budget closer to $100k. This allowed them to rid themselves of debt. It also allowed them to fund their employer retirement plans fully. And now, because they had done the hard work, they were able to retire into the lifestyle they had become accustomed to. That day, they became clients, but my hard work had been five years before.

Easy faith is just that, easy. A mature faith, a real walk of faith, is more challenging and rewarding. It is a matter of awareness and a willingness to follow the Spirit, even when it's not easy.

My journey includes leaps of Faith and nudging by the Spirit. Sometimes, God's Love, through The Spirit, nudges us along. Sometimes, it pushes us, and sometimes, we have to get out of the boat and walk.

Throughout my life, I have had many "ah ha" moments when it was undeniable that God's Spirit was at work in my life. The first was the night my mother confronted me about accepting Christ over and over again. It was a breakthrough moment when God's love swept over me, and I was forever changed.

Then, when God's Spirit nudged me to think of being in ministry, I resisted but eventually gave in and took that next step.

I had an "ah ha" moment when I asked The Spirit to guide me to the Seminary. I had to take a "leap of faith" that time, choosing before receiving confirmation that it was where I was supposed to be. It was so tough at the time, but then Southern Seminary opened 20 additional spots, and I was #20. You just can't make this stuff up. The Spirit is always way ahead of us, nudging, moving us along.

I had another moment when I felt that God wanted me in Texas. That affirmation came the same week I was going to Vermont. If I had gone to Vermont as originally planned, my health issues might very well have killed me (small town, proximity to major hospitals, etc.) and/or taken the small non-profit down. Only later did I realize the Spirit had guided me the way I should go.

I knew God sent me home after my intestinal surgery to be with Mom before her sister died. That one was hard, but it was still something I needed to do; be there for my mother in her time of grief as she was struggling with her faith.

I struggled with my decision to leave the ministry. I didn't want to go, but God interceded with people of impeccable integrity who urged me to reconsider. That time, the easy answer was to stay put. But I needed a push to do the hard thing, the mature thing and leave the University.

I had an "ah ha" moment when confronted by a nurse whom I worked with about the truth of my being gay. I rejected her statements and refused to accept them, though years later, I had to admit she had spoken the truth in love. I would have been better off if I had accepted the truth when it was spoken, and taken that leap of faith, but I still had more growing to do. God kept working with me as I peeled away layer after layer of misinformation and self-loathing. The Spirit never gave up on me.

I accepted another nudge of faith when I returned to Tampa after seeing an advertisement for the Gay Chamber of Commerce Job Fair. It was the only time that RJ had a recruiter at the Job Fair in my 25 years with the company. I know because I was a member of the Gay Chamber of Commerce for all those years, even serving on the Board of Directors and once as president.

Another step of faith was joining with Michael Ragsdale to form M2 Financial Advisors of RJ. This one was more him than me. He was nervous about leaving a salaried position for commissions. With his partnership, we landed our largest account.

The most interesting thing is that God had directed me to Mobile College, now the University of Mobile *before* I went to OBU. I did not want to go there, but if I hadn't, Dr. Hazel Petersen, from whom I learned so much, never would have caught me dancing in the Canteen. She and I reconnected at Mobile College years later and again after she moved to Florida during her retirement. She was an amazing woman; a person of deep faith and she had a tremendous influence on my career development and life.

There are many more examples, but the point is clear. God's Spirit doesn't walk with us sometimes, it's with us always. But we are not always attuned to The Spirit. God knows our path from beginning to end. We only know right now. As the saying goes, faith requires us to only take *One Day at A Time, Sweet Jesus.*

Life Is Good, Even with Struggles

Now it is easy for me to see what I could not see most of my life. In The Amplified Bible in Mark 8:18 it says, *"Though you have eyes, do you not see? And though having ears, you do not hear..."* That was me. I was blind and deaf to the truth for much of my life. I especially disliked the truth that homosexuality was an unchangeable part of me. Yet, whether we want the truth or not, it will set us free (John 8:32, NIV) as John said in his gospel.

I have learned much, with much still to learn. But one thing I can tell you for sure is that The Spirit will walk with you, no matter how bumpy the path. Following Christ is tough, the scripture never promises "an easy road," just the opposite. My great disappointments and victories came at the most challenging moments. From them, I learned the most important lessons. This book started on the darkest night of my life: The Dark Night of My Soul, a reference from St. John of the Cross, an early Christian mystic.

The mystery of faith is love. Love is the central commandment of scripture. *"Love the Lord your God with all your heart and with all your soul and with all your mind and ... the second is like unto it, love your neighbor as yourself."* (Matthew 22:37-40, NIV). It took me years to learn the truth of this passage. You can't love others until you love yourself. I did not love myself for many years, but God loved me and guided me. I finally came to understand that they, the nay-sayers, are not the arbiters of God's love or grace or the dispenser of God's forgiveness.

Last, The Spirit promises to always be with us. Upon learning of Jesus' impending death, the disciples worried about what life would be like without him. The promise was that The Spirit would always be there for them. That has been true in my life. I am sure that the next 5, 10, or 15 years, whatever time I have, will include struggles. There is no promise of life without challenges. Scripture does not say everything is good. The scriptures say, *"All things work together for good."* (Romans

8:28, KJV). God can bring good out of bad; my life has proven that. If it can happen to me, it can happen in your life too.

2024: A Living Test: Life is good even with struggles

With age, hopefully, comes a little wisdom. By now, I know that sometimes what I preach and believe will be put to the test and that the values I hold will be challenged by life events. In the last chapter, I wrote, "Life is good even with struggles." 2024 put that declaration to the test.

I know that some years will always be remembered because of how wonderful they were. For instance, I remember 2011 and 2012 as two of my very best, most enjoyable years. In 2011, I reclaimed the President's Club after missing it the year before for the first time since 2007. I met and started dating Rick, and in 2012, he proposed to me on New Year's Eve in Paris, France. Other great years included 1980 (I graduated from college), 1984 (I graduated from Seminary and went to West Germany), and 1999 (I moved to Tampa and began the last phase of my final career at Raymond James).

But sure enough, there are also difficult years. This book is filled with examples, including 1968, when my mother, Dr. Martin Luther King, Jr., and Robert F. Kennedy all died. In 1983, my roommate was killed in an accident, and I was diagnosed with Crohn's disease. In 1985, I left New York for Texas, only to be terminated from my new job after having two life-threatening surgeries for Crohn's Disease and then my wonderful Auntie died. Very tough years indeed.

When my belief that "LIFE is GOOD even with struggles" was put to the test in 2024, I should have known that the Spirit of God was not finished with my life or this book. 2024 was supposed to be my Victory Lap year as I concluded my 25-year career with RJ. And it started out well. By agreement, I was scheduled to get three months of vacation this last year, and I planned to use it all in a glorious "going out in style" retirement. We made plans for travel with friends to our beloved Canadian Rockies followed by a trip to Alaska. Rick had never been there, so with much anticipation, we went in early May. Alaska was Beautiful. However, both Rick and I got sick on the ship with flu (Rick) and

COVID (me) but not diagnosed until we returned to Tacoma. Then I came down with Rick's flu as well. May and June were pretty difficult.

In the fall, we returned to the Canadian Rockies but had to cut the trip short to get back to the United States because Hurricane Helene was headed for Tampa Bay. The day we crossed back into the United States, Helene slammed into the coast of Pinellas County, where we live.

Tampa Bay had been spared a direct hit for 103 years, and it was said the Seminole Indian Burial Grounds had always protected us. But the year I retired, we took a direct hit. Of course, being away when Helene's eye wall moved ashore, we could only watch and wait to hear how our friends and property faired.

Life is good even with struggles, I reminded myself repeatedly over those days. I realized as we waited to find out how bad it was, we were blessed and in a significantly better situation than many others. First, we have enough resources to weather this storm financially. Second, we had many friends reach out to help us in this very difficult time, such as Kay & Floss, who let us use their car while they weren't in town. We received support from Ashley, Dianne & Bill, Judy, Bradley, Dee, Jason & Anthony, and Vivian, among others. And both of our families reached out and checked in on us to see if there was anything they could do to help. Of special note is that Carol & Roy offered us their RV to use. So many others do not have such a robust and generous support network. We are fortunate. Even the hotel I stayed in, the Fairfield Inn in Riverview, and Delta Airlines gave me special considerations and waived some fees. Of course, my church family, Pass-a-Grill Beach Community Church, was there for us as well.

Our condo indeed flooded, and the next day, I was forced to purchase a plane ticket to return to St. Petersburg for an early morning Condo Association "hurricane remediation meeting" on October 4th. In that meeting, I learned that we and all other first-floor residents were under mandatory evacuation orders and had to be out of our condos by Friday, October 11th, or risk "anything left being discarded" so mold remediation work could begin. Over the next four days, I spent 56 hours gathering what was savable and packing it in boxes. In the meantime, our assistant at RJ informed me I needed to pay attention to a new storm in the Gulf of Mexico. I paid little attention at first as I was under a strict deadline. With Judy's help I hired storage and movers to pick up our belongings on Tuesday, Oct. 8th at 8 am, the soonest I could find anyone available.

By Monday, October 7th, *the new hurricane*, Milton, grew from Category 1 to a Category 5 storm in 18 hours, the quickest on record. As I frantically packed, we agreed that Rick should stay in Tacoma to coordinate logistics, including working to get our ruined cars settled with insurance. This proved very difficult as the titles were packed away among our sixty boxes of things to be put in storage. But Rick is tenacious and prevailed via another route. He also had the thankless task of coordinating with our Flood Policy Insurance adjuster to meet with me on Friday, October 11th. This, too, proved challenging as circumstances on the ground were changing dramatically hour by hour. Then, of course, he also had to get the Homeowner's Policy adjuster out to see the property. I finally met with the Homeowner's adjuster on Sunday, October 13th before I was scheduled to fly back to Tacoma.

Initially it looked like I had succeeded in getting movers, finding storage, and having an exit strategy before the second hurricane hit Tampa Bay. The timeline had been pushed back a day or two but still looked doable. Then things fell apart. Monday October 7th in the afternoon the moving company that had confirmed *twice* that morning, texted me at 3 pm to say they had to cancel my Tuesday morning pick up date. To make matters worse, Tampa International Airport (TIA) decided to close at 9 am on Tuesday, one full day earlier than anyone expected. This meant I couldn't get our belongings moved to safety *AND* leave the area before Hurricane Milton hit because, of course, my flight was now canceled as it was scheduled for Tuesday at 5pm.

Anxiety was high on both coasts, Rick on the Pacific and me on the Gulf of Mexico. On Tuesday we waited for the storm, currently predicted to have a catastrophic wave surge of 15 to 20 feet in Tampa

Bay. We anticipated losing all the little things that helped make our lives special: like the Lightning Strike Picture I bought Rick for our second anniversary. Or Rick's antique moonshine jugs from his relatives in southeastern Ohio. But at least we were both safe for now.

On Wednesday, October 9th, we hoped to hear that the hurricane track was shifting enough to the south to save Tampa Bay from the worst possible outcome. If Hurricane Milton came ashore at or north of Tampa Bay, we would experience a catastrophic surge of up to 23 feet in St. Petersburg and Tampa. Metro Tampa has more than 2 ½ million residents. The potential death and destruction were unimaginable. If it came ashore south of Tampa Bay, while still bringing misery across the state, it would be far less damaging and directly impact fewer people.

In times like this, my faith in God's Love sustains me. I can't tell you that this particular week wasn't among the most difficult of my life, because it was. I can tell you that God provided what I needed to survive. When the movers canceled the Tuesday pick-up, I knew I had to find lodging in Tampa Bay or a flight out to anywhere. After living through Hurricane Camille in 1969, I choose to never again stay for a hurricane if I can help it. But here I was with a storm stronger than Camille, on a potentially more dangerous and destructive path through my adopted hometown.

I called Delta first to find a replacement flight for the one I had booked for after the movers (who were no longer coming) completed the pick-up. But by this time there were no seats available out of Tampa/St. Petersburg or Orlando going anywhere: not Atlanta, Minneapolis, Cincinnati, Denver, Detroit, Chicago, Las Vegas, Phoenix, Los Angeles, Seattle, Portland, Boston, Philly, D.C., New Orleans or NYC with Delta. After striking out with them, I did the same with Southwest and American Airlines. Twice I almost had a seat, but hundreds of people were doing the same thing I was simultaneously; at least two people beat me to the finish. I wasn't flying anywhere.

By this time, my friends and neighbors who were leaving were already gone. I panicked just as Bill and Dianne called and agreed to help with one final hour of packing before they headed off to Charleston, South Carolina for a "Getaway from Milton" Vacation.

They calmed me down and helped me locate a hotel room in Riverview, Florida, 29 miles from our home. Family and friends were worried that I had been foolish staying. Yet this new location proved to be exactly what I needed. I arrived Monday evening after a two-hour drive to discover the hotel was not in a flood plain and even better, Telemundo TV crews and FEMA personnel had rooms there too (surely a good sign)! That plus no big trees close to the hotel made us feel safer. But most importantly, there were no big debris piles here from Hurricane Helene, like there were on Sunny Lane where our condo is located. This area of Riverview had not flooded when Hurricane Helene hit.

So, from this hotel room in Riverview, Florida, with wind whipping outside, rain slashing against the windows, and the sound of rhythmic scraping against the building, I finished writing this book. Oh, I'm still stressed out. I am still worried about our unlivable condo. But I still believe LIFE is GOOD, even with struggles!

CHAPTER 10

Epilogue

This book tells the story of my life, but more than that, it tells of the times in which I grew up. It was a time some are now attempting to recreate. It was 1950s-1980s America.

This book is for a time like this in our Nation's history, where we are facing well-funded efforts to roll back progress made over the last 60+ years on Civil Rights for women, African Americans, seniors, immigrants, First Nations peoples, and the LGBTQIA+ community, among many others There are too few voices raising concerns and discussing the real-life implications of the societal restructuring being signed into law through President Trump's executive orders, following the *Project 2025* roadmap to Autocracy created by a Christian Nationalist think tank. Their goal is to drag us back to the "good ole days" of the 1950s, where women stay home and raise children, gay and transgender people remain deep in the closet, and wealthy white straight men hold almost total power in society.[1]

Harvey Milk, the first openly gay politician in American History, a member of the San Francisco Board of Supervisors in 1977 and 1978, said, "Gay people, we will not win our rights by staying quiet in our closets....We are coming out to fight the lies, the myths, the distortions. We are coming out to tell the truths about gays, for I am tired of the conspiracy of silence, so I'm going to talk about it." Like Harvey, I can't remain silent. The next generation of LGBTQ+ people need us adults to step up, take the risk of speaking up for them, and have their backs when they speak for themselves.

I know that feeling, it is reminiscent of my own era when discrimination was encouraged in the deep South towards African Americans and anyone the authorities (church, police, government, etc.) considered deviant.

Making matters worse, the 988 federally mandated suicide and crisis line, supported by the Substance Abuse and Mental Health Services (SAMHSA), has been defunded by the Trump Administration.

Trump's budget would cut all funding to specialized services for LGBTQ+ youth, including the 988 Suicide and Crisis Lifeline. LGBTQ+ youth are at an elevated risk for suicide.

Mark Henson, director of federal advocacy and government affairs for The Trevor Project, emphasized that the LGBTQ+ 988 subnetwork has been a vital tool since its launch three years ago.

"LGBTQ+ youth are four times as likely as their peers to consider attempting suicide," Henson told *The Advocate* in an interview. "The specialized LGBTQ+ services within 988 were designed because of this elevated risk, much like the separate support track for veterans. It's about meeting people where they are with someone who understands their lived experiences." Mental health experts agree that affirming services save lives — and that general crisis lines often fail to meet the specific needs of LGBTQ+ youth.

Critical funding changes for federally mandated programs like the Suicide and Crisis Lifeline mentioned above leave me deeply concerned that if the Trump administration and Christian Nationalists get their way, we are going back to a time of less freedom and more restrictions, which means many gay, lesbian, trans, queer + youth will give up on life. According to the Trevor Project's 2024 U.S. National Survey on the Mental Health of LGBTQ+ Young People, 39% of LGBTQ+ young people seriously considered attempting suicide in the past year — including 46% of transgender and nonbinary young people. LGBTQ+ youth of color reported higher rates than their white peers.

For my fellow LGBTQIA+ friends, this means they will attempt to move us out of sight again and back into the closet, and with that closet comes despair! Do not despair, trust your faith in God. Whenever I was at my lowest, God always provided someone for me to lean on for support, and not always someone I expected. Reach out to GLSEN, PFLAG, and other Resources listed at the end of this book to find allies who can help support you in your local community.

We adults must help instill courage and provide support to these young people coming of age in these challenging times. We can't let the code of silence 'disappear' their voices, our voices, as it did in my day!

To the young readers of this book, I hope it gives you the courage to be your authentic self (and, hopefully, you had a chuckle or two at my expense). Think of courage not as the absence of fear, but as action in the face of it!

There is a list of resources included at the end of this section with places you can turn to for help if you, like I once did, think it's no longer worth the struggle and suicide seems the only way out. There are resources available today that weren't around in my youth. Google is a fantastic starting point. There are LGBTQIA+ books, movies, documentaries, legal organizations, LGBT+ community centers, mental health services, open and affirming Churches, hot lines, and even organizations like PFLAG which will help you find support and educational tools for your family and friends, and GLESN which can help you connect with other schools and like-minded students, to name just a few. Please take a look at the attached resource list to get a sense of what's out there.

I am a part of the grand coalition of Americans of goodwill towards all, who stand up for people not favored by our society, as Christ taught us. I add my voice to the chorus of men and women who say Be yourself as God created you to be.

NOTES

1.   https://en.wikipedia.org/wiki/Project_2025

RESOURCES

LGBTQIA+ Friendly Resources

- Information provided by ComprehensiveLifeRescourses.org and organization websites
- Trevor Project (text 678-678 or call 866-488-7386): The Trevor Project is the leading suicide prevention and crisis intervention nonprofit organization for LGBTQ+ young people. We provide information & support to LGBTQ+ young people 24/7, year-round.
- LGBT National Hotline (over 25 call 888-843-4564; under 25: 888-246-7743)
- National AIDS Hotline (English: 800-342-2437, Spanish: 800-344-7432)\
- Find an LGBTQAI+ community center near you: Center-Link LGBTQ Community Center Member Directory (May be reached via the internet: *www.lgbtqcenters.org/LGBTCenters*
- PFLAG is the nation's largest organization dedicated to supporting, educating and advocating for LGBTQ+ people and those who love them. Many PFLAG materials available for free download or at nominal cost (including Parents: Quick Tips for Supporting Your LGBTQ Kids – and YOURSELF – During the Coming-Out Process; Our Trans Loved Ones, PFLAG Academy On-Demand, toolkits, and easy to read and understand resource materials. For more information, visit: *www.pflag.org/about-us*.

- GLSEN's mission is to ensure that every member of every school community is valued and respected regardless of sexual orientation, gender identity or gender expression. For more information, visit: *www.glsen.org/about-us.*

WHO'S WHO IN THE FAMILY

Our Family Tree (Branches)

<u>Dad's Branch</u>

Carl William Brill, Dad
Carol, my sister
Carl William, Jr. (a.k.a. Billy or Little Billy), my older brother
Charles Michael Brill, me
David, my younger brother
Uncle Donnie, Dad's brother
Aunt Beverly, Dad's sister
Nanny Brill, Dad's mother
Pawpaw (Oscar) Brill, Dad's father
Mickey, Aunt Beverly's daughter
Bobby, Aunt Beverly's son
Gary, Nanny and Pawpaw's foster son
Susan, Nanny and Pawpaw's foster daughter

<u>Mother's (Anne's) Branch</u>

Anne Claire Lindsey Brill, Mom
Nanny Shaw, Mom's mother
Aunt Julie, Mom's Aunt
Uncle Winston, Aunt Julie's Son

Mother's (Ruby's) Branch

Rudy D. Brill, stepmother
Debbie, oldest stepsister
Renae, middle stepsister
DiAnne, youngest stepsister
Aunt Finley or Auntie, Ruby/mother's sister
Uncle Earl, Ruby/mother's brother-in-law
Uncle Jerry, Ruby/mother's brother-in-law
Gina, daughter to Auntie and Uncle Jerry

Other Branches

Richard (Rick), my husband
Becky, my husband's sister, my sister-in-law
Two half-sisters I do not know very well (referenced but not named in the book)

APPENDIX: THEOLOGICAL REFLECTIONS

The 4 Big S's

There are four BIG S's I had to deal with before I could make peace with myself and accept that this, a gay man, is who God made me to be: **S**ex, **S**in, **S**outhern Baptist, and The **S**criptures. I almost killed myself before I took a hard look at what my Church, Southern Baptist, and my personal faith taught me about these issues. I previously refused to study these issues in the Bible because I didn't want to be right or wrong. I didn't want to be right and therefore condemned. I didn't want to be wrong because I would no longer have a reason to not accept myself the way God made me. I would have to be honest about my attraction to men. That is a trap that I, and many gay Southern Baptist and Evangelical youth, find themselves in. It often leads to despair, substance abuse, self-harm and suicide.

Sex: Sex is a good gift from God, a beautiful part of life. When done responsibly it is wonderful. It is not dirty or something to be ashamed of. In fact, the Bible makes reference to the beauty of sex and love, the most well-known is *The Song of Solomon* located between Ecclesiastes and Isaiah in the Old Testament. It is a love poem.

The silence and/or fear around sex causes young people especially to view it as wrong and dirty. I thought that way for many years. Most straight youth eventually get over this as they have opportunities to openly discuss this contradiction within the Church, when talking with their friends, watching sexualized content on TV or in the movies, or by looking at pornographic magazines (like my friends showed me). Therefore, when the Church teaches or implies sex is wrong until marriage, many straight youth ignore the church.

Most Gay, Bi, and Trans youth do not have nearly as many opportunities to openly discuss their questions about sexuality for fear of rejection or retribution from their spiritual leaders, teachers or peers. In recent years, many schools around the country, especially in more progressive areas, started supporting LGBTQIA+ student groups by providing a safe space where these youth and their allies can discuss their questions and concerns with peers, teachers and counselors. Sadly, the Heritage Foundation's *Project 2025*, President Trump's roadmap for his second presidency, spells out areas to be eliminated and high on that list is supportive environments in schools for LGBTQIA+ youth and their allies (https://en.wikipedia.org/wiki/Project_2025).

As one of those closeted gay youth, I struggled to accept the idea of sex as a beautiful gift from God. I put it off for a long time. What a shame. I missed out on this gift from God until much later. Our body tells us, through puberty, when our sexual awakening is taking place. I was 13 when I had my first sexual urges. Not understanding them and afraid to ask about them, I buried them. I wasted my youth and early adult years sexually out of ignorance and fear. I had no one willing to tell me the truth about this important part of life. Instead, my Christian counselors instructed abstinence.

Sin: Sin is anything that breaks our relationship with God, others, or ourselves. The Hebrew (*khata'*) and Greek (*hamartia*) are words that are translated as sin. The literal translation is "to miss the mark." Both are word pictures of an archer shooting an arrow and missing the bull's eye. For example, when we gossip, and the person we gossiped about finds out or is harmed by our gossip, our comments miss the mark, and it hurts our relationship with the other person and with God. This is an example of sin. In this regard, we are sinners all the time. Oh yeah, I know we would prefer a clear set of unambiguous rules. I did. I was a great rule follower (remember me driving 65mph on I-65?). But the rules themselves are not the heart of the matter. Rules are easy. You can keep all the rules and still not be like Jesus: kind or compassionate. The story of the rich young ruler (Matthew 19:16-26, NIV) comes to mind. He claimed to have kept all the commandments. Yet when Jesus told him he still lacked one thing, the rich young man walked away sad because he was unwilling to follow Jesus' command. Behaving in ways that are kind, promote justice, show patience with others, etc. are much more difficult than just keeping the rules. Living the teachings of Jesus is harder. Jesus' sermon on the mount is a good place to start for a practical application of Jesus' teachings on how to live a moral and ethical life.

According to Jesus, these are the two greatest commandments *"...Love the Lord your God with all your heart, with all your soul and with all your mind. This is the first and greatest commandment. And the second is like it: Love your neighbor as yourself. All the Law and the Prophets hang on these two"* (Matthew 22:37-40, NIV).

Sin is part of life. We continuously sin (hurting our relationships with ourselves, others and God) by missing the mark. But God, through the Holy Spirit, is continuously moving us forward to mend those broken relationships as modeled by Jesus, who came to restore our relationship with God the Father, our creator.

Southern Baptists, in my experience, are an uptight people. I sincerely believe most want to live Holy and do what is right. But in the area of sexuality, they are so uptight that everything becomes "against the rules," whether it has a biblical basis or not. Take, for instance, masturbation. Most evangelical Christian groups, including Southern Baptist, consider it a sin. And yet, there is no specific reference to masturbation in the Bible, just a reference in the Old Testament to "spilling seed" and several generic references to "sexual immorality," which relate to abstinence, not having a wicked heart and not associating with those who are "sexually immoral."

Southern Baptists also preach that sex before marriage is a sin. But magically, once married, sex is beautiful and a gift from God for the purpose of procreation. Other sex is recreational and, therefore, a sin. This idea ironically came not from the Bible, but from the Catholic Theologian St. Augustine in the 5th Century, Kathy Baldock reminds us in her book, *Walking the Bridgeless Canyon*. I say ironically because Baptists do not usually follow Catholic theological teachings.

Nothing in the Bible says sex is only for procreation, but some churches, including Southern Baptist, Catholic and many evangelical churches preach this stricter view. As a youth, these teachings confused me and basically led me to believe sex was wrong all or nearly all the time.

Even if I were straight, I would have struggled with sex because I couldn't go from being taught it is totally wrong to "now that you are married, enjoy." Marriages have failed, especially among the deeply devout, because one person in the marriage can't stop thinking that sex is wrong and impure, as they had been taught for years by the church. The other reaction, of course, is to say, "To heck with the church" and its rules, just go wild. Neither extreme is healthy. These church teachings miss the mark, in my opinion.

Just read the Bible, it has a lot of sex in it. Of course, having concubines and multiple wives in Old Testament times adds confusion too, but we won't address that here.

The Scriptures: This was the most difficult part of my journey to self-acceptance. As I believe the scriptures are the living word of God, as Bonhoeffer and other theologians have said, my story includes my understanding of both the literal translation, historical context and my understanding of the verses at the time I was coming out.

Let's look at some of these sexual issues from scripture, starting with masturbation. I was taught that masturbation is wrong. The most common reference used to support this is from an Old Testament passage regarding "spilling seed" (Genesis 38:8-10). Onan was required by law to provide an heir for his dead brother. But Onan, having his own family, did not want to do this and "pulled out early," thereby spilling his seed. (This is hardly "masturbation" as the term is understood today).

For violating the law by intentionally refusing to get his dead brother's wife pregnant, he was condemned.

I tried my best to be faithful in this regard, but I was a miserable failure. But contrary to my church's teaching, masturbation is commonly practiced today by men (92%), gay or straight, regardless of what you hear from them, according to one of the foremost sex researchers in American History, Alfred Kinsey (1894-1956), who published his book *"Sexual Behaviors in the Human Male in 1948."* Some people, including professional Christian counselors, now believe masturbation is healthy and describe it as a release valve.

One also has to keep in mind that rules regarding sexuality have changed from culture to culture and through the centuries. Remember the Bible was written over several hundred years. Think about our own culture. Has it not changed since the founding of the country? Of course it has. The same is true for the timeframe in which the Bible was written. Some cultures and time periods were more relaxed than others, but the consistent message throughout was that excess was generally frowned upon.

Scripture does imply, however, that unwanted sex leads to broken relationships. The Old Testament, which I prefer to call The Hebrew Scriptures, is full of stories of sex outside of a relationship ending badly. The most recognized such story in the Old Testament is probably King David and Bathsheba (2 Samuel 11:1ff). Relationships in King David's time were very different from relationships today. Women had essentially no rights. The expectation in King David's time was that if he (a powerful man) wanted something he got it. Only the prophet, Nathan, challenged this assumption (2 Samuel 12:1ff). Even by Jesus' time, a woman could be put away (divorced) for any reason. (This view of women's rights was largely still true in the 1930's in the Jim Crow South!) Bathsheba had NO CONTROL over what was happening to her or her husband, and it is David, not Bathsheba, who was confronted by the Prophet Nathan for his sins. Another lesson that can be taken from this story is the damage that can be done when the powerful exploit those who are vulnerable and without power, as Bathsheba was here.

LEVITICUS

When I was coming out, some of the Leviticus Biblical passages bothered me a great deal. For instance, in the Leviticus passages (Lev. 18:8-22ff, NKJV) of the Hebrew Scripture, there is a lot of sex going on. *Do not have sex with your father's wife (*Lev. 18:8, *NKJV). Do not have sex with your sister* (Lev. 18:9, NKJV). *Do not have sex with your son's daughter* (Lev.18:10, NKJV*). Do not have sex with your father's sister* (Lev.18:11, NKJV). *Do not have sex with your neighbor's wife* (Lev. 18:20, NKJV). And it goes on and on. Finally, Lev. 18:22, NKJV says, *"Do not lie with a man as one lies with a woman"* after the key passage that clarifies all this: *"Do not give any of your children to be sacrificed to Molech..."* (Lev.18:21, NKJV). I could not in a clear conscience accept being gay if I couldn't reconcile myself to the scriptures that specifically said a man should not lie with a man as one lies with a woman.

Without context, the Leviticus section of the Bible makes no sense. In 1997 I started researching and studying these passages. I found scholarly answers. My question was "Where was all this sex taking place?" Most people don't go around looking to have sex with their sisters, their sons' daughters and their neighbors' wives. At the time the Hebrew texts were written, Yahweh, the new Hebrew God, had many rivals. Molech, Baal, and Ashtoreth (each mentioned in the Hebrew Bible) were Canaanite gods considered to be Yahweh's key rivals. Canaanite religious practices of the day were polytheistic, meaning they worshiped multiple gods simultaneously. When Yahweh was introduced to the Canaanites, they simply thought of him as another god among many, (The Canaanites did not originally consider him the supreme deity). Canaanite religious practices included sexuality, fertility rites and human sacrifice, among many others. In these early years, some of the Israelites were undoubtedly attracted to the Canaanite temples, gods and rituals and began participating in the fertility cults of their day, which included both male and female prostitutes, lots of sex, and in some cases, human sacrifice. After all, even King Solomon was fascinated and built a temple for Molech east of Jerusalem (1 Kings 11:7). This, my new understanding (in 1997), satisfied my quest to make peace with this passage in Leviticus.

Today, conservative scholars will maintain that it says literally that homosexuality is wrong no matter what I say about the context! To the conservative scholars, I disagree and believe context as well as literal translation matters in understanding the true meaning of any verse, including these.

Other Biblical scholars might question my conclusions on this matter (fertility cult worship as not really the best conclusion to draw). They maintain the whole of these Leviticus passages has more to do with societal order, inheritance law, and the role of males in sexual activity.

My secular friends who study law and different cultures bristle at this explanation. They have pointed out to me that all law, whether written by religions or government, are about maintaining societal order (Controlling the masses to do what you say rather than another government or religion says), Inheritance law (Property Law & Family Law), and the role of males in sexuality activity (Criminal and Civil Law)—has been true in every society.

While all of this about maintaining societal order makes sense, I am not sure this explanation would have satisfied me when I was coming to terms with being gay. I have more research to do on this matter.

However, for me a stronger response came from Jesus himself when he said *"...Love the Lord your God with all your heart, with all your soul and with all your mind. This is the first and greatest commandment. And the second is like it: Love your neighbor as yourself. All the Law and the Prophets hang on these two"* (Matthew 22:37-40 NIV).

These same (Leviticus) passages include other prohibitions: engaging in sex with a woman while she is having her period, requiring that males be circumcised, charging interest on loans, etc.

These passages also use the term "abomination," with regard to more than just men sleeping with men. And let's face it – that word sounds sinister! But in Leviticus it also says that eating shellfish, clothing made from more than one kind of fabric, sowing mixed crops, etc. are also abominations. Hmmm. These, prohibitions and abominations, are regularly ignored today by Christians and our larger society. So why do we cling to ONE prohibition/abomination, while discarding the others?

Either we are required to keep ALL of the LAW or we are not under the law anymore.

In the end, it comes down to this: the Old Testament law, including Leviticus, is no longer binding on Christians. *See* Romans 7:6 (Christians are "released from the law"). *See, also,* Galatians 3:23-25 and Ephesians 2:15 (emphasizing Old Testament law is no longer in effect for believers).

SODOM & GOMORRAH

Now the biggie, Sodom & Gomorrah (Gen. 19:4-5). This is the primary, some would argue "most important, most preached" Old Testament Biblical passage used to substantiate the claim that homosexuality is a sin. Way back in Part 6, Chapter entitled Lou-uh-vul I specifically discuss this passage, so I won't repeat myself now. This passage isn't about men who want to have sex with men, but about sex being used to humiliate, belittle and control. This is about gang rape. One of the greatest sins of the Old Testament was inhospitality. When the scriptures tell you what something is, one should take the scripture's word for it. Ezekiel 16:49 (NIV) tells us exactly what the sin of Sodom was: *"...Sodom: She and her daughters were arrogant, overfed and unconcerned; they did not help the poor and the needy, were haughty, and did detestable things before God."*

Do you notice **what is missing** from Ezekiel's description of what happened in Sodom and the reason it was destroyed? Any mention of men having sex with men? That's because the story of Sodom & Gomorrah has nothing to do with homosexuality. They lived in the desert.

If a stranger (poor or needy) came to you, you were expected to treat them with respect, take care of their needs and put them up. Only Lot showed the strangers hospitality, the rest of Sodom did not. For their lack of hospitality, they were destroyed.

By the way, Leviticus has a similar passage found one chapter *AFTER* the one with all the sexual prohibitions. It says:

When a foreigner resides among you in your land, do not mistreat them. The foreigner residing among you must be treated as your native-born. Love them as yourself, for you were foreigners in Egypt. I am the Lord your God. (Leviticus 19:33-34, NIV)

It seems clear many Americans, including our current President and those running our federal government, are not following this humanitarian commandment today.

NEW TESTAMENT PASSAGES

Did you know the word "homosexual" did not appear in the Bible for the first time until 1952? This passage *"Do not be deceived; neither the immoral, nor idolaters, nor adulterers, nor homosexuals, nor thieves, nor the greedy, nor drunkards, nor revilers, nor robbers will inherit the kingdom of God."* (Revised Standard Version of 1952, 1 Corinthians 6:9-10). This passage made me detest being that awful thing called a "HOMO-SEXUAL." As a youth I read the Bible but didn't know anything about a change in the Bible's translation. The Revised Standard Version of the Bible was changed to say that homosexuals will not inherit the Kingdom of God ... and I believed it word for word! It didn't help that many preachers preached it from the podium also.

Below is some background information I did not have growing up. "Homosexuality" has galvanized the Christian Right since 1946 when the word "homosexual" was first added to the Revised Standard Version of the New Testament (The entire Revised Standard Version of the Bible wasn't published until 1952). I use the term "homosexual" throughout this book because it is the language I knew and understood from the Baptist Church throughout my young adult years. I believed "homosexuals," especially gay men, were dangerous and bad. Those stereotypes filled my mind throughout my formative years.

With this history, let's look at two different translations of I Corinthians 6:9-10, one an older translation (American Standard Version of 1901) and one a modern translation, meaning after the Revised Standard Version came out in 1952:

"Do you not know that the unrighteous will not inherit the kingdom of God? Do not be deceived; neither the immoral, nor idolaters, nor adulterers, nor sexual perverts, nor thieves, nor the greedy, nor drunkards, nor revilers, nor robbers will inherit the kingdom of God." (ASV of 1901)

"Do you not know that the wrongdoers will not inherit the kingdom of God? Do not be deceived: Neither the sexually immoral, nor idolaters, nor adulterers, nor male prostitutes, nor homosexual offenders, nor thieves, nor the greedy, nor drunkards, nor slanderers will inherit the kingdom of God." (New International Version-1978)

Prior to 1946, the word "homosexual" did not appear anywhere in the New Testament. Since "homosexual" was added to the Bible (The whole RSV Bible published in 1952), there has been a debate among Biblical Scholars about the "new" interpretation of the Greek words (*malakoi* and *arsenokoitai*) now translated in many post-1952 Bibles as "homosexual." This second word, *arsenokoitai*, is a Paul word, meaning it is a word found in his writings but not found in general use via other writings of the period, except in rare cases (fewer than 100 times in other writings over 600 years and found nowhere in scripture except in Paul's writings: 1 Corinthians 6:9-10 and 1 Timothy 1:9-10). In other literature, the word seems to imply "men having sex with young boys."

The 2022 documentary film *1946: The Mistranslation That Shifted Culture,* engages in an in-depth analysis of the revised translation and concludes it is an inaccurate mistranslation. The book *What the Bible Really Says About Homosexuality* by Dr. Daniel Helminiak devotes ten pages to the different interpretations of the Greek words used in the passages above. The word translated as "homosexual" in the Revised

APPENDIX: THEOLOGICAL REFLECTIONS – 273

Standard Version of 1952, approved by the committee in 1939, takes the two Greek words referenced above and makes them one: homosexual. The 1977 updated RSV version translates it as sexual perverts. The 1989 New Revised Standard Version translates the two words separately: male prostitutes and sodomites.

Dr. Helminiak, wrote, the "1985 New Jerusalem Bible provides the most accurate translation: "the self-indulgent." He goes on to say that "...until the Reformation in the 16th century and in Roman Catholicism until the 20th Century, the word *malakoi* was thought to mean "masturbators." It seems that as prejudices changed, so have Bible translations.

Even if you use the 1989 NRSV translation with "sodomites and male prostitutes," sodomites were men who raped men in my reading of that passage. And unless you are a rapist or male prostitute, then this doesn't apply to you.

But putting that aside, immorality in the first century included prostitution, so the scriptures discourage that pretty strongly. I am a married man in a committed gay relationship, this passage doesn't speak about that, in my reading of it.

ORIENTATION OR PREFERENCE

Romans 1:26 was the hardest for me to come to terms with: *"God gave them over to shameful lusts. Even their women exchanged natural relations for unnatural ones. In the same way, the men also abandoned natural relationships with women and were inflamed with lust for one another. Men committed indecent acts with other men and received in themselves the due penalty for their perversion."* (Romans 1:26, NIV)

I prayed and read, prayed and read some more. I studied these verses. Then one day it dawned on me. While previous generations would not even have a term for this, I did now due to science and research that there was a thing called orientation. Having established that all people are sexual beings, it is time to focus on orientation. Language matters in how the issue is framed. Many Southern Baptists and other evangelicals use the term *sexual **preference,*** implying choice. I had no choice in the matter. I was born gay. Making it a preference implies I can choose or not choose to be gay. I believed this for much of my life. Unfortunately, that is not how it works. My preference was always to be straight. But God, the Creator, made me gay. This is an important theological point. Sin is an act, an action. It is something we do. It is not something we are. I can reject God's gift (sex). I can deny my sexuality (be celibate), but at the end of the day, I am still a gay man.

God revealed I had committed the sin, or at least nearly did, when I dated women with the intent to be sexual, because I would have been "exchanging my natural relationship," (gay), for an unnatural one (heterosexual)!

Faking it is painful, just ask Betsy, Vanessa, or Diana about that. My dishonesty (an act), not my natural sexual orientation, was my sin in the sight of God. God forgives but deceiving another is a serious breach of relationship. For most people, this would be true if straight men or women sought out gay sex for sex's sake. But for me, being gay is my natural orientation.

Early in my time back in Mobile, I met a Gay man through the Baptist Church who was just coming out to his wife of 30 years. She was supportive but deeply wounded by the dishonesty of their relationship. She supported him through his coming out, eventually forgiving him. But she was hurt badly by the experience. They ended their marriage, as one might expect. She went on to study and graduate from Asbury Theological Seminary in Kentucky and pastored several small Methodist Churches until her retirement, setting an example of God's love. From her experience, she advocated for the Methodist Church to become open and affirming towards gay people. Still, it did not take away the pain of her experience.

Let me be clear, the Apostle Paul wrote this verse with a different audience in mind (Roman Gentiles). He didn't know what sexual orientation was, as that concept did not yet exist in the world. But he did know about Nero's Roman Empire. He knew of the powerful taking advantage of weaker parties in sexual relations (Master and Slave, Citizen-non-citizen) etc. I believe he was opposed to these over/under power arrangements where the less powerful person had no choice. The Church of Jesus Christ was to live differently in the world, according to Paul.

While I didn't know it growing up, and was scared to even seek information about sexual orientation, there are resources where one can learn more about gay sexuality and the scriptures. I encourage those with questions to read Matthew Vines' *God and the Gay Christian* or Rev. Dr. Mel White's *Clobber the Passages: Seven Deadly Verses* and *What the Bible Really Says About Homosexuality,* by Daniel A. Helminiak. These are great resources on this topic.

I now know that gay men, like most men, are sexual beings. Some act in inappropriate ways, like the man in my church in Kentucky who sexually abused minors in exchange for "gifts." This is wrong, immoral and against the law. The same is true for the youth minister, Pastor or Priest who entices young girls to have sex with them. The Catholic Church has been rocked by these accusations for years, damaging and/ or destroying tens of thousands of young lives and costing the church millions of dollars in compensation. Some of them were gay Priests picking up altar boys, but many were Priests preying on young girls. The principle is the same: having unwelcome sex or sex with underage children is immoral, illegal, and wrong. The Catholic Church is not alone in this. Society is aware of the Catholic church's problems, but Southern Baptists have avoided the same degree of scrutiny and have only recently begun to come to terms with their own sexual abuse scandals and coverups.

Ironically, the two architects of the original 1979 SBC takeover, Dr. Paige Patterson and former Texas Judge Paul Pressler were both later exposed for problems related to their own handling of sex related issues. Patterson mishandled student rape/sexual assault allegations and engaged in coverups, leading to a demotion from his position as President of Southwestern Baptist Theological Seminary in 2018. A few months later he was terminated altogether and stripped of his retirement benefits after the Board learned he had lied to them about a prior student sexual assault allegation that occurred during his tenure as President of Southeastern Baptist Seminary.*

Meanwhile, in 2017, former Texas judge, lawmaker and fellow architect of so called "conservative resurgence" or as I call it "the fundamentalist takeover," Paul Pressler, was accused of sexually assaulting a male teen for years beginning when the youth was just 14-years-old. Following years of high-profile litigation which by 2024 included evidence of Pressler's sexual assault of seven additional young men. The SBC and others entered into a confidential settlement of the matter. Remember Jesus said *"He that is without sin among you, let him cast the first stone..."* (John 8:7-8, ASV). So, while Pressler and Patterson were rallying fundamentalists about immorality, they themselves were far from guilt free.

In 2022 at the Southern Baptist Annual Convention, SBC officially admitted for the first time that they had a serious sexual abuse problem and began working to create accountability on the part of the church, its pastors and other church leaders.

This was a brutal fight won by dedicated Christians who believed it was past time to deal with this plague on the denomination. However, the next year, in 2023, a reincarnation of the original fundamentalist coup group that launched the 1979 attacks against the SBC nominated a pastor whose goal was to prevent the newly adopted sexual abuse reforms from ever taking place.

Thankfully, the extreme fundamentalists lost, and the reforms have gone forward. Sexual abuse among clergy is a significant problem, be it Catholic, Southern Baptist, Methodist, Pentecostal or any other religious tradition.

CONCLUSION

My Church, Southern Baptist, taught very little about sexuality except that sex is wrong and dirty outside of marriage of one man to one woman. This warped my view. I went to my pastor for help and was given materials to read, all of which reaffirmed that homosexuality is wrong, as was masturbation, pre-marital sex, and recreational sex. Oh, how I wish I had the ability to think critically back then. So much of my lack of comfort as a sexual being would have dissipated. I'm the person God created me to be. Once I was honest about this, I could finally be my whole self. Others might still tell you that you are a sinner. And they'd be right. You are a sinner. We all are. Not because of who we love, but because we are continuously breaking our relationships. God, through Spirit, is the mender of broken relationships. Thank God we have Jesus as our model. He came to mend our broken relationship with God because God loves us so much!

NOTES

*For further information see: Shellnut, Kate *Christianity Today* "Paige Patterson Fired by Southwestern, Stripped of Retirement Benefits" May 30, 2018 *(Patterson lied to the board of Southwestern Baptist Theological Seminary about rape allegation that came before him at another seminary)*; Neuman, Scott *National Public Radio*, "Seminary Votes to Fire"; Pulliam Bailey, Sarah *The Washington Post* "Southern Baptist Seminary Drops Bombshell: Why Paige Patterson was Fired" *(Jun 3, 2018)(lied about treatment of alleged rape victim in 2003 and in 2015 tried to isolate a female student, an alleged sexual assault victim, from chief of security so he could "break her down")*.

Platoff, Emma, *The Texas Tribune*, "Paul Pressler, former Texas judge and religious right leader, accused of sexually assaulting teen for years" (Dec. 12, 2017).

Pulliam Bailey, Sarah, *The New York Times*, "Paul Pressler, Disgraced Christian Conservative Leader, Dies at 94" (A former judge, he helped steer the Southern Baptist Convention to the Right, but at least seven men accused him of sexual abuse; Described by publisher of Baptist News Global as the "Steve Bannon of the Southern Baptist Convention.") (June 16, 2024; Updated June 17, 2024); Downen, Robert, *The Texas Tribune*, "Paul Pressler, a Former Southern Baptist Leader Accused of Sexual Abuse, Dead at 94,"(June 15, 2024).

Charles Michael Brill was born during the early days of the Civil Rights Movement in Mobile, Alabama. He accepted Christ at 13, called into ministry during high school, and was ordained while in college. He graduated from Oklahoma Baptist University and Southern Baptist Theological Seminary. For most of the first decade and a half he worked within the Southern Baptist Convention in various ministry positions. Eventually, he left the SBC as the convention moved more conservatively. With that change came the freedom to finally be his authentic self. For the last 30 years was a financial advisor with New York Life (five years) and then Raymond James (25 years) until his retirement in 2024. He is now happily retired and living his best life with Richard, his husband, serving his church and community in various volunteer roles.

www.ingramcontent.com/pod-product-compliance
Lightning Source LLC
Chambersburg PA
CBHW060412130626
46555CB00005B/2034